RADICAL VOICES

A Decade of Feminist Resistance

Women's Studies International Forum

the ATHENE series

General Editors

Gloria Bowles

Renate Klein

Janice Raymond

Consulting Editor

Dale Spender

The ATHENE SERIES assumes that all those who are concerned with formulating explanations of the way the world works need to know and appreciate the significance of basic feminist principles.

The growth of feminist research has challenged almost all aspects of social organization in our culture. The ATHENE SERIES focuses on the construction of knowledge and the exclusion of women from the process — both as theorists and subjects of study — and offers innovative studies that challenge established theories and research.

ON ATHENE — When Metis, goddess of wisdom who presided over all knowledge was pregnant with ATHENE, she was swallowed up by Zeus who then gave birth to ATHENE from his head. The original ATHENE is thus the parthenogenetic daughter of a strong mother and as the feminist myth goes, at the "third birth" of ATHENE she stops being Zeus' obedient mouthpiece and returns to her real source: the science and wisdom of womankind.

Pergamon Related Journals

(Free sample copies available on request)

Women's Studies International Forum

Reproductive and Genetic Engineering

RADICAL VOICES

A Decade of Feminist Resistance

from

Women's Studies International Forum

Edited by

Renate D. Klein

and

Deborah Lynn Steinberg

PERGAMON PRESS

OXFORD · NEW YORK · BEIJING · FRANKFURT
SÃO PAULO · SYDNEY · TOKYO · TORONTO

U.K.	Pergamon Press plc, Headington Hill Hall, Oxford OX3 0BW, England
U.S.A.	Pergamon Press, Inc., Maxwell House, Fairview Park, Elmsford, New York 10523, U.S.A.
PEOPLE'S REPUBLIC OF CHINA	Pergamon Press, Room 4037, Qianmen Hotel, Beijing, People's Republic of China
FEDERAL REPUBLIC OF GERMANY	Pergamon Press GmbH, Hammerweg 6, D-6242 Kronberg, Federal Republic of Germany
BRAZIL	Pergamon Editora Ltda, Rua Eça de Queiros, 346, CEP 04011, Paraiso, São Paulo, Brazil
AUSTRALIA	Pergamon Press Australia Pty Ltd., P.O. Box 544, Potts Point, N.S.W. 2011, Australia
JAPAN	Pergamon Press, 5th Floor, Matsuoka Central Building, 1-7-1 Nishishinjuku, Shinjuku-ku, Tokyo 160, Japan
CANADA	Pergamon Press Canada Ltd., Suite No. 271, 253 College Street, Toronto, Ontario, Canada M5T 1R5

Copyright © 1989 Renate D. Klein and Deborah Lynn Steinberg

First edition 1989

Library of Congress Cataloging-in-Publication Data
Radical voices.
(The Athene series)
1. Feminism. 2. Women's rights. I. Klein,
Renate D. II. Steinberg, Deborah Lynn. III. Series.
HQ1154.R27   1988   305.4'2   88-29006

British Library Cataloguing in Publication Data
Radical voices: a decade of feminist resistance
studies international forum. – (The Athene series)
1. Feminism
I. Klein, Renate D. II. Steinberg, Deborah Lynn
III. Spender, Dale IV. Series
305.4'2

ISBN 0-08-036484-5 Hardcover
ISBN 0-08-036483-7 Flexicover

Printed in Great Britain by A. Wheaton & Co. Ltd., Exeter

*To Dale Spender, without whose
inspirational encouragement
many women's words would not
be available in print*

Contents

Section III   Feminist ethics and vision: the meaning of feminism

Preface

Dale Spender

Each one of the papers included in this volume is to be valued for its contribution to the task of accounting for and of transforming women's oppression. But together, these papers are of greater value than the sum of their individual parts; together they constitute a new entity and provide a history of ideas within Women's Studies as it has developed over the last ten years.

It is appropriate that the collection should begin with Dorothy Smith's classic contribution on the extent to which women have been excluded from legitimated knowledge—and the nature and extent of the effort required if women are to occupy a central place in the generation of knowledge. And appropriate too, that the collection should conclude, with Shulamit Reinharz's admirable appraisal of the achievements—and the potential—of feminist conceptualizations. In between come some of the many radical articles from *Women's Studies International Forum* which reveal the intellectual diversity, dynamism and direction of a decade of feminist resistance in action and theory.

Apart from the significant pattern of growth and development which appears when these articles are placed together, this collection also provides an important reminder of the quantity and quality of ground-breaking contributions that have been produced within Women's Studies over the last ten years. But if there is cause for celebration and congratulation, there is also cause for concern; in some areas women are now no closer to sustaining satisfactory strategies or solutions for ending their subordination than they were when many of these articles were first written. This is why such a collection is crucially important; for while it stands as a testimony to the excellence of feminist academic endeavor, it also serves as a reminder that this writing and research has been undertaken in a male-dominated world. While it shows women as active subjects, it also points to the parameters of women's subordination.

It was with great pride that I was associated with the journal which helped to legitimate and communicate some of the most radical feminist ideas over the last ten years; it is with great pleasure that I commend this collection which supports and extends the achievements of women and Women's Studies.

Coogee, Australia
August 1988

Introduction

Deborah Lynn Steinberg
and Renate D. Klein

Our idea to compile this collection originated long before we actually began to do it. Both of us, through personal and shared experiences of feminist scholarship and feminist activism, have depended upon, learned from and been deeply inspired by the radical ideas of friends, colleagues and sisters in the women's liberation movement. We have felt for ourselves the generative power of the interweaving of ideas, action and visionary ethics that are the process of women's liberation.

This collection is one outcome of our shared and long-standing concern to preserve the development of radical thinking by keeping the original and visionary ideas of feminists in circulation. Since we began working together three years ago (mainly on a feminist critique of reproductive and genetic technologies), we have felt the need for writings that discuss the origins and developments of both feminist scholarship and the women's liberation movement; how they interconnect, what forms their interaction takes. When we had to read through all the past issues of *Women's Studies International Forum* to find papers for a Women's Studies course, we were delighted to find that we had such a collection of work at hand.

In putting together this anthology, we address several concerns we both have in relation to feminism in general. We are both becoming increasingly disturbed about the growing alienation of women's academic writing from the spirit, history and goals of the women's liberation movement, and indeed with the fundamental subversion of the *feminist* meaning of women's liberation. We feel that this fragmentation and subversion of feminism in part reflects a reaction to a shifting political climate where economic and political policies are being built on more overt foundations of bigotry and woman-hating. It is a shift that has impacted to the direct detriment of women's lives, feminist activism and feminist education.

It is within this context that we have seen, particularly in relation to women's struggle for sexual and reproductive autonomy through resistance to pornography and new reproductive technologies, the (re)emergence of 'me-istic' liberal and libertarian ideologies which forward individual consumerism and personal pleasure as the index of 'liberation,' including women's 'liberation.' We are concerned in particular about emerging 'feminist' ideologies of sexual libertarianism, manifested in writings and movements which defend or forward the consumption of pornography and enaction of sadomasochism and which have located sexual pleasure alone as the central arena for women's struggles for sexual self-discovery, selfhood and emancipation.[1]

We contend that because women have been and continue to be systematically subordinated within nearly all aspects of our cultures, pleasure, like all women's experiences, is experienced within the specific contexts of our oppression. That is, we cannot have acontextual experiences; we live, act and feel within the world, and within the living context of the systematic subordination of women. Consequently, it should be evident that experiencing personal pleasure does not in and of itself change the world and is not, by itself, evidence of the breakdown of social, cultural, political and economic relations which oppress women. We believe that the individualized and acontextual focus on sensations and personal pleasure and the position that they intrinsically constitute women's liberation and therefore justify and even call for the preservation and consumption of pornography and sadomasochistic sexual relations by and among women undermines the meaning of feminism. By encouraging a limited self-centered analysis of women's experience, this thinking marginalizes the historical struggle of women to investigate the social, political and economic ideologies and institutions which promote and entrench disenfranchisement of and violence against women, and women's efforts both to generate a women-centered world view and to achieve the realization of that world view by acting *against* the oppression of women. The libertarian position trivializes and shifts focus away from understanding women's subordination as a structural and social phenomenon and understanding women's resistance as political action for *all* women's social liberation. We are concerned that such thinking has been increasingly promoted and published within so-called 'feminist' scholarship.

In recognizing and experiencing this libertarian 'feminism' as in fact an ideological, political and economic backlash *against* feminism and therefore

---

[1]We refer in particular to such publications as *Coming to Power*, SAMOIS, 1981, 1982, USA, Alyson Publications, and *On Our Backs* (a 'lesbian' S/M magazine) published in San Francisco, California, USA. These publications forward sadomasochism as 'liberation' and as a movement of an 'oppressed' minority. *Coming to Power* explicitly names sadomasochism as a 'feminist' process. Although these sources we list are from the United States, the topic of sadomasochism is by no means limited to there. It is becoming increasingly visible in Britain, for example. Among West German feminists there are women who claim an S/M component in art celebrating sexual violence (Maria Mies, personal communication, Cologne 1985).

against women, we emphasize that there is a *need* for articulated feminist ethics. By feminist ethics we mean a process and system of values and priorities that are oriented from women's experiences and toward the eradication of the oppression of women. We use the term feminist ethics to represent three fundamental processes which we see as integral to women's liberation and which are the conceptual and conscious underpinnings of feminist politics and feminist scholarship. We define feminist ethics as:

1. *A system and process* of personal and political priorities and values that have emerged from women's experiences of oppression; they are women-centered, women's lives and feminist perspectives being the basis of research and politics.
2. *A process of analysis* from a women-centered perspective of the nature of the agencies and ideologies which do violence to and socially dispossess women.
3. *A process and world-view* which inform and inspire women's personal and political goals to end the oppression of women, and *generate* the enaction of visionary feminist ethics in theory and practice as feminist politics and strategies.[2]

Our criteria for selecting articles for this collection emerged out of our commitment to feminist ethics and to re-covering and re-circulating radical feminist scholarship. We feel that the articles in this collection, many of which were written some years ago, particularly reflect this commitment and are as relevant and necessary to understanding the social climate and subordination of women in the late 1980s as they were when originally published.

We have structured this book to reflect the conceptual processes we have defined as feminist ethics by dividing it into three sections. Each section addresses what we see as fundamental feminist questions: What is the cultural meaning of 'woman' and how does this meaning underpin the oppression of women? What are the components of patriarchy and how do they oppress women? What is feminism and how does it function to end the oppression of women?

The first section is entitled 'The Cultural Construction/Consciousness of Women: the Meaning of Woman.' The articles in this section address on the one hand the question of what is 'woman' as a cultural personification and on the other how women see themselves (i.e., women's self-consciousness). Articles in this section address, for example, the exclusion of women from the making of culture, therefore from the making of the cultural meaning of

---

[2] We derive our concept of feminist ethics here from a discussion of the idea power (conceptual origins) of Women's Studies which is discussed in *The Dynamics of Women's Studies: An Exploratory Study of Its International Ideas and Practices in Higher Education*, a PhD thesis by Renate Klein, 1986, University of London, Institute of Education.

ourselves as women, which in turn excludes women from the expression of culture (e.g., art, literature and ideas). The meaning of 'fatness' and race are discussed as culturally constructed identities for women within the context of the subordination of women. And finally, women's negotiation for our survival and resistance to oppression is examined in relation to women's decision whether or not to identify as feminists.

The second section, 'Feminist Re-vision: the Meaning of Patriarchal Institutions and Theories from a Feminist Perspective' focuses on the meaning and operation of the agencies and ideologies that disenfranchise and inflict violence on women. This section begins with articles addressing patriarchal scholarship and praxis including the ideologies of rape, sociobiology, and sexual deviance. The latter part of this section includes articles examining patriarchal political and social institutions, including the New Right, men as intruders and obstacles to the production of feminist scholarship and education, the social control of and traffic in women through new reproductive technologies, paternity 'rights' and pornography.

The third section is entitled 'Feminist Ethics and Vision: The Meaning of Feminism.' The last part of this book is devoted to articles which focus on feminist ethics and politics including philosophical definitions of the meanings, concerns and priorities of feminists in relation to such issues as a feminist world view, female friendships, feminist education, lesbian feminism, black feminism, and feminism and aging.

We invited the contributors to add, if they chose, a comment on their papers. Those who did, contextualize their past work within current politics, bring it up to date, add new ideas and share their present feelings about the way they presented their ideas some years ago.

We were very excited and greatly inspired by the hundreds of wonderful articles that have been published in *Women's Studies International Forum* over the past decade and found the selection of articles for this collection very difficult. It was encouraging for us to see that there were many types of anthologies which could have been compiled. For example, we could have drawn on the international aspect that *Women's Studies International Forum* has always emphasized and thus created a collection about women's social positions and experiences in different countries around the world. We could also have done an anthology of articles discussing the development of Women's Studies. These possibilities might still be explored in further publications.

Thinking ahead, we hope that a similar collection after the *second* decade of *Women's Studies International Forum* will include many more papers on feminist ethics by and for women of different ethnic, cultural and racial backgrounds. We are very excited by the current flourishing of writings, for example, from the rapidly expanding fields of black feminist and Jewish feminist theory, to name but two. We hope that many of the writers will choose to contribute their work to *Women's Studies International Forum* in the future.

Finally, we would like to express our gratitude to Dale Spender without whose vision and hard work *Women's Studies International Forum* would never have begun. It is our hope that the articles in this collection will inspire readers to continue formulating their own feminist ethics and lend their radical voices and visions to the future of feminism.

I

The cultural construction/consciousness of women: the meaning of woman

1

A Peculiar Eclipsing: Women's Exclusion from Man's Culture[1]

Dorothy E. Smith

I

In the kind of society we have, a great deal gets done in words (or other symbolic terms) and on paper. The work of administration, of management, of government, is a *communicative* work. Organizational and political processes are forms of action in words. It is an *ideologically* structured work of action—images, vocabularies, concepts, abstract terms of knowledge, are integral to the practice of power, to getting things done.

Further, the ways in which we think about ourselves and one another and about our society—our images of how we should look, our homes, our lives, even our inner worlds—are given shape and distributed by the specialized work of people in universities and schools, in television, radio and newspapers, in advertising agencies, in book publishing and other organizations forming the 'ideological apparatus' of the society.

This way of organizing society began to develop in Western Europe some 400 or 500 years ago. It is an integral aspect of the development of a capitalist mode of production. Women have been at work in its making as much as men, though their work has been of a different kind and location. But women have been largely excluded from the work of producing the forms of thought and the images and symbols in which thought is expressed and ordered. There is a circle effect. Men attend to and treat as significant only what men say. The circle of men whose writing and talk was significant to each other extends backwards in time as far as our records reach. What men were doing was

[1] An earlier version of this paper was published in the *Canadian Review of Sociology and Anthropology*, 'Women in the Canadian Social Structures,' November 1975, part one. It was titled, 'Ideological Structures and How Women are Excluded.' The phrase 'a peculiar eclipsing' is Tillie Olsen's.

relevant to men, was written by men about men for men. Men listened and listen to what one another said.

This is how a tradition is formed. A way of thinking develops in this discourse through the medium of the written and printed word as well as in speech. It has questions, solutions, themes, styles, standards, ways of looking at the world. These are formed as the circle of those present builds on the work of the past. From these circles women have been excluded or admitted only by a special license granted to a woman as an individual and never as a representative of her sex. Throughout this period in which ideologies become of increasing importance, first as a mode of thinking, legitimating and sanctioning a social order, and then as integral in the organization of society, women have been deprived of the means to participate in creating forms of thought relevant or adequate to express their own experience or to define and raise social consciousness about their situation and concerns. They have never controlled the material or social means to the making of a tradition among themselves or to acting as equals in the ongoing discourse of intellectuals. They have had no economic status independent of men. They have not had, until very recently, access to the educational skills necessary to develop, sustain and participate in the making of a common culture.

Women have, of course, had access to and used the limited and largely domestic zone of women's magazines, television programs, women's novels, poetry, soap operas, etc. But this is a limited zone. It follows the contours of their restricted role in the society. The universe of ideas, images and themes— the symbolic modes which are *the general currency* of thought—have been either produced by men or controlled by them. In so far as women's work and experience has been entered into it, it has been on terms decided by men and because it has been approved by men.

This is why women have had no written history until very recently, no share in making religious thoughts, no political philosophy, no representation of society from their view, no poetic tradition, no tradition in art.

II

It is important to recognize that in this kind of society people generally do not participate in the making of its culture. The forms of thought and images we use do not arise directly or spontaneously out of people's everyday lived relations. Rather, they are the product of the work of specialists occupying positions in the ideological apparatus (the educational system, communications, etc.). Our culture does not arise spontaneously; it is 'manufactured.'

These organizations are part of the larger apparatus of ruling the society, the apparatus which puts it together, co-ordinates its work, manages its economic processes, generally keeps it running, and regulates and controls it.

This means that the forms of thought we make use of to think about ourselves and our society originate in special positions of dominance. Since these positions of dominance are occupied by men (almost exclusively), this means that our forms of thought put together a view of the world from a place women do not occupy. Hence, the means women have had available to them to think, image and make actionable their experience have been made for us and not by us. It means that our experience has not been represented in the making of our culture. There is a *gap* between where we are and the means we have to express and act. It means that the concerns, interests, experiences forming 'our' culture are those of men in positions of dominance whose perspectives are built on the *silence* of women (and of others).

As a result the perspectives, concerns, interests of only one sex and one class are represented as general. Only one sex and class are directly and actively involved in producing, debating, developing its ideas, in creating its art, in the formation of its medical and psychological conceptions, in the framing of its laws and political principles and its educational values and objectives. It is thus that a one-sided standpoint comes to be seen as natural, obvious and general. It is thus that a one-sided set of interests preoccupies intellectual and creative work. Simone de Beauvoir describes the effect for women in this way:

> 'A man never begins by presenting himself as an individual of a certain sex; it goes without saying that he is a man. The terms *masculine* and *feminine* are used symmetrically only as a matter of form, as on legal paper. In actuality the relation of the two sexes is not quite like that of two electrical poles, for man represents both the positive and the neutral, as is indicated by the common use of *man* to designate human beings in general; whereas woman represents only the negative, defined by limiting criteria, without reciprocity' (de Beauvoir, 1961:xv).

Issues such as the uses of the male pronouns to represent the general are not trivial after all. They express exactly this relation.

Let us be clear that we are not talking about prejudice or sexism as a particular bias against women or as a negative stereotype of women. We are talking about the consequences of women's exclusion from a full share in the making of what becomes treated as *our* culture. We are talking about the consequences of silence, an absence, a non-presence. What is there—spoken, sung, written, made emblematic in art—and treated as general, universal, unrelated to a particular position or a particular sex as its source and standpoint, is in fact partial, limited, located in a particular position and permeated by special interests and concerns.

For example, listening recently to the radio, I heard an account with excerpts of a musical made from Barry Broadbent's book on the depression years. Broadbent's book contains the reminiscences of both women and men. But the musical as it was described and excerpted on the radio, had the voices only of men. Hence only men's viewpoint, men's experience of that time were there for all or any of us to hear. Women's experience and viewpoint were altogether missing.

Or again, a radio program concerning violence between husbands and wives spent most of the time discussing violence of wives against husbands, though violence of husbands against wives constitutes by far the most frequent and most serious form of violence between husbands and wives.

The biases of beginning from the experience of men enters in all kinds of ways into our thinking. Take for example the Freudian conception of sexuality. It is clearly based on the man's experience of his body and his sexuality. Hence we have a conception of sexuality based on male genital sexuality and of woman's body as deviating from this so that her psychosexual development must be thought of somehow as an attempt to do away with this fundamental defect. Her child, particularly her male child, is represented as a substitute for a missing penis. How extraordinary this is if you don't treat a man's body as normative. Think for a moment what it might be like to construct an account of our psycho-sexual being beginning from women's experience of our bodies and sexuality as a norm. How odd *that* would be if it were imposed upon men as normative. And how is it that we could not have an account which begins indeed from the actualities of our experience and recognizes the difference as just that, or perhaps indeed as complementary, rather than treating the sexuality of one sex as deviant *vis-à-vis* that of the other?

The enormous literature on the relation of family socialization and educational attainment, in which the role of the mother takes on such a prominent part, can be seen also to have its distinctive biases. Virtually the whole treatment of mothering in this literature is in various ways evaluative, critical or instructive with respect to the practices and relations which are conducive to educational attainment or the psycho-social well-being of children. Virtually the whole of this literature presupposes a one-way relation between school and family whereby family practices, organization and in particular mothering practices are seen as consequential for the child's behaviour at school. The phenomenon of school phobia as it is vulgarly described is one notorious example, whereby the protectiveness of the mother is understood as creating a dependency in the child and hence the child's fearfulness at school (Kahn and Nurstein, 1964:13–15). Or take the psychiatric literature on the family and mental illness in which the mother is continually the focus of an inescapable indictment (see King, 1975).

Who has thought to take up the issue of these relations from the standpoint of women? Might we not then have studies concerned with the consequences of the school and the educational process for how the child matures in the family and for the family itself? Where are those studies which show the disastrous consequences of the school for the families of immigrants, particularly non-English-speaking immigrants? Where are the studies which suggest that mothers' protectiveness to children who are terrified of school arises as a protective response to what is perceived as a source of damage and harm to the child? Where are the studies which tell us anything about the consequences for family organization of societal processes which 'sub-contract' educational responsibilities for homework, etc., to the family and in particular to the mother? What effects does this odd role—lacking authority and overburdened with responsibility for outcomes over which in fact she has little control—have on women? What are the implications of this role for family relations, particularly for relations between mothers and children? [Consider in this light Pauline Bart's work on depression among middle-aged Jewish housewives (Bart, 1971).]

In the field of educational research itself, our assumptions are those of a world seen from men's position in it. Turn to that classic of our times, Aries's *Centuries of Childhood*. Interrogate it seriously from the standpoint of women. Ask, should this book not be retitled *Centuries of the Childhood of Men?* Or take Jencks's influential book on *Inequality*. Should this not be described as an examination of the educational system with respect to its implications for *inequality among men*. The very terms in which inequality is conceived are based on men's occupations, men's typical patterns of career and advancement. Women's experience of work in this kind of society is located in standstill jobs, lacking career structure and in a status system in which their position is derived from that of men. A work examining the educational system with respect to the inequality of women would be focused quite differently. It would, among other matters, be concerned with the educational system as systematically producing a differential of competence among women and men in almost every educational dimension, including that of physical development. It would focus on inequality between the sexes as a systematically organized product of the educational process.

These only illustrate the outcomes of women's absence. We cannot inventory them fully. It is not a special unfortunate and accidental omission of this or that field. It is a general feature of how our society is organized.

III

The exclusion of women from the making of our culture is not the product of a biological deficiency or a biological configuration of some kind. As we learn more of our (women's) history we discover that a powerful intellectual and artistic current moves like an underground stream through the history of the last few centuries. It appears sometimes merely as a missing potentiality, as in the stories of women mathematicians whose biographies show in almost every case the effect of a general deprivation of education for in almost every case they have discovered mathematics by accident, sharing a brother's lessons, the interest of a family friend, the paper covered with calculus used to paper a child's room—some special incident or relation which introduced them to the territory of their art (Osen, 1974). Lacking such accident, there was no provision, no systematic training, no opening of an intellectual universe. Or we find that the intellectual or artistic practice itself was appropriated by a man, as Caroline Herschel's major work in astronomy in association with her brother William Herschel is treated as his. We learn of the subordination of genius to the discipline of service in the home and in relation to children and of the fragmentary realization of extraordinary powers of mind and dedication, as in the lives of Charlotte and Emily Brontë, of Emily Dickinson and in our time, of Tillie Olsen—among others, known and unknown.

We can see also the submerged folk-tradition of a true art sustained and perpetuated by women when the emergence of a high art excluded them and surely excluded distinctively feminine materials. Thus the artists of quilting have used forms, materials and practices unlike those taken for granted in the organization and form of art (until recently). Though if you see the quilts and read the accounts, you are clearly in the presence of artists of high technical excellence and quality of design who were not treated or recognized as artists until the women's movement. A quilt was made to be used. It was integrated into particularistic relations—the piece of her grandmother's dress, her daughter's pinafore—and was often made by a group of women working together. The making itself and the friendships were built into the design, the collection of fabrics, the stitching. A quilt was not a piece of art, therefore, to be seen in isolation from its history and the social relations of its making. It was not made to be set in the high walls of gallery or museum, detached from everything except its visual effect. It was always a moment in the moving skein of family and tradition, raising suspicion against time and its powers of separation.

We have evidence now also of a submerged and repressed political and spiritual intelligentsia dating at least from that moment when in Europe the translation of the Bible into the vernacular made the authoritative book available to anyone who could read—among them women of course. We have as yet fragmentary intuitions of an emerging female intelligentsia and the repressions to which they were subject—we hear for example of women such as Joan Boughton and her daughter Lady Yonge who were burned at the stake in the late fifteenth century because they held fast to their right to direct interpretation of the scriptures and to speak and express their own under-standing of the Bible rather than on the authority of the clergy (Thrupp, 1962). We can see a similar phenomenon in the reign of Henry VIII when the reformation enlivened the intellectual possibilities for women as well as for men and women such as Sara Ann Askew were tortured and martyred for heresy. In the founding and organization of the Quaker sect Margaret Fell (later to be Margaret Fox) played a leading and important role. Her influence was such that the Quaker sect was one of the few to grant a position of equality to women in religious matters. She herself, imprisoned many times for her beliefs, wrote in the seventeenth century a powerful pamphlet arguing the scriptural justification for the right of women to preach and teach (Fox, 1713). Those however who actually took up such responsibility, as many women have in many forms, were not always received as leaders, as was Margaret Fell. In the seventeenth century also, Anne Hutchinson was banished from the Massachusetts Bay Colony because she chose to preach and teach religion and claimed the right to do so as a woman (Rowbotham, 1973). Again, the struggle emerges from its underground existence during the French Revolution when women were active in women's revolutionary organization. Again it is repressed. The clubs were proscribed and at least two of their leaders, Olympes de Gouges and Manon Roland, were guillotined as an example to other women of what happened to those women who stepped so far out of their place as to claim wisdom, learning and political leadership (des Jacques, 1973). The underground movement surfaces again in Mrs. Packard's struggle against her Calvinist husband who had committed her (as under the law of that time he could) to the Illinois Insane Asylum on the grounds not only that she held religious opinions different from his, but that she insisted on her right to do so (Szasz, 1973). Closer to our own time, as women in the 1960s began actively to take up women's issues in the civil rights movement, they encountered ridicule, vilification and an opposition from men which exhibited to them for the first time how they were despised (Mitchell, 1971).

Let us be clear that what we are hearing in these brief biographical moments is the emergence into our view, into the view of a history written largely by men and with men's concerns in mind, of a continuing and active struggle renewed continually in different times and places by women who often had no knowledge of their predecessors or of their contemporary sisterhood.

The repression of the continuing underground sources of intellectual power and assertion among women shows us the rough stuff. There is an actively enforced barrier of which we were unaware until we looked at these kinds of examples. But as work begins to accumulate telling us of our history and breaking the silence of our past, we can see that other forces were at work, more conventional, seemingly more rational, but no less powerful and effective in ensuring the silence of women.

For example, we now have well-documented history of midwives both in England and the United States, showing how over a period of 200 years they were reduced to an ancillary role in childbirth or eliminated altogether. This was a struggle fought by the medical profession consciously and deliberately. It was concerned to eliminate the competition not only of women, but of a continuing native tradition of learning which was at odds with the technical

apparatus and technical knowledge of the emerging profession of gynaecology. In the suppression of that art or the bringing of English midwives into
a subordinate relation to the medical profession, the traditions perpetuated
by the older art have been lost (we cannot now of course evaluate their
possible importance). Further direct access to women's own knowledge of
their sexual and procreative functions was cut off (Donnison, 1977).

We now know also that women were systematically and consciously
excluded from the growing profession of medicine in the United States,
where admission to medical school for women was restricted to a very small
number. Those who were trained found that the kinds of jobs open to them
were largely in public health or institutional medicine. Again we find an
organizational process which by excluding women also excludes their knowledge, experience, interests and perspectives, and prevents them becoming
part of the systematic knowledge and techniques of a profession. This has of
course been of fundamental significance in the formation of practice and
knowledge in gynaecology. Its current practices are distinctively marked by
the silence of women in its making (Walsh, 1977).

These are some of the forms in which women's silence and exclusion has
been practiced. Some have arisen inadvertently as a concommitant of
women's location in the world, some have been a process of active repression
or strong social disapproval of the exercise by women of a role of intellectual
or political leadership; others have been the product of an organizational
process. It is this last form of exclusion I shall focus on now, for in our society
we see less of the rough stuff (though do not assume that it is not there) and
more of a steady institutional process, equally effective and much less visible
in its exclusionary force.

IV

The exclusion of women from participating in creating the culture of the
society is in this day and age largely organized by the ordinary social
processes of socialization, education, work and communication. These
perform a routine, generalized, and effective repression. The educational
system is an important aspect of this. It trains people in skills they need to
participate at various levels in the ideological structuring of the society (they
must be able to read at least); it teaches them the ideas, the vocabularies,
images, beliefs; it trains them to recognize and approve ideologically sanctioned forms of relations and how to identify authoritative ideological
sources (what kinds of books, newspapers, etc., to credit, what to discredit,
who are the authoritative writers or speakers and who are not). It is part of
the system which distributes ideas and ensures the dissemination of new
ideological forms as these are produced by the intelligentsia. It is also active
itself in producing ideology, both in forms of knowledge in the social

sciences, psychology, and education, and in the forms of critical ideas and theories in philosophy and literature.

Prior to the late nineteenth century, women were almost completely denied access to any form of higher education beyond the skills of reading and writing. One of the first major feminist works, Mary Wollstonecraft's *Vindication of the Rights of Women*, places their right to education at the center of her argument. She is responding specifically to Rousseau's prescriptions for educating women aimed at training them for dependency, for permanent childishness and for permanent incapacity for the autonomous exercise of mind (Wollstonecraft, 1967). During the latter part of the nineteenth century, in both Europe and North America, opportunities for women in higher education were a major focus of women's struggle. Though women's participation in the educational process at all levels has increased in this century, this participation remains within marked boundaries. Among the most important of these boundaries, I would argue, is that which reserves to men control of the policy-making and decision-making apparatus in the educational system.

When we look at where women are in the educational system, our focus should go beyond issues of social justice. Equality of opportunity is only one aspect of the problem. I want rather to draw attention to the significance of the inequalities we find for how women are located in the processes of setting standards, producing social knowledge, acting as 'gate-keepers' over what is admitted into the systems of distribution, innovating in thought or knowledge or values and in other ways participating as authorities in the ideological work done in the educational process.

We can look at the statistics from two points of view—education itself has a status structure organizing its internal relations so far as sources of knowledge and academic standards are concerned. Though there are of course other aspects of schools and community colleges of social significance which are not related to the university, the university is important as a source of intellectual leadership *vis-à-vis* the rest of the educational system. Secondly, these differing levels of the educational system are related to the age structure of the educational process. Generally more advanced training for older students has a higher status than education for younger and less advanced students. This status structure has little to do with the skills required or the social importance of this work. It has a great deal to do with control over the standards and substance of education. As we go up to the Canadian educational hierarchy from elementary to secondary to community college to university we find a lower proportion of women teachers at each step.

At each level upward in the hierarchy of control and influence over the educational process, the proportion of women declines. At the elementary level, women are the majority (although the proportion has declined to 74 per

DOROTHY E. SMITH

% Women at different levels of the educational system, various years 1969–1973		
Elementary teachers (ex. Quebec)	78.0%	(72–73)
Secondary teachers (ex. Quebec)	37.0%	(72–73)
Community college teaching staff (ex. Quebec)	19.5%	(70–71)
University (all ranks)	15.0%	(69–70)

cent in 1975/1976), but at the secondary school level they are already a minority and their share of the educational process is lowest at the university level.

Further, within each level we find women markedly unrepresented in administrative positions and positions of professional leadership.

In elementary and secondary schools women's relative share of administrative positions is much lower than their share of teaching positions. It shows generally the same pattern of decline at each next position upward in the hierarchy as we have seen in the overall educational structure.

% Women in positions in elementary and secondary schools (ex. Quebec) 1972/1973*		
	Elementary	Secondary
Teacher	78	37
Department head	42	21
Vice-principal	20	7
Principal	20	4

*From *The Declining Majority*, A Canadian Teachers' Federation Status of Women Publication, 1978.

A similar pattern in the figures for community colleges and universities is evident in the following tables:

% Women educational staff in community colleges by position (ex. Quebec) 1970/1971*	
Teaching staff	19.5
Academic administrative	11.9

*From *Women in the Labour Force, Facts and Figures 1973*, Labour Canada, Women's Bureau, Table 7.

The inverse relation between status level and proportion of women is obvious at every level. Women are most heavily concentrated in the positions of lecturer and instructor which are not part of the promotional system leading

% Women holding academic positions, by rank 1969/1970*	
Lecturers and instructors	31
Assistant professors	14
Associate professors	8
Professors	3

*From *But Can You Type?*, J. Vickers and J. Adam, 1977.

to professorial rank (the so-called 'ladder' positions) and are usually held on only a 1-year contract. There is an appreciable drop even to the next level of junior positions, the assistant professors—the first step on the promotion ladder. Women form a very small proportion of full professors.

It is important to keep in mind that we are looking at rather powerful structures of professional control. It is through this structure of ranks and the procedures by which people are advanced from one to another that the professions maintain control over the nature and quality of work that is done and the kinds of people who are admitted to its ranks and to influential positions within it. Two points are of special importance: first the concentration of women in the relatively temporary non-ladder positions. This means that they are largely restricted to teaching, that their work is subject to continual review and that reappointment is conditional upon conformity. The second point to note is the marked break in the proportion of women between tenured and non-tenured positions.

The tenured faculty to a large extent control who shall be admitted to its ranks and what shall be recognized as properly scholarly work. This minimal 'voting power' of women helps us to understand why women in more senior positions in the university do not ordinarily represent women's perspectives. They are those who have been passed through this very rigorous filter. They are those whose work and style of work and conduct have met the approval of judges who are largely men. And, in any case, they are very few.

In sum, the statistics show a highly inequitable distribution of women throughout the educational system. Though women are more than half of all teachers, they are very under-represented in the ranks of principals; there are very, very few women superintendents. In the educational bureaucracies, women appear almost exclusively in secretarial and clerical roles. In universities and community colleges, women are very markedly under-represented in the academic staff. They are clustered in the lower ranks with the greatest turnover and in a very limited range of subjects (think of who taught you and who taught what subjects). The officers of organizations representing educators are also predominantly men. We find in general that the closer positions come to policy-making or innovation in the ideological forms, the smaller the proportion of women. Power and authority in the educational process are the prerogatives of men.

V

Men have authority in the world of thought as members of a social category and not as individuals. Authority is a form of power which is a distinctive capacity to get things done in words. What is said or written merely means what the words mean until and unless it is given force by the authority attributed to its 'author.' When we speak of authority we are speaking of what makes what one person says count. Men are invested with authority as individuals, not because they have as individuals special competencies or expertise, but because as men they appear as representative of the power and authority of the institutionalized structures which govern the society. Their authority as individuals in actual situations of action is generated by a social organization. They do not appear as themselves alone. They are those whose words count, both for each other and for those who are not members of this category. The circle I spoke of earlier is formed of those whose words count for one another. It excludes those whose words do not count, whose speakers have no authority.

We have by now and in various forms a good deal of evidence of the ways in which this social effect works. It is one which Mary Ellman has described as a distinction between women and men in intellectual matters, which is both obvious and unnoticed. A man's body gives credibility to his utterance whereas a woman's body takes it away from hers (Ellman, 1968). A study done by Philip Goldberg which was concerned with finding out whether women were prejudiced against women demonstrates this effect very clearly (Goldberg, 1969). Here is Jo Freeman's description: 'He gave college girls sets of booklets containing six identical professional articles in traditional male, female and neutral fields. The articles were identical, but the names of the authors were not. For example, an article in one set would bear the name John T. McKay and in another set the same article would be authored Joan T. McKay. Each booklet contained three articles by "women" and three by "men" '. Questions at the end of each article asked the students to rate the articles on value, persuasiveness and profundity and the authors on writing style and competence. *The male authors fared better in every field*, even in such 'feminine' areas as 'Art History and Dietetics' (Freeman, 1970—my emphasis). There seems to be something like a plus factor which adds force and persuasiveness to what men say and a minus factor which depreciates and weakens what is said by women.

The way in which the sex of the speaker modifies the authority of the message has been observed in other ideological fields. Lucy Komisar points out that in advertising it is men who give instructions to women on how to do their housework. Men tell women why one detergent or soap powder or floor polish is better than another. The reason for this, according to a leading advertising agency executive, is that the male voice is the voice of authority (Komisar, 1972).

Chesler's study of preferences among psychotherapists and their patients shows that the majority of women patients prefer male therapists and that the majority of male psychotherapists prefer women patients. The reasons women give for preferring male psychotherapists are that they generally feel more comfortable with them and that they have more respect for and confidence in a man's competence and authority. Chesler reports that both men and women in her sample said that they trusted and respected men as people and as authorities more than they did women (Chesler, 1972).

A study done by Fidell on sex discrimination in university hiring practices in psychology shows the intersection of this effect with the educational system of controls described in the preceding section. She used an approach very similar to Goldberg's, constructing two sets of fictional descriptions of academic background and qualifications (including the Ph.D.). Identical descriptions in one set had a women's name attached and in the other a man's. The sets of descriptions were sent to chairpersons of all colleges and universities in the United States offering graduate degrees in psychology. They were asked to estimate the chance of the individuals described getting an offer of a position and at what level, etc. Her findings supported the hypothesis of discrimination on the basis of sex. Men were likely to be suggested for higher levels of appointment. They received more regular academic positions of the kind which lead to promotion and tenure; and only men were offered full professorships (Fidell, 1970). It seems as though the attribution of authority which increases the value of men's work constitutes something rather like a special title to the positions of control and influence and hence to full active membership in the intelligentsia.

It seems that woman as a social category lack proper title to membership in the circle of those who count for one another in the making of ideological forms. To identify a women novelist as a women novelist is to place her in a special class outside that of novelists in general. Doris Lessing is described as one of the greatest *women* novelists of this century—rather than just as one of the greatest novelists. Among the professional problems confronted by women writers, Tillie Olsen cites this:

'Devaluation: Still in our century, women's books of great worth suffer the death of being unknown, or at best a peculiar eclipsing, far outnumbering the similar fate of the few such books by men. I think of Kate Chopin, Mary Austin, Dorothy Richardson, Henry Handel Richardson (*Ultima Thule*), Jean Rhys, Storm Jameson, Christina Stead, Elizabeth Madox Roberts (*The Time of Man*), Janet Lewis, Mary Sarton, Harriette Arnouw (*The Dollmaker*), Agnes Smedley (*Daughter of Earth*), Djuna Barnes (*Nightwood*), Kay Boyle—every one of whom is rewarding, and some with the stamp of enduring. Considering their stature, how comparatively unread, untaught are Glasgow, Glaspell, Bowen, Parker, Stein, Mansfield—even Cather and Porter' (Olsen, 1977).

And she points out further how work by women is treated quite differently from that by men. She describes:

> 'the injurious reaction to a book not for its quality or content, but on the basis of its having been written by a woman, with consequent misreading, mistreatment' (Olsen, 1977).

These effects are not confined to literature written by women. They are rather special instances of a general social organization of relations among women and men when the medium is communicative. Men have title of entry to the circle of those who count for one another. Women do not. The minus factor attached to what women say, write or image is another way of seeing how what they say, write or image is not a 'natural' part of the discourse.

The examples so far given have been mainly of the written word. But the metaphor of a game points to our experience in actual everyday interactional settings. We can and have observed these patterns ourselves, which serve to fill out our description of how male control over the topics and themes of discourse is maintained in actual situations of interaction. For example, Strodtbeck and Mann in their study of jury deliberations report that men talked considerably more than women. These differences, however, were more than quantitative. They also described what seems to be a general pattern of interaction between women and men. Men's talk was more directed towards the group task while women reacted with agreement, passive acceptance and understanding (Strodtbeck and Mann, 1956). The pattern I have observed also involves women becoming virtually an audience, facilitating with support or comments, but not becoming among those who carry the talk and whose remarks are directed towards one another.

It is like a game in which there are more presences than actors. Some are engaged in tossing a ball between them, the others are consigned to the roles of audience and supporter, who pick the ball up if it is dropped and pass it back to the players. They support, facilitate, encourage but their action does not become part of the play. In ordinary situations of meeting and working together we can find these same patterns. What women have to say may simply remain unsaid. Or it is treated as a byplay—not really integral to the game. If it comes into play at all it is because a male player has picked it up and brought it into play *as his*.

Characteristically women talking with men use styles of talk which throw the control to others. As for example by interspersing their words with interjections which reassign the responsibility for its meaning to others, by saying 'you know' or failing to name objects or things or to complete sentences. Expectations of how much men and women should talk and for how long have an effect on how much and how long they are seen to talk. Caudill describes a supervisor of nurses as an assertive person, willing to express her opinion in unequivocal terms. Yet his data show that in meetings she spoke less on the average than the hospital administrative and psychiatric personnel, including a resident described as 'passive and withdrawn' (Caudill, 1958:249).

Candace West has made a study of differences between single-sex and mixed-sex conversations which focuses upon the differential rights to speak of men and women. She observed a variety of different 'devices' used by men, apparently with women's consent, which serve to maintain male control of the topics of conversation. For example, men tended to complete women's sentences, to give minimal responses to topics initiated and carried by women, and to interrupt without being sanctioned. Her study describes how men control conversation through the use of interruption and by withdrawing active participation when women are developing their topics (West, 1974).

In professional conversations we can also identify a collection of devices which may be used to restrict women's control of the development of topics. Among them are devices which are used to recognize or enter what women have said into the discourse under male sanction. For example, a suggestion or point contributed by a woman may be ignored at its point of origin. When it is re-introduced at a later point by a man, it is then 'recognized' and becomes part of the topic. Or if it is recognized at the time, it is re-attributed by the responder to another male (in the minutes of the meeting, it will appear as having been said by someone else). Or the next speaker after the woman may use a device such as, 'What Dorothy really means is . . .'. Or the woman's turn is followed by a pause, following which the topic is picked up at the previous speaker's turn as if she had not spoken.

Celia Gilbert makes a vivid symbolic presence of this circle and the practices which exclude women in her poem 'On Refusing Your Invitation to Come to Dinner.' The dinner table reflects (both metaphorically and actually) the unspoken presence of women. Gilbert looks back on it from the standpoint of one who has already learned another practice of her being. She writes:

> 'But I am forgetting the language,
> sitting has become difficult,
> and the speaking, intolerable,
> to say, 'how interesting'
> makes me weep.
> I can no longer bear to hear
> the men around the table laugh,
> argue, agree,
> then pause, politely
> while we speak,
> their breath held in, exhaled
> when we've finished,
> politely,
> then turn to the real conversation,
> the unspoken expectation of applause' (Gilbert, 1979).

The interpersonal is symbolic of the circle of men across time and space whose discourse has excluded women. But it is also the actual practice of the circle. It is a practice we can and probably have experienced in our working and our personal lives. At the interpersonal level it is not a conspiracy among men which they impose on women. It is a complementary social process between women and men. Women are complicit in the social practices of their silence.

The practices extend to women's participation in art, music, literature, science, in the health sciences, in education. The figures which show us where women are in education, represent an organization of social relations at a deeper level, extending throughout the educational structure and its articulation to the society which it both serves and structures. In the educational system at all levels, and in all aspects, women have access and participate so that they may be present as subordinates, as marginal. Their training and education ensure that *at every level of competence and leadership* there will be a place for them which is inferior and subordinate to the positions of men.

VI

It is important to recognize that the deprivation of authority and the ways in which women have been trained to practise the complement of male controlled 'topic development' (West, 1974), have the effect of making it difficult for women to treat one another as relevant figures. We have difficulty in asserting authority for ourselves. We have difficulty in grasping authority for women's voices and for what women have to say. We are thus deprived of the essential basis for developing among ourselves the forms of thought and images which express the situations we share and make it possible to begin to work together. Women have taken for granted that our thinking is to be authorized by an external source of authority. Bostock tells us that this is because we live in a world dominated intellectually by men. As a consequence women's opinions tend to conform to the approved standards and these in the last analysis are men's. This means that women's opinions are sharply separated from their lived experience and that as they begin to develop their own opinions, they have to check them against their collective experience as women rather than merely their personal experience (Bostock, 1972). But it has not been easy for women to find their own voices convincing. It is hard for us to listen to each other. The voice of our own experience is equally defective.

Lack of authority, then, is lack of authority for ourselves and for other women. We have become familiar in the women's movement with the importance of women learning to relate to one another. We need also to learn how to treat what other women say as a source and basis for our own work and thinking. We need to learn to treat one another as the authoritative speakers of our experience and concerns.

It is only when as women we can treat one another, and ourselves, as those who count for one another that we can break out of our silence—to make ourselves heard; to protest against the violence done to women (and there is violence done); to organize politically for justice and equality in law, to work together to become more effective in the organizations which represent us; to work together to resist the unloading of economic crisis on to women and, as educators, to advance, develop and pass on to our children (our daughters and our sons) a knowledge of women's history and experience, of our poetry, our art, our political skills and confidence. This is the road to full and equal membership in our society for women.

The institutionalized practices of excluding women from the ideological work of society are the reason we have a history constructed largely from the perspective of men, and largely about men. This is why we have so few women poets and why the records of those who survived the hazards of attempting poetry are so imperfect (Bernikow, 1974). This is why we know so little of women visionaries, thinkers and political organizers (Rowbotham, 1973). This is why we have an anthropology which tells us about other societies from the perspective of men and hence has so distorted the cross-cultural record that it may now be impossible to learn what we might have known about how women lived in other forms of society. This is why we have a sociology which is written from the perspective of positions in a male-dominated ruling class and is set up in terms of the relevances of the institutional power structures which constitute those positions (Bernard, 1973). This is why in English literature there is a corner called 'women in literature' or 'women novelists' or the like, but an over-all critical approach to literature which assumes that it is written by men and perhaps even largely for men. This is why the assumptions of psychological research (Sherif, 1977) and of educational research and philosophy take for granted male experience, male orientation and concerns, and treat as normative masculine modes of being.

The ideological practices of our society provide women with forms of thought and knowledge which constrain us to treat ourselves as objects. We have learned to practise, as Rowbotham points out, a nihilistic relation to our own subjectivity and experience (Rowbotham, 1974). We have learned to live inside a discourse which is not ours and which expresses and describes a landscape in which we are alienated and which preserves that alienation as integral to its practice. In a short story Doris Lessing describes a girl growing up in Africa whose consciousness has been wholly formed within traditional British literary culture. Her landscape, her cosmology, her moral relations, her botany, are those of the English novels and fairytales. Her own landscape, its forms of life, her immediate everyday world do not fully penetrate and occupy her consciousness. They are not named (Lessing, 1966). Lessing's story is a paradigm of the situation of women in our society. Its general culture is not ours.

Clearly the issue is more than bias. It is more than simply an omission of certain kinds of topics. It involves taking up the standpoint of women as an experience of being, of society, of social and personal process which must be given form and expression in the culture, whether as knowledge, as art or literature or politically. This is the work we see now in progress in many forms in the women's movement and beyond. When we speak of 'women's studies' we are identifying a broad range of work which develops and makes way for research, philosophic and theological thinking, poetry, literature, the study of art, history, sociology, law and other fields giving expression to and building essential knowledge of this whole range of seeing the world from women's place in it. Women's studies identifies space in universities, colleges and schools making room for these developments and opening a conduit into the educational system for the astonishing work that is now being done by women in art, philosophy, poetry, scholarship and in political and social theory.

REFERENCES

Aries, Philippe. 1975. *Centuries of Childhood*. Penguin Books, Harmondsworth, Middlesex.
Bart, Pauline. 1971. Depression in middle-aged women. In: Gornick, V. and Moran, Barbara K. (eds), *Women in Sexist Society*. New American Library, New York.
de Beauvoir, Simone. 1961. *The Second Sex*. Bantam Books, New York.
Bernard, Jessie. 1964. *Academic Women*. New American Library, New York.
Bernikow, Louise. 1974. *The World Split Open: Four Centuries of Women Poets in England and America* 1552–1950. Vintage Books, New York.
Bostock, Anya. 1972. Talk on BBC Third Programme published in *The Listener* (August).
Canadian Teachers' Federation Status of Women Committee. 1978. *The Declining Majority*. Canadian Teachers' Federation (April).
Caudill, William. 1958. *The Psychiatric Hospital as a Small Society*. Harvard University Press, Cambridge, Mass.
Chesler, Phyllis. 1972. Patient and Patriarch: women in the psychotherapeutic relationship. In: Gornick, Vivian and Moran, Barbara (eds), *Women in Sexist Society: Studies in Power and Powerlessness*, pp. 362–92. Signet Books, New York.
Donnison, Jean. 1977. *Midwives and Medical Men: A History of Inter-Professional Rivalries and Women's Rights*. Heinemann, London.
Ellman, Mary. 1968. *Thinking about Women*. Harcourt Brace Jovanovich, New York.
Fidell, L. S. 1970. Empirical verification of sex discrimination in hiring practices in psychology. *American Psychologist* 25(12), 1094–7.
Freeman, Jo. 1971. The social construction of the second sex. In: Garskof, Michele Hoffnung (ed.), *Roles Women Play: Readings Towards Women's Liberation*, pp. 123–41. Brooks/Cole Publishing, Belmont, California.
Fox, Margaret, 1710. *A Brief Collection of Remarkable Passages & Occurrences*. London.
Gilbert, Celia. 1977. *Queen of Darkness*. Viking Press, New York.
Goldberg, Philip. 1969. Are women prejudiced against women? *Transaction* (April), 28–30.
Gornick, V. 1972. Woman as outsider. In: Gornick, Vivian and Moran, Barbara (eds), *Women in Sexist Society: Studies in Power and Powerlessness*, pp. 126–44. Signet Books, New York.
des Jacques, Smache. 1972. Women in the French Revolution: the thirteenth brumaire of Olympe De Gouges, with notes on French amazon battalions. In: Ann Forfreedom (ed.), *Women Out of History: A Herstory*, pp. 131–40. Peace Press, Culver City, California.
Jencks, Christopher *et al.* 1972. *Inequality: A Reassessment of the Effect of Family & Schooling in America*. Basic Books, New York.

Kahn, J. and Nurstein, J. 1964. *Unwillingly to School*. Pergamon Press, London.

King, Elinor, Smith, D. E. and David, S. J. (eds). 1975. *Women Look at Psychiatry*.

Komisar, Lucy. 1972. The image of woman in advertising. In: Gornick, Vivian and Moran, Barbara (eds), *Women in Sexist Society: Studies in Power and Powerlessness*, pp. 304–17. Signet Books, New York.

Labour Canada Women's Bureau. 1973. *Women in the Labour Force, Facts and Figures*, 1973. Queen's Printer, Ottawa.

Millett, Kate. 1971. *Sexual Politics*. Avon Books, New York.

Mitchell, Juliet. 1972. *Women's Estate*. Penguin Books, Harmondsworth, Middlesex.

Olsen, Tillie. 1977. One out of twelve: women who are writers in our century. In: Ruddick, Sara and Daniel, Pamela (eds), *Working It Out: 23 Women Writers, Artists, Scientists and Scholars Talk About Their Lives and Work*. Pantheon Books, New York.

Osen, Lynn M. 1974. *Women in Mathematics*. MIT Press, Cambridge, Mass.

Rowbotham, Sheila. 1973. *Women, Resistance and Revolution*. Penguin Books, Harmondsworth, Middlesex.

Rowbotham, Sheila. 1974. *Women's Consciousness, Man's World*. Penguin Books, Harmondsworth, Middlesex.

Sherif, Carolyn Woods. 1977. Bias in psychology, paper presented at a conference on The Prism of Sex, Women's Research Centre, Wisconsin, November.

Strodtbeck, F. I. and Mann, R. D. 1956. Sex role differentiation in jury deliberations. *Sociometry* **19** (March), 9–10.

Szasz, Thomas S. (ed.) 1973. *The Age of Madness: The History of Involuntary Hospitalization* presented in selected texts. Doubleday Anchor Books, Garden City, New York.

Thrupp, Sylvia L. 1962. *The Merchant Class of Mediaeval London* 1300–1500. Ann Arbor Paperbacks, University of Michigan Press, Ann Arbor, Michigan.

Walsh, Mary Roth. 1977. *Doctors Wanted, No Women Need Apply: Sexual Barriers in the Medical Profession*, 1835–975. Yale University Press, New Haven.

Vickers, Jill McCalla and Adam, June. 1977. *But Can You Type? Canadian Universities and the Status of Women*. Clarke Irwin and Co. and Canadian Association of University Teachers.

West, Candy. 1973. Sexism and conversation: everything you always wanted to know about Sachs (But were afraid to ask), MA thesis, Department of Sociology, University of California, Santa Barbara, California.

Wollstonecraft, Mary. 1967. *A Vindication of the Rights of Women*. W. W. Norton, New York.

2

Obesity and Women—II. A Neglected Feminist Topic

Orland W. Wooley,
Susan C. Wooley
and Sue R. Dyrenforth

'At the next light, the ricksha "boy" who pulls alongside the car has gray hair, and his stubbly face is streaming with sweat. He is very thin, except for his left leg below the knee, which elephantiasis has made thick as the trunk of a tree. The traffic moves. He half-stumbles, half-jogs ahead, pulling a comely, very fat Indian woman. As the ricksha begins to move, she reaches into the shawl of her sari, extracts a sweet, which she carefully unwraps, and eats. In Calcutta, the relationship between rich and poor always has been as obvious as that.'

In this excerpt from an article (Allman, 1977) on Calcutta, a lazy fat woman becomes, for the American observer, the symbol of the callous selfishness of an entire civilization. This familiar moral criticism of obesity is peculiarly inappropriate to American society, where in fact, obesity is a condition not of the rich and powerful, but of the poor and especially of women. As the Duchess of Windsor's famous quip, 'A woman can never be too rich or too thin,' implies, slenderness has become an elitist value in Western society.

'We are not exactly slender at Paris, but few of us are as fat as those grand New Yorkers. It is especially pitiable to watch the eyes of the ladies grow round with greed as pheasants and lobsters, sorbets and desserts, are presented them. Even those who do not betray their appetite by staring, who continue to talk with animation of other subjects, give themselves away when, without warning, a polite and cultivated syllable will drown in an excess of saliva' (Gore Vidal, 1976).

It is precisely because thinness is unattainable by more than a fortunate few in our society that it is so valued. As the Vidal quote (1976) suggests, women who aspire to success must somehow transcend, deny or suppress appetite. And yet, there is no evidence that obesity is due to unusual appetite or abnormal food intake. Scientific study has, so far, failed to uncover the causes of obesity or to provide an effective cure. Not surprisingly, attempts to sustain semi-starvation in the pursuit of increasingly stringent ideals of slenderness usually fail, frequently creating new problems. A few feminists and other writers, whose work will be reviewed in this paper, have begun to articulate some of the important political implications of these facts. Essential to an understanding of their thesis are the documented failure of reducing diets to achieve their purpose (Wooley and Wooley, 1979), the stigmatization of overweight, and the selective pressure on women to achieve unrealistic cultural ideals.

THE STIGMA OF OBESITY: HATRED OF FAT CHILDREN

The intensity of shame engendered by overweight can only be understood by recognizing the extreme ostracism and hatred to which overweight children are subjected. Perhaps nothing can better illustrate that prejudice than studies of attitudes toward children of different body builds. These studies show that, at an early age, children of both sexes develop distinct aversions to chubby bodies and preferences for athletic or lean ones. The child whose build is socially 'deviant' comes, early in life, to be regarded by others as responsible for his/her 'condition,' and deserving of social disapproval and, sooner or later, is subjected to pressures to restrict food intake in order to 'correct' his/her condition. Failure to do so is seen as 'weakness,' 'wanting to be fat,' or even as a masochistic desire for rejection.

In a report of the attitudes of mesomorphic, endomorphic and ectomorphic[1] children toward body builds, Staffieri (1967) reports that 6-10-year-old male children responded in a uniformly favorable way to silhouettes of mesomorphic male children, and a uniformly unfavorable way to endomorphic silhouettes. They used the following words to describe the endomorphic silhouette: cheats, dirty, argues, gets teased, forgets, lazy, lies, sloppy, mean, ugly, stupid. Words applied to the ectomorph were: quiet, (does not) fight, afraid, weak. Words reserved for the mesomorph: strong, best friend, (does not) worry, lots of friends, (not) nervous, happy, helps others, polite, (not) lonely, (not) sick, healthy, honest, brave, good looking, (not) sad, smart, (not) tired, neat. Female children (Staffieri, 1972) attribute virtually all the same negative characteristics to the obese body build as do males but add: worries, fights, naughty, sad, and lonely, suggesting an even greater recognition of the social isolation which accompanies overweight. The attitudes of

---

[1] Throughout this chapter the words used to describe heavier vs slimmer persons are those used by the original researchers. For example, endomorphic is used by some investigators as a synonym for fat, chubby, or a 'roundness and plumpness' of physique; 'mesomorphic' and 'ectomorphic' are used as synonyms of 'average' and 'thin' respectively. These three terms are descriptive and correspond only in a rough, general way to Sheldon's (1940) somatotypes. Other terms such as obese, overweight, chubby and fat will be used to designate the relatively heavier groups examined in the studies being described and reflect the researcher's own descriptions of them.

overweight children toward the three different body builds were the same as those of the non-overweight children. Sixty-seven per cent of the girls preferred to look mesomorphic and 33 per cent to look ectomorphic; none preferred the endomorphic shape.

In another study, Lerner reports that males, 10-20 years of age, believed an endomorphic adult male to: 'be the poorest athlete,' 'drink the most,' 'smoke three packs of cigarettes a day,' 'eat the most,' 'be the least likely to be chosen leader,' and 'make the worst soldier.' Ectomorphs were believed to 'eat the least' and 'make a poor father.' Mesomorphy was almost exclusively positive. 'There is considerable overlap in the socially negative stereotypes associated with the endomorph and ectomorph body builds' (Lerner, 1969: 139). This finding is in contrast to the studies (to be discussed in a following section) which show that females almost always like 'small.'

Lerner and Gelbert (1969) in a study of 45 white, urban kindergarten children, 5-6 years of age, report that '86 per cent of those children who were consistent in their choices showed an aversion for "chubbiness" when tested with headless photographs of chubby, average and thin children in bathing suits.'

Lerner and Korn report that both 'chubby' and 'average' 5-year-old, 15-year-old and 20-year-old males assign to endomorphic drawings descriptive phrases which they themselves judge 'bad' and, to mesomorphic drawings phrases which they judge 'good.' 'One may conclude that both chubby and average Ss share a common body-build stereotype' (Lerner and Korn, 1972: 915). Furthermore: 'In all age groups, chubby Ss viewed themselves as having more of the attributes they associated with body types other than the endomorph, [suggesting] that these Ss have a rejecting attitude towards their own physique and [implying] a negative body concept' (op. cit. 915). Of the 90 'chubby' and 90 average males who were subjects in this study, only three (each of whom was an 'average' 5-year-old) indicated a desire to look like the endomorphic drawing.

Lerner (1973) found that 66 first, second and third grade children from a school in a semi-rural setting preferred to maintain a greater 'personal space distance' from an endomorphic than from a mesomorphic or ectomorphic child. The children indicated how close they wanted to come to endo-, meso- and ectomorphic children by placing a marker along a line at one end of which were placed side-view drawings of these three body-types.

Two reports (Richardson et al., 1961; Goodman et al., 1963) comparing children's attitudes to various kinds of handicaps reveal that drawings of obese children were consistently ranked lower than those of a child with crutches and a brace, a child sitting in a wheelchair with a blanket covering both legs, a child with the left hand missing, or a child with a facial disfigurement on the left side of the mouth. Out of eight samples of mentally normal children, 10–11 years of age (sample size ranging from 42 to 163), 7 samples ranked the obese child last. Only a sample of 'white Jewish' children of low socio-economic status in New York City ranked the obese child anywhere but last (i.e., third). The authors speculate that Jewish cultural practices and values associated with eating are different from those of other Americans: 'The well-fed stockily built Jewish child is often viewed by other Jews as one who is both healthy and *loved*' (Goodman *et al.*, 1963: 434. Goodman *et al.*'s emphasis).

Particularly revealing are the rankings of a 9th sample, consisting of 72 adults including nurses, physical and occupational therapists, physicians, psychologists and social workers who ranked the obese child last.

In another study by an independent group of investigators (Maddox *et al.*, 1968) using the same drawings, 200 adults, 'deliberately chosen to sample populations presumed to value fatness, or at least to be tolerant of over-weight,' i.e., people of low socioeconomic status, including blacks and overweight people, ranked the obese child last. Additional data suggested that it is because the obese are held responsible for their condition that they are disliked.

Matthews and Westie (1966) report that 144 high school students in a small midwestern city preferred to be at a greater 'social distance' from an obese child than from handicapped children depicted by drawings. 'Social distance' was assessed by a scale of graded statements ranging from 'would exclude this type of person from my school,' to 'would be willing to marry this type of person.'

These studies document the hatred of obese children by other children and by adults. The impact this hatred has on the individual child is probably irreversible. It is not only the obese child who suffers from this hatred; anti-fat attitudes learned in childhood no doubt become the basis for self-hatred among those who become overweight at later ages, and a source of anxiety and self-doubt for anyone fearful of becoming overweight.

As Maddox *et al.* state, 'the incidence of socially deviant overweight is a function of shared definitions of *best* weight and tolerable deviations from that standard' (Maddox *et al.*, 1968: 297). The papers reviewed below attack the current standards and the assumptions implicit in them. Three themes emerge:

(1) Fat is a woman's problem.
(2) Fat is an ethical, political problem more than a medical, psychiatric or behavioral problem.
(3) A call for different attitudes toward and treatments of obesity.

FAT IS A WOMAN'S PROBLEM

Studies of attitudes toward endomorphic children reveal that children of both sexes, and of all body builds, adopt the prevailing negative stereotypes associated with endomorphy. However, at later ages, beginning with adolescence, females are more affected than males by this prejudicial climate.

Kurtz had 89 male and 80 female white middle-class college students rate themselves (using the Semantic Differential[2]) on 30 'body concepts' (including profile; size of bust/chest, hips, waist; body build; weight). He concluded: 'The hypothesis was confirmed that college women have a more clearly differentiated body concept than men. This finding suggests a greater awareness and concern over bodily appearance may be more acceptable in the female than in the male' (Kurtz, 1969: 628). He also found that the females rated their bodies higher on the 'evaluative' dimension of the Semantic Differential than the men, but saw their bodies as less 'potent,' and less 'active.' He speculates that 'greater body differentiation and high evaluation in the female is related to her lack of actual social or political power in American society' (op. cit. 628).

Clifford reports that 194 adolescent females, 11–19 years of age, were more dissatisfied with, or more critical of their bodies, than were 146 male adolescents of the same age range. These subjects rated 45 'body-satisfaction' items; the females rated weight, looks, legs, waist, and hips lowest, while the five features least liked by the males were weight, waist, teeth, running and posture. 'Females may be more critical of their bodies because of the relatively greater amount of emphasis placed on buying clothing, personal adornment, and standards of beauty and appearance for women' (op. cit. 124).

Jourard and Secord present evidence that there is a shared 'ideal female figure' and that, among 60 female college students, satisfaction with one's own height, weight, bust, waist, and hips was a function of how closely matched perceived and ideal dimensions were. As a group, these women perceived themselves as too tall, as weighing too much, as too big in the waist and hips, but not big enough in the bust. 'The size specifications of the ideal female figure in our culture seem to be rather restrictive, i.e., they are difficult to attain. In general, the ideal could be paraphrased: "It is good to be smaller than you are in all dimensions except bust". None of the women in our sample had physical dimensions that were identical with all of their ideal self-ratings, and none of the women rated positively all of their body parts. . . . [A] woman's status and security [may be] highly conditioned by perceived and demonstrated attractiveness to males—irrespective of her skills, interests, values, etc.; hence, if she does not feel or appear "beautiful," she feels a loss of self-esteem, i.e. insecure. . . . Since "ideal" proportions appear to be difficult for many women fully to attain in our culture, it seems warranted to assert that the ideal, insofar as it is internalized by women, is indirectly responsible for much anxiety and insecurity among

[2] C. Osgood, G. Suci, and P. Tannenbaum, 1957. The Measurement of Meaning. University of Illinois Press, Urbana.

members of that sex. . . . [The] ideal . . . produces self-hate, guilt, and insecurity when it is not fulfilled [and this accounts] for the apparently widespread efforts among women in American society to mold and sculpture their bodies toward the ideal, by corsetry, dieting, exercise, and camouflage' (Jourard and Secord, 1955: 246).

Douty *et al.* (1974) report that 54 of 91 (59 per cent) female college students rated themselves low on 'satisfaction with figure,' even though 'few of these *Ss* would attract negative attention because they were obviously different from societal expectations.' If these women, who as a group were within the 'desirable weight' limits used by medical and behavioral investigators and therapists to define obesity, are dissatisfied with the way they look and are presumably adversely affected by this dissatisfaction, then it is a safe bet that women whose weight is higher than these limits are even more dissatisfied and adversely affected.

Beck *et al.* report that 115 college women rated silhouettes of female figures with large buttocks, large breasts, and a 'proportionately "large" overall' female figure as less preferred than silhouettes of figures with small buttocks, 'moderately small' breasts, and a 'proportionately "moderate" overall (standard)' female figure. On the basis of these results and of personality tests scores, the authors speculate: 'Women who select smaller female breasts and buttocks are, in general, less traditionally feminine individuals who desire to achieve in many ways and to pursue academic goals. . . . The women of this study may associate the more ample female body with a culturally stereotyped picture of the woman as "wife and mother," while the smaller (thinner) female body is associated with greater personal career freedom' (Beck *et al.*, 1976: 1209). These results show that college females prefer smallness in women. A study by Halmi *et al.* (1977) showed that 86 10–18-year-old females (from Iowa City schools) consistently *overestimated* the width of their own face, chest, waist, hips, and 'the greatest depth from front to back of the body below the waist.' These last two studies together suggest that, in general, young females see smallness as an ideal, but perceive themselves as falling short of that ideal.

The studies reviewed thus far show that fat is a woman's more than a man's problem because less deviation from 'ideal' is allowed women. A study by Monello and Mayer reveals the psychological/emotional price paid by women whose body builds are not within acceptable limits. Responses to projective tests of 100 obese girls, 13–17 years of age, attending a weight reduction camp were compared to those of 75 nonobese girls (same age range) attending a 'typical summer camp next door.' Highly statistically significant differences between the two groups were found; the obese girls scored higher on items measuring 'passivity,' 'withdrawal,' 'blocking responses,' 'family conflict' and 'concern about weight status.' These authors note the close similarity of this pattern of characteristics with that shown by ethnic and racial minorities: 'When obese subjects demonstrate attitudes similar to those resulting from ethnic and racial prejudice, it is not far fetched to say that obese persons in the United States may form a minority group suffering from prejudice and discrimination' (Monello and Mayer, 1963: 38). They compare the obese girls' 'obsessive concern' with weight to chronic feelings of helplessness, anxiety, and impending doom experienced by victims of racial discrimination and anti-Semitism.

One of the authors' patients made the following entries in her journal:

'How did I every arrive at this severe state of self-hatred? Little by little over the years. I had been prodded, badgered, passed judgement on by so many people who had been important in my environment. Mother, sister, brother, husband, children, in-laws, distant relatives, and friends. Soon it seemed everyone had to be thinking the same thing. Until my self-esteem eroded to a point almost beyond tolerating' (15 November). 'The more I hated myself the better a job I thought I was doing. The hate snowballed until I was so encumbered by lack of self-esteem that I entered a state of inertia' (16 November). 'A mountain of fat, great volumes of larded flab, covered with over-stretched and sagging skin. Buried deep within is a bit of joy slowly drowning in the emolient folds. Hope too is suffering the death-agony, going down for the third time in the enormous body of fat. There is only one cure for the indignities. . . . Marking time, counting calories, recording activities, avoiding people, hiding misery, extravagantly wasting my life' (29 December).

Two additional studies show that the price paid by women having a 'deviant' body build can be more than just psychological/emotional. Goldblatt *et al.* report data (collected from 1660 adult residents of 'Midtown Manhattan') which demonstrate that compared to nonobese women, overweight women are much less likely to achieve a higher socio-economic status, and much more likely to achieve a lower status than their parents. No such relationship was found among the men studied. They also report that, although the percentage of *men* who were 'thin' was the same for all three social classes (i.e., 10 per cent, 9 per cent and 12 per cent for low, middle and high SES, respectively), the percentage of *women* who were 'thin' was directly proportional to the social class level (i.e., 9 per cent, 19 per cent and 37 per cent for low, middle and high SES, respectively). The authors state; 'In the Midtown [Manhattan] society we do not have to look far to see the image of the slim, attractive female as portrayed throughout the popular culture. . . . A selection process may operate so that in any status-conferring situation, such as a promotion at work or marriage to a higher status male, thinner women may be preferentially selected over their competitors' (Goldblatt *et al.,* 1965: 1042–1043).

Canning and Mayer found that among the 1964 graduating classes in the high schools of a large middle-class suburban community, 23.3 per cent of the females were overweight ('ponderal-index ratio,' or height in inches divided by the cube root of weight in pounds, less than 12.4), but only 11.2 per cent of the female college freshmen in 'one of the Seven Sister Colleges' in 1964 were overweight. Moreover, while 51.9 per cent of the nonobese high school women went to college the year after graduation, only 31.6 per cent of the obese girls did. The obese and nonobese women did *not* differ on objective measures of intellectual ability and achievement or on the percentage who applied for college admission. The corresponding figures for men were: 18 per cent of the high school seniors and 13 per cent of the college freshmen at an unspecified Ivy League school were obese; 53.3 per cent of the non-obese and 49.9 per cent of the obese high school students went to college (difference not statistically significant).

Canning and Mayer state: 'If obese adolescents have difficulty in attending college, a substantial proportion may experience a drop in social class, or fail to advance beyond present levels. Education, occupation, and income are social-class variables that are strongly interrelated. A vicious circle, therefore, may begin as a result of college-admission discrimination, preventing the obese from rising in the social-class system' (Canning and Mayer, 1966: 1174).

The articles discussed so far have been primarily empirical and conclusions have been more or less constrained by the findings. There are a number of papers which, although they do not include new data, reach similar conclusions and take stronger stands on the issues raised by this knowledge.

Cahnman, in a paper entitled 'The stigma of obesity,' concludes on the basis of the last two studies discussed above that 'obesity, especially as far as girls are concerned, is not so much a mark of low SES as a condemnation to it' (Cahnman, 1968: 290).

Margaret Mackenzie (1975): 'As a cultural disease, obesity is not limited to those who weigh more than the ideal. Especially among women there are those who believe they are obese when they weigh less than the insurance norms. Usually, their ideas of the normal for themselves come from their notion of what their husbands or lovers expect of them.'

Ann Scott Beller writes: 'The fact that females are, from birth onward, fatter than their male counterparts may seem on the face of it a biological injustice as undeserved as any social or economic injustice exercised upon women by a male-dominated social system—especially to women who tend to run [sic] to more than their fair share of fat in the first place. We live in a culture that values leanness in both sexes; if there is any particular lesson for feminists in this preference it may be that the ideal of feminine beauty has thus come increasingly, within the span of the past half century, to reflect a male ideal model in preference to a typically female one. The status assumptions implicit in this choice are interesting. People tend to ape their betters, and women's aspirations to the unmodulated physiques of men express unvoiced, and until recently probably largely unconscious, judgements about the nature of male status and privilege as compared to their own. But from an anthropometric point of view the trend is a dubious one: female fleshiness is a fact of biological life and one that has every appearance of having been programmed into the species long ago by nature. . . . In the context of the new feminism, therefore, it may be well to remember that, for whatever reasons, the present model is one that has by and large been imposed on women by women: men's pinup magazines have usually dealt in somewhat more biometrically realistic images and ideals' (Beller, 1977: 57–58).

Robin Morgan, in an article in *Ms*. magazine entitled 'The politics of body-image,' writes: 'And what about confronting the very space our bodies inhabit; who defines it? In this patriarchial world, space-taking by a woman is seen as unattractive and attraction is the one bargaining power she is allowed.' Men have assigned to women 'the realm of the physical. The result [is] that women feel at once mired in and alienated from [their] bodies . . .' (Morgan, September 1977: 47).

Boskind-Lodahl, in 'Cinderella's stepsisters: a feminist perspective of anorexia nervosa and bulimia,' a paper dealing with 'bulimarexia,' a syndrome of alternating binge-ing and starving, quite common among college women, believes that bulimarexics accept the 'stereotype of femininity—that of the accommodating, passive dependent woman' (Boskind-Lodahl, 1976: 345). 'I came to understand that their obsessive pursuit of thinness constitutes not only an acceptance of this ideal but an exaggerated striving to achieve it' (*ibid*. 346). 'Why is it that the bulimarexic gives men the power to reject her? Why does she give up her own power and make men larger than life? A reasonable answer . . . lies in our heritage of sexual inequality' (*ibid*. 354).

Boskind-Lodahl and Sirlin write: 'We came to understand that the bulimarexic's problem is that she identifies *too* strongly with what she perceives as the proper female role. She doesn't reject her femininity; she becomes a caricature of it (Boskind-Lodahl and Sirlin, 1977: 52).

Aldebaran, in an article which appeared in the *Journal of Radical Therapy*, writes: 'Most people who worry about their weight are women, and fat is a women's problem. The current standards of beauty are set so thin that there is hardly any woman who does not consider herself "overweight." And women are brought up to regard [their] bodies as objects to be sacrificed for beauty. There is no doubt that a chief reason why the truth about fat and eating is ignored by doctors and psychotherapists is because fat is seen as a "trivial" woman's issue. Mass starvation of women is the modern American culture's equivalent of foot-binding, lip-stretching, and other forms of woman-mutilation' (Aldebaran, 1975: 6).

Susie Orbach takes a position which is *politically* compatible with those of Boskind-Lodahl and Sirlin and Aldebaran, i.e., fat is part of the greater problem of sexual inequality, but, implicitly assuming that they are 'compulsive eaters,' she hypothesizes that fat women overeat *because* of, or *in response to*, the conditions of sexual aggression.

'Fat is a social disease, and fat is a feminist issue. Fat is *not* about lack of self-control or lack of will power. . . . It is a response to the inequality of the sexes' (Susie Orbach, 1978: 18). 'For many women, compulsive eating and being fat have become one way to avoid being marketed or seen as the ideal women: "My fat says 'screw you' to all who want me to be the perfect mom, sweetheart, maid and whore . . ." ' (*ibid.* 21).

FAT IS AN ETHICAL OR POLITICAL PROBLEM MORE THAN A MEDICAL, PSYCHIATRIC OR BEHAVIORAL PROBLEM

This theme takes three forms:

(1) *Questioning the assumptions that the obese 'overeat' and are not healthy*

Cahnman quotes *Obesity and Health*, a government publication (1966): 'The association of body fat and mortality below the level of frank obesity is not clear.' He says a 'moral problem is posed, if those who are not in fact responsible for their condition, nevertheless are held responsible for it' (Cahnman, 1968: 286). He speaks of a 'moralistic diagnosis' which includes the 'unspoken assumption that what is needed first and foremost in the treatment of the "immature" obese is the repression of ravenous appetites; the corresponding materialistic therapy consists in a strict dietary regimen, with or without the assistance of drugs' (*ibid.* 287).

Aldebaran: 'It is incredible that no one has protested how psychological assumptions about fat people contradict material evidence. Most fat people do *not* eat more than most slim people. Most fat people do *not* want to be fat' (Aldebaran, 1975: 5).

Later she writes: 'When the PhDs and MDs . . . talk about "hyperphagia" or "overeating" they get into a mind-fuck where aesthetics, instead of hunger, is the reference point for what fat people should eat. Both a fat person and a slim person would feel constant hunger trying to live on 1600 calories per day. But whereas this food intake would be considered "under-eating" or "semi-starvation" for a slim person, it is exactly what nutritionists mean by "overeating" for a fat person—who remains fat on it' (*ibid.* 5).

In another article 'Fat liberation—a luxury?' (1977), Aldebaran says: 'There is no way to know at this time whether fat is inherently healthy or unhealthy because virtually all studies quoted as evidence that fat is unhealthy were done on fat people who were severely persecuted for their weight, and in most cases were chronic dieters.'

(2) *Rejection of obesity as a psychiatric problem*

Boskind-Lodahl and Sirlin: 'We concluded that we weren't dealing with a strictly psychiatric problem but with a problem of female socialization and its reinforcement by the media's steady bombardment of "ideal" female images' (Boskind-Lodahl and Sirlin, 1977: 52).

Aldebaran (1977) in an open letter to therapists with fat clients writes: 'You see fat as suicide, I see weight loss as murder—genocide, to be precise—the systematic murder of a biological minority by organized medicine, acting on behalf of the law- and custom-makers of this society.'

Aldebaran: 'Psychotherapy observes our problems and tells us we overeat to compensate for them. True, some of us are lonely, sexually-repressed, and dependent on the approval of other people. Aren't some thin people, too? And who wouldn't be, if other people shun you, jeer at your body and label you "disgusting," if you are embarrassed and hungry almost every day of your life? Who wouldn't be obsessed with food after being told that all her problems are due to her not being *in control* of food?' (Aldebaran, 1975: 5; original emphasis).

(3) *Questioning the belief that fat people should diet*

Aldebaran, in the letter to therapists of fat clients (1977): 'You see your role as therapist to help fat people follow doctors' advice to reduce by helping us stay on reducing diets. I want to impress on you how much harm you are doing. . . . Reducing programs are . . . *ineffective* at producing permanent weight loss, and this . . . failure is well-known in the medical literature' (original emphasis).

Later in the same article: 'The assumption that making fat people lose weight will make fat people's mortality rate the same as slim people's is absurd. To assume so is to ignore enormous amounts of evidence that fat people differ genetically, and metabolically from slim people. A fat person who loses weight is no more a real slim person than a white person who gets a suntan is a real black person. . . . By relying on weight loss as a cure for serious disease, the medical profession plays statistical roulette with fat people's lives.'

In the same paper: 'The . . . failure of reducing diets is fat people's collective experience, and therapy tells us to ignore it. *You* can lose weight if *you* try hard enough. If *you* failed *you* were not motivated enough' (original emphasis).

Susie Orbach: 'Doctors are no less susceptible than other people to cultural ideas about beauty and thinness and frequently feel entitled to comment on the size of their patient's body even when their medical problems are not related to it. But women came to know that diets and guilt do not work, whether they come from doctors or magazines' (Orbach, 1978: 176).

CALLS FOR NEW ATTITUDES AND TREATMENTS

Deborah Berson and someone who calls herself Cathy Fatwoman writing in the *Radical Therapist* (1974) seek to change the attitudes of thin women who want to 'help' fat women: 'Perhaps thin women are not aware quite how humiliating and powerless a position it is to be defended from persecution, supported and encouraged in a diet by a thin friend who someplace in her caring soul still knows she's better and luckier than you.'

Boskind-Lodahl and Sirlin used group therapy, 'a social cure for a social neurosis. Female therapists were essential. They served as models for the younger women struggling to define new selves, and they share their own struggles with problems of self-worth, body image, and acceptability to men. . . . We wanted the therapy to illustrate the limited ways in which our culture teaches women to see and use their bodies. . . . Since their low opinion of themselves seemed crucial, we encouraged the women to become more assertive . . . [and] to develop their own interests and activities independent of men in their lives' (Boskind-Lodahl and Sirlin, 1977: 52). 'The therapists point out how women give men the power to demolish their self-respect by assuming that men define their worth in the first place. . . . [Eventually] the discussion drifted away from anger and fear toward the joyous discoveries that it is possible to live without desperately needing a man and that it is possible to like men' (*ibid*. 82).

Cahnman: 'In the case of the obese adolescent, especially the obese girl, the social fall from grace cannot be counteracted except by a change in the social-psychological environment, that is, by a removal of the prevailing stigmatizing attitude against the deviant "minority." The trouble is that this change is hard to bring about.' Later: 'If the disability of the obese rests with the pervasive sense of inadequacy which has been instilled in them, the cure will have to consist in a generous amount of confidence in their abilities. . . . As in other problem areas, so in the area of body shape and appearance, what is needed is an agreement of mutual respect for the common humanity of each and every one of us. That is the *irreducible minimum*' (Cahnman, 1968: 298–299, original emphasis).

Robin Morgan (1977) recommends that women:

> (1) 'Confront those medical practitioners, drug manufacturers, and chemical corporations who sell us our own disfigurements and deaths.'
> (2) 'Continue saying the unmentionable—cry rape and cry pornography . . . proclaim the existence of fat, vaginal fungus, dandruff, and other unspeakables great and small. Discover new ones and keep harping away at the old ones, because their unmentionability grows back, reinforced daily by our every waking moment.'

Susie Orbach believes the solution to the problem of obesity will come from women not medicine (doctors and drugs): 'Doctors, who are frequently male, overworked, untrained to see the social issues that have produced distress in their women patients and unlikely to face this kind of distress themselves, recommend tranquillizers and psycho-active drugs to lift the spirits of these women so that they can function well enough again to clean up their own kitchens and not be a nuisance to anyone. The underlying social cause of distress is not dealt with. Medication is offered, the women are drugged. The situation requires a major reorientation of medical and scientific education, organization and practice based on the demands of the women's health improvement' (Orbach, 1978: 184–185).

Aldebaran: 'Finally fat people are beginning to say we have a right to eat as much as we want, and no one has the right to persecute us for what we eat. This position is absolutely basic to fat liberation.

'Along with the right to eat, fat people are saying that we have a right to be fat. This is a powerful assertion for a fat person to make, in light of the mystification surrounding fat, and the persecution of fat. However, the right to be fat is only a theoretical right, for rightful or not, we are fat and our efforts to change ourselves almost always fail.

'One problem with the "right" to be fat is that it requires fat people to "choose" to remain fat in order to justify no longer dieting. Because of our conditioning we have to develop a way to move from self-hatred to self-love. Part of the process could be, "I want to be slim, and I recognize that my want is because of all the persecution I get for my weight." Nevertheless, I know that dieting oppresses fat people, and I'm not going to collude any more with my own oppression.

'The "right" to be fat leaves all sorts of loopholes for liberal bullshit like, "Sure you have a right to be fat, but don't you think there are better ways of solving your problems than eating them into oblivion?" We need proud emotions when dealing with these arguments. But when we're attacked by "scientific claims", we'd better be prepared to defend ourselves with knowledge and reasoning' (Aldebaran, 1975: 6).

CLOSING QUOTE FROM JUDITH THURMAN'S (*Ms.*, SEPTEMBER 1977) 'NEVER TOO THIN TO FEEL FAT'

'[E]ating, like dreaming, is a moment of true feeling. The body seizes that moment and keeps it for us tangibly, undeniably, unforgettably—as flesh. But that feeling is taken away from us at a certain age—subjected to language, interpreted by culture, assimilated by the values of other people. And what we "get back", what we finally "understand", is not our own. Fatness is an idea we consume at face value and which subsequently distracts us from the real experiences' (p. 48).

REFERENCES

Aldebaran. 1975. Uptight and hungry, the contradiction in psychology of fat. *RT: J. Radical Therapy* 5, 5–6.
Aldebaran. 1977. Fat liberation—A luxury? An open letter to radical (and other) therapists. Quotes taken from an unpublished manuscript supplied by the author; this article subsequently appeared in *State and Mind* 5, 34.
Allman, T. D. 1977. Calcutta's bounty. *Harper's* 255, 17.
Beck, S. B., Ward-Hull, C. I. and McLear, P. M. 1976. Variables related to women's somatic preferences of the male and female body. *J. Personality soc. Psychol.* 34, 1200–1210.
Beller, A. S. 1977. *Fat and Thin: A Natural History of Obesity*. Farrar, Straus & Giroux, New York.
Boskind-Lodahl, M. 1976. Cinderella's stepsisters: a feminist perspective on anorexia nervosa and bulimia. *Signs: J. Women Culture Soc.* 2, 341–356.

Boskind-Lodahl, M. and Sirlin J. 1977. The gorging-purging syndrome. *Psychology Today* **10**, 50.

Cahnman, W. J. 1968. The stigma of obesity. *Sociological* Q.**9**, 283–299.

Canning, H. and Mayer, J. 1966. Obesity—Its possible effect on college acceptance. *New Engl. J. Med.* **275**, 1172–1174.

Clifford, E. 1971. Body satisfaction in adolescence. *Percept. Mot. Skills* **33**, 119–125

Douty, H. I., Moore, J. B. and Hartford, D. 1974. Body characteristics in relation to life adjustment, body-image and attitudes of college females. *Percept. Mot Skills* **39**, 499–521.

Fatwoman, C. and Berson, D. 1974. The fat story on eating as an act of revolution. *RT: J. Radical Therapy* (formerly: *The Radical Therapist/Rough Times*) **4**, 16–17.

Goldblatt, P. B., Moore, M. E. and Stunkard, A. J. 1965. Social factors in obesity. *J. Am. med. Ass.* **192**, 1039–1044.

Goodman, N., Dornbusch, S. M., Richardson, S. A. and Hastorf, A. H. 1963. Variant reactions to physical disabilities. *Am. sociol. Rev.* **28**, 429–435.

Halmi, K. A., Goldberg, S. C. and Cunningham, S. 1977. Perceptual distortion of body image in adolescent girls: distortion of body image in adolescence. *Psychol. Med.* **7**, 253–257.

Jourard, S. M. and Secord, P. R. 1955. Body-cathexis and the ideal female figure. *J. abnorm. soc. Psychol.* **50**, 243–246.

Kurtz, R. M. 1969. Sex differences and variations in body attitudes. *J. consult. clin. Psychol.* **33**, 625–629.

Lerner, R. M. 1969. The development of stereotyped expectancies of body build-behavior relations. *Child Dev.* **40**, 137–141.

Lerner, R. M. 1973. The development of personal space schemata toward body build. *J. Psychol.* **84**, 229–235.

Lerner, R. M. and Gellert, E. 1969. Body build identification, preference, and aversion in children. *Devl. Psychol.* **5**, 256–462.

Lerner, R. M. and Korn, S. J. 1972. The development of body-build stereotypes in males. *Child Dev.* **43**, 908, 920.

Mackenzie, M. 1975. Self-control and moral responsibility, competence rationality: obesity as failure in American culture. Paper presented at American Anthropological Association Meeting.

Maddox, G. L., Beck, K. W. and Liederman, V. R. 1968. Overweight as social deviance and disability. *J. Hlth soc. Behavior* **9**, 287–298.

Mathews, V. and Westie, C. 1966. A preferred method for obtaining rankings: reactions to physical handicaps. *Am. sociol. Rev.* **31**, 851–854.

Monello, L. F. and Mayer, J. 1963. Obese adolescent girls: an unrecognized 'minority' group? *Am. J. clin. Nutr.* **13**, 35–39.

Morgan, R. 1977. The politics of body-image. *Ms. Magazine* **6**, 47–49.

Obesity and Health. 1966. (Published by the U.S. Department of Health, Education and Welfare—U.S. Public Health Service, 1966; quote taken from p. 6, according to Cahnman, reference above.)

Orbach, S. 1978. *Fat Is a Feminist Issue: The Anti-Diet Guide to Permanent Weight Loss.* Paddington Press, New York and London.

Richardson, S. A., Goodman, N. Hastorf, A. H. and Dornbusch, S. M. 1961. Cultural uniformity in reaction to physical disabilities. *A. Sociol. Rev.* **26**, 241–247.

Sheldon, W. H. 1940. *The Varieties of Human Physique.* Harper, New York.

Staffieri, J. R. 1967. A study of social stereotype of body image in children. *J. Personality soc. Psychol.* **7**, 101–104.

Staffieri, J. R. 1972. Body build and behavioral expectancies in young females. *Devl. Psychol.* **6**, 125–127.

Thurman, J. 1977. Never too thin to feel fat. *Ms. Magazine* **6**, 48–51; 82–84.

Vidal, Gore. 1976. *1876.* Random House, New York.

Wooley, S. C. and Wooley, O. W. 1979. Obesity and women—I. A closer look at the facts. *Women's Studies Int. Quart.* **2**, 69–79.

3

Black Woman
Professor—White University

Nellie McKay

The history of black people in America in relationship to their exclusion from many of the opportunities and institutions that make up the 'given' for the 'others' in the population, has been a topic of much discussion for a long time, and therefore raises no new subject here. However, the specific roles and place of black women in our society have come under greater scrutiny, and have been open for more evaluation within the past decade, partly because of the momentum of the women's movement. For the larger number of years of our national history, the lives, work and worth of black women have been ignored and under-rated by the larger society, but during the last several years, black women in all areas of life and work have been making their voices heard, and insisting that this social erasure and invisibility end. Black women in the academy have been in the forefront of this new revolutionary political stance.

Until the late 1960s when the positive effects of the black discontent of that decade became apparent, black women were almost totally absent from the academy, except as students preparing to become elementary and secondary school teachers, mainly in the South and for the South. Of the few names we know from among what was no doubt many brilliant black women in the nineteenth and early twentieth centuries, whom posterity can never honor because they are nameless to us, two are worth special mention here as victims of the social limitations that were placed on their intellectual potentials. Anna Julia Cooper, who graduated from Oberlin College in the 1870s and later earned a PhD at the Sorbonne, and Jessie Remond Fauset, who graduated Phi Beta Kappa from Cornell University in 1905, and also studied at the Sorbonne, exemplify the fate of black women who were sufficiently audacious to choose education and scholarship as areas of interest and work. For them, teaching was restricted to the secondary level.

When white universities began to admit an appreciable number of black graduate students to their ranks in the 1960s, predictably, a significant number of their applicants were black women. Since many black women had always been involved in education, this younger generation of women was ready to take advantage of the wider opportunities. In the graduate school I attended which was white, Northern and prestigious, the total number of black students may have been small, but there were an equal or larger number of black women as men in English and American Literature. Many of the college trained black men and women who went on to white graduate schools between the end of the 1960s and the early years of the 1970s with teaching as their goal are now largely employed in white colleges and universities, mainly in the North, West and Midwest, where the majority of these institutions can boast at least a token black faculty member, most of whom endure a fishbowl existence.

At the beginning of the 1980s, to be a black professor in a white university is, above all, never to be able to forget it. For one thing, our numbers are very small. At the University of Wisconsin, Madison, where I teach, there are approximately twenty black faculty members (tenured and untenured) out of a total of almost three thousand. One third of this group teaches in Afro-American Studies, but to the University's credit, almost a half of us are women.

Black men and women who entered graduate schools in the 1960s and 1970s, intending to be college professors, were in the vanguard of the changing attitudes of black intellectuals to white America. Most of them were the young people who came of age in the wake of the Civil Rights Movement of the 1950s and 1960s; they were assertive and aggressive, unashamed and unapologetic for their blackness—biologically, philosophically, or politically—and were no longer willing to live within the limitations that had been imposed on black older scholars. In characterizing this group I would venture to say that it embodied a strange blend of nationalism, radicalism, and intellectual ferment, and that it was determined to change the status quo in higher education. Now these young people are college professors and facing new challenges. For blacks and other minorities, the struggles against discrimination and racism have only as yet scratched the surface of our American way of life and thinking, and minority women face all the problems of minorities and women. It is extremely difficult to be a black woman professor in a white university.

On one hand, there is isolation. Most black professors are singular persons in academic departments outside of Afro-American Studies. In the early years of my teaching career, when I worked in a small New England women's college, I was not only the only black person in my department, but for a while, I was also the lone full-time woman. This was not an unusual situation. The feelings of isolation on the departmental level expand when one considers the whole picture on almost any white college or university campus. Again, to look at my home institution—all of the black women professors (and almost all black professors) are in different disciplines. One constantly feels the pressure of a double-edged sword; simultaneously, a perverse visibility and a convenient invisibility. The small number makes it easy for others to ignore our presence, or be aware of it. We are treated as blacks, on one hand, as women, on the other. We are left constantly taking stock of the landscape as different issues arise and we have to determine on which side, women or non-white, we wish to be identified. Since a black woman professor is highly visible in any group of professors, and since we are so few, many demands are made on the few. Each is asked to serve on many committees. Each is asked to represent various interests. Many community groups place demands on our time, many times and in many places we provide the token black or black woman. We must do all these things and our work too.

Shifting from the general to the specific, there is the role of the black woman professor and her students. In my experience, the relationships are different based on the sex and/or race of the students. Each black woman professor is a role model for every black woman student on campus. This does not mean that black women students necessarily like their black women professors. But we represent something special to them, and they identify us with possibilities for themselves that otherwise they could not envision. Again, this does not always mean long-term possibilities. Quite often, it is the present that is most important.

A graduating black woman in the School of Agriculture comes to me in the eighth week of the semester and pours out a tale of woe. She needs three more credits this semester to replace those she just lost because of a course she dropped. She had problems in that course because of a personality conflict with the white male professor. She asks if she might do an independent study with me. She loves to read, she tells me, adding that she has read a number of black women writers but never had a chance to discuss them with anyone. She apologises for asking me to do this work with her, but a friend suggested to her that I was a 'kind lady,' and maybe I can see my way to help her out of her dilemma.

I try to present an impassive face and think quickly. I'm swamped with work. It is late in the semester. I've been on this campus for more than 2 years and I've never seen this student before! Why me? I'm tired! I have not had a chance to look at my own writing (tenure desperation!!!) since the weekend before fall registration! What special favors did I get in college? I never even had a black professor! It's a tough world kid, and you might as well learn one thing all black professional women must learn: how to deal with personality conflicts with white men!

Out loud, I ask what she has read and what she would like to read for the study she proposes. I do not agree to do it then, but ask that she return in a couple of days with a list of books and a schedule for reading and discussion. Then I make phone calls. I discover she is a bright student, avid reader, and able to write. She has had some difficulties through school, but deserves help if that is possible.

Her paper—on *Sula* and an Alice Childress story—a paper on friendships between women—was not profound, but intelligible and reasonably well written. She gained three credits and escaped the financial and psychological burdens of another semester in school for want of those three credits. She came to me when she did because I represented an important possibility at that time.

Black men students are often less direct in their approaches for special treatment than black women. For the most part, they make fewer personal demands, but more often use verbal persuasion as their method of trying to gain what they want. They expect sympathy for their status as black men in a white world, and that means special understanding, which often they do not think they need to articulate: understanding of why the paper was not done on time, or why it was not typed, etc. As a group, both black men and women students expect a special sympathy from black women professors, who, after all, are their mothers and sisters, and as everyone knows, all black women nurture all black people all of the time.

On the surface it seems that white women students make few 'special' demands on black women professors. They do not identify racially with the professor and seldom manifest hostility toward her. Nor do they take it for granted that the grade they will get in the course is the one they want. But appearances can be deceptive, and seeming objectivity often masks deep-felt anxiety. Many white women students come to my classes carrying the burden of the guilt of privilege and the fear that ignorance and unconscious insensitivity will mar the close encounter for me, for them, and especially for black women in the course. To their credit, I suspect that most white women in my courses honestly want to bridge the gap that separates them from women of color.

White male students are the most difficult of the groups. They often express open hostility towards the authority of the black woman on the opposite side of the lectern. In New England, once, in a large urban university in which I was a Visiting Lecturer, at the end of the term, a white male student informed me that at the beginning of the course he had often been angry at many of the things I had said, and that he had considered confronting me and 'punching' me in the nose several times. When he told the story he was congratulating himself on not having taken such a drastic action—after all, because he was patient he had learned some things from the course.

Students do get angry at professors, and most likely often feel like retaliating in a violent manner. I had many such thoughts, especially as a graduate student, and I understand them. But how many times does the student articulate this kind of feeling to the professor?

At the University of Wisconsin, Madison, during the time that I have been there, several white male students have angrily challenged my authority in relationship to the grades they receive in my classes. In an age of grade inflation, and when students need the best grades in order to go on to post-college work in professional schools, I understand their frustrations and chagrin. I even understand the expressions of thinking they deserve more for their efforts. But I have a difficult time in understanding angry verbal attacks on my authority and qualifications to administer the grades. I ask myself—am I paranoid or is it because I am a black woman that they respond this way? And finally, the ultimate assault on my vulnerability, the expression of greatest disrespect for me came in the sexual advances of a white male student.

As for white colleagues, between those who ignore me and those who attempt to compensate for the former, there are those who make a serious effort to treat me like a human being, sensitive to my race and sex. Unfortunately, many white people are unaware of their racism, and much too often, their blindness impinges on me. While I find a larger number of white women more aware and sensitive to racism than white men, on the whole, both white men and women in our profession have a great deal to learn, or perhaps even more, to unlearn, in our struggle for justice and equality for all. My white friends are learning and unlearning.

What is it like to be a black women professor in a white university? It is difficult, mainly because one can never take one's self for granted. One never forgets that she is black and a women. But it is a difficulty that has exciting challenges. I do the work I love and want to do, and I don't spend time unnecessarily lamenting my situation. I sometimes like to think that in a small way I contribute to a better understanding of a shared humanity between my colleagues and myself, and that some of my students will better comprehend the nature of race and sex for having come in contact with me.

Until 10 or 15 years ago there were only a very few black professors in a very few white colleges and universities. Now there are a few more of us in many of these institutions. Black women professors note that in hiring and retention practices, many institutions seem to think that black equals male, and women equals white. This is another battle for black women in a shrinking job market, and an even more shrinking tenure market. One pitfall we will avoid is falling prey to the accusation that black women deprive black men of jobs when they compete in the same market. We reject it as a tactic of the oppression of black women. Black people, as a group, can ill afford to stifle the talents, skills, and creativity of black women in any area of our life and work. In fair competition we will not be willingly shunted aside for the benefit of white women or black men. Black women of this generation will make sure that the lists of black professors on the faculties of white colleges and universities in the closing decades of this century will include the names of black women. As we fight racism, we will do similarly with sexism.

Life in America has always been difficult for black people, and survival has always presented challenges. There are those who claim that it has always been more so for black women. In widening the arena of struggle to the halls of academe, black women professors are doing no more than to stake out a claim for options otherwise denied them—and they are here to stay.

Job competition between black men and women, and between white and black women is an unfortunate part of our present reality, but one that must be honestly faced. We will no longer accept the role of token passively, or the expectations that we must be sensitive to everybody's problems at our expense, or be always unselfish at the same price. We want to teach, to write, to publish like all other scholars and intellectuals, and we are no longer anyone's Dilseys. These are some of the challenges of the 1980s. We hope they can be resolved in an atmosphere in which there is mutual respect between ourselves and everyone else. This is important because we can't go back.

To be a black women professor in a white university is difficult and challenging, but it is exciting and rewarding, and black women professors like it here. We aim to stay!

4

Women Who Do and Women Who Don't Join the Women's Movement

Robyn Rowland

It seems appropriate that when discussing 'strategies for empowerment' we look closely at the position of the women's movement currently in terms of *all* women. It must be true that full liberation for women cannot be achieved while we are constantly divided among ourselves. This is not to say that diversity should not exist, but that fragmentation of women's strength should be ended and reconciliation sought if at all possible, with those women who hate feminism out of their fear that what they term 'women's power' will be lost in the moves for equality. Adrienne Rich has said that:

> 'It is pointless to write off the antifeminist woman as brainwashed, or self-hating, or the like. I believe that feminism must imply an imaginative identification with all women (and with the ghostly woman in all men) and that the feminist must, because she can, extend this act of the imagination as far as possible' (1980:71).

There is new interest emerging within feminism about antifeminist women for a number of reasons. First, it is difficult for us to understand how a woman who is intelligent, articulate and strong, as many ardent antifeminists are, could ignore the vast catalog of oppressive acts against women and will fight changes which would end that oppression. As Andrea Dworkin questions: 'Why do right-wing women agitate for their own subordination?' (1983: xiii).[1]

Second, in terms of power, the divide-and-rule technique which patriarchy has always applied to women continues to function, as witnessed, for example, in the defeat of the ERA in North America. The hatred of

[1] Although Dworkin discusses right-wing women only, it is difficult to clarify divisions between feminists and antifeminists on those grounds. Antifeminist women are generally seen to be those belonging to groups or espousing their platforms, which are antagonistic to any changes towards equality and liberation for women in feminist terms.

antifeminist women is representative of a self-hatred imposed upon all women by patriarchy which leads us to loathe our bodies, leave our minds fallow, continue to exist within silence in language and history, and to court the powerful (male) forces in order to survive. In surviving within oppression and repression, women must of necessity reject other women to prove their allegiances to male power. The virulent anti-woman attacks by antifeminists indicate a continuing need to build positive self-valued identification for women. No woman like Marabel Morgan, who would recommend to the 'Total Woman,' acts totally devoid of self-respect in order to 'keep her man happy,' can have a real and lasting sense of her own self-value. Hélène Cixous has written:

> 'Men have committed the greatest crime against women. Insidiously, violently, they have led them to hate women, to be their own enemies, to mobilize their immense strength against themselves, to be the executants of their virile needs. They have made for women an antinarcissism! A narcissism which loves itself only to be loved for what women haven't got! They have constructed the infamous logic of antilove' (1980: 248).

Antifeminists are women too, who need to find themselves, to love themselves, and to cast off their fear. Their rage at difference or change represents the rage and hate they feel toward their own oppression and their fear of a loss of what power they feel they have. Having no courage to risk or rebel, they displace their anxiety and hate, finding in other women easier targets than men. Their anger makes them, in Dworkin's view, 'easily controlled and manipulated' by male antifeminists (1983: 34).

Thirdly, in terms of the future of women, it is necessary to approach some reconciliation. Feminist understanding of the way the world operates in its more subtle forms has increased. Where once we fought for the vote or for equal rights legislation with a belief that change would follow, we now understand that, necessary though these reforms are, they cannot combat the subtleties of male power. Every wolf whistle educates us about the lack of real change in woman's position, as our minds chain-react, linking this experience to 'woman as object,' male violence, rape, suffering, and back to woman's silence as she continues to walk through the air thick with whistling. Our minds are so attuned to the precision of oppression that we see it in the non-verbal language of the sexes, hear it in the silences of women writers, and feel it in our broken bonding.

This more intimate understanding of our oppression leads us to perceive separatism as an avoidance of the difficulty of tackling the real experience of most women, yet we have kept ourselves separate from antifeminist women. Separatism of this kind is a non-political act, though it may well be a self-preserving one. Rich has commented on the difficulty of 'the lifelong process of separating ourselves from the patriarchal elements in our own thinking, such as the use of phallic language and the fear of any difference from our own "correct" positions' (1980: 229).

There are indications now that the future holds a great threat to women in the area of reproductive technology, and may wrench from women our last uniqueness—the power to create life (see Arditti *et al.*, 1984). Men have managed to gain control over women's bodies but will soon have control of creation itself. With the coming of the 'glass womb,' the position of *all* women is threatened. No longer necessary in a childbearing or sexual capacity, what is our future? These technologies demand a new assessment by feminists and we may well find ourselves aligned with antifeminists on some of these issues. That coalition may be the beginning of a new bonding among women. In Zoë Fairbairn's novel *Benefits*, the unlikely and the 'improbable feminist—FAMILY alliance that called itself The Women' was created to fight such a threat. Understanding at last the manipulation of women in the FAMILY political party, Isabel is terrified to see the imposition on women of new reproductive controls: 'How,' she says, 'had it happened, this descent from an ideal family life, to control and contempt. *Same thing*, she heard the feminists hiss, and knew she could not go to them, even if she wanted to, even if she knew where they were' (1979: 175, her stress). If in reality we can build some common bridges of communication, when the time comes perhaps it will be easier to find each other. It is this bonding of women that patriarchy works to dissolve daily, that 'intense, powerful surge toward female community and woman-to-woman commitment,' which threatens the foundations of male dominance (Rich, 1980: 225).

Women Who Do and Women Who Don't Join the Women's Movement is a book that gathers together the experiences of feminists and antifeminists in relation to the women's movement, aiming to clarify points of difference and similarity. Twenty-four women from five countries contributed and their backgrounds varied in class, race, age and sexual preference. Before discussing the emerging points of difference and similarity, I'll summarize briefly the major issues in the platforms of both the women's movement and the antifeminist backlash.

The membership of feminist and antifeminist groups emerges from differing political backgrounds. Many feminists still have affinities with the socialist Left, though many are disillusioned with the New Left's platform of male-class success. The women's movement contains as many diverse groups as do most social movements, though they are united in their aims for challenges which will create choice for women, fulfilment of their individual potential, and will improve the class position of women to one equitable with that of men. Firestone's (1972) delineation of the women's movement based primarily on ideological approaches to social change is still useful in general terms. Her 'conservative feminists' are often labelled 'femocrats,' working within the political and institutional setting towards change through reform. The 'politicos' have primarily a Black or Left allegiance, with feminism representing part of the changes incorporated in race and class struggles.

'Radical' feminists see women's issues as the *first* priority and liberation necessitates a total overhauling of existing social systems.

The antifeminists emerge primarily from the New Right (particularly in North America) which itself is a coalition of three basic groups: business groups threatened by changes in the capitalist system; groups joined through moral issues and traditional values; and groups fighting specific issues, like abortion. Most of the groups in the coalition are led by men, motivated either by the threat they detect from feminism to their right to male preserves of power, i.e., the right to power over *some* men and *all* women; or by their belief in the traditional relations between the sexes; or by an antagonism to women in general. In addition to being antifeminist, these groups are anti-social welfare, and against what they see as the invasion of the state into the private sphere of the family.

Antifeminist women form two groups. The first fear that change will aggravate their situation rather than improve it. They perceive feminists to be devaluing the work of mother and wife and feel threatened by this. The second group is ideologically opposed to the women's movement. There are three sub groups here. The Professional Traditional Woman has been successful within the traditional role and finds it comfortable, though she often professionalizes the role, travelling to lecture on its benefits. The Specific Issues Antagonists are those who object to one or two feminist platforms, e.g., they may be pro-child care but oppose abortion. The third group are the Queen Bees, who have achieved success in a 'man's world' while also raising a family. Motivated by self-interest they keep in with the male power system by devaluing other women. There are also women who have not consciously experienced discrimination and cannot understand the claims of the women's movement.

Apart from feminists and antifeminists, there are great numbers of women who are too tired, too oppressed and too concerned with the survival of themselves and their children to be involved with feminism, and there are still those who have had no contact with the ideas of liberation and equality.

There are three basic ideological differences between feminists and antifeminists. Feminists work to eliminate sexism, while antifeminists reject the theory of male oppression as a feminist paranoia, and see no sexism operating. Secondly, feminists stress the social conditioning of the sexes and reject innate and immutable sex differences; while antifeminists stress the 'naturalness' of sex differences based on biological differences. Thirdly, feminists see women as part of a social group sharing the experience of oppression. Antifeminists see the individual woman as responsible for her situation and her life. Therefore, any problems experienced by a woman are *her* problems and not representative of a shared powerlessness.

There are a number of major issues which recur as platforms within the women's movement. These are: abortion and the right of the individual woman to control her own body; sexuality and the rights of choice, satisfaction and sex of partner within sexual relationships; social class and the realization of the differences in the degree of powerlessness experienced by women in differing classes; and race, and the position of white women as oppressors of women of color. Finally, there is the triumvirate of family, motherhood and work, with its accompanying understanding that the patriarchal nuclear family leads to domestic slavery for women; that 'maternal instinct,' i.e., the mandate that women breed, leads to an equating of child-bearing with child-rearing for women; and that paid work increases both the status and self-esteem of women. A belief in the rights of women to have access to workforce participation, leads to demands, for example, that adequate child care facilities be available for workforce and home-working mothers.

The issues debated by antifeminists are in direct reaction to these platforms. Abortion, sexuality, motherhood, family and workforce participation are primary. Class and race issues are rarely mentioned, but religion is important. Antifeminists believe that woman's rightful place is in the family; that the male should be the breadwinner; and that woman's job is to 'appreciate and admire her husband' (Schlafly, 1977: 54). So if a woman 'chooses' to work in the workforce, she should also carry the burden of home duties. Women have the right to be protected and supported financially by their husbands. Abortion is abhorred as murder and the rights of the unborn are seen to predominate over the rights of a woman. The sexual drive is stronger in men and her husband's satisfaction is pleasure enough, a woman's sexuality being mainly related to the maternal drive. Orgasm is therefore not necessary for her. Lesbian women are seen as unnatural and deviant because their sexuality does not lead to the fulfilment of maternity. Dworkin has pointed out that antifeminists fear lesbian women because they have been convinced that they are violent, dirty, and child molestors. Religion forms a moral creed for antifeminists and their positions on family and motherhood are frequently supported by biblical quotation. Schlafly, for example, points out that the female body with its 'baby-producing organs was not designed by a conspiracy of men but by the Divine Architect of the human race' (1977: 12).

Though these issues are easy to delineate, when we look at the statements by contributors to *Women Who Do and Women Who Don't*, the boundaries are more confusing and the interaction of issues more complex. Some of these issues are summarized in the following pages.

Antifeminists *do* argue that sex differences are innate and biologically determined, and feminists claim social conditioning as causal. This issue is important because it determines the position taken by both groups concerning the concept of equality.

Antifeminists want to be 'equal but different' and see feminists as wanting to be the *same* as men; as forfeiting their uniqueness. This leads antifeminists to scorn the use of non-sexist language and the implementation of similar education for girls and boys. They are ignorant of the arguments with respect to sexist language, and fear a sameness between girls and boys, girls thus losing sight of the values of motherhood and the power within that role as perceived by antifeminists.

Antifeminists often claim to be the true feminists and that they represent stage III of the women's movement. Stage I was emancipation, stage II is liberation (equal pay and opportunities) and stage III is recognition for 'uniquely female roles.' They express no understanding of oppression and have no sense of being part of the social group 'woman,' which, Juliet Mitchell points out in her chapter, is a prerequisite for feminist conscious-ness. Antifeminists see their own success in terms of their individual merit, and the assumption is strong that if a woman has 'failed' or is unhappy, there is something wrong with her, and not with society.

Feminists reject the idea of 'uniquely' sex-typed roles, seeing this as a ploy by which men opt out of child-rearing and women are excluded from the workforce. They have experienced the oppression of women as individuals and as a group, and have a group consciousness and a belief in co-operative action.

Relationships with men were discussed. Antifeminists argue that feminists hate men and marriage. They invariably describe their husbands as 'wonder-ful' and 'loving.' They profess to like men, yet see them as untrustworthy, less worthy and moral, 'slightly inferior,' and as users of women. They express the fear that the removal of the protective role from men would lead to 'risks to the group, in particular the female, from the isolated non-responsible male.' Men thus need the moral guidance and control of women and family, otherwise they are a threat. Any woman, therefore, who threatens that view of woman as moral, would place that power base, and therefore antifeminists, at risk. There is a naïve division of men into two groups: the married, loving and controlled husbands; and the unmarried, childless and irresponsible men. Dworkin has suggested that the right-wing woman sees the violence in man and has devised a way of controlling it. She bargains continuously with the male not to use his power over her. In my book the antifeminists certainly give the impression that 'good' husbands are the result of good management and a reflection, therefore, of their own greater worth as women.

For feminists too, men are a problem. Contrary to the antifeminist belief, most of the feminists expressed a desire to relate to men, but at differing levels, and not at a cost to their selfhood. The experiences of some contribu-tors with incest, man's violence during and after war, and the study of rape, illuminate the reality of woman as victim. It is the violence and cruelty of men which feminists loathe. Antifeminists seem either to ignore this, or believe it only exists in the 'odd' case. As Scutt points out in the book, 'the real problem for the women's liberation movement is that we care about men too much' (p. 220). In fact, if women were strong enough to withdraw support from men, change would be easier to effect.

Men's attitudes to sexuality offend feminists and antifeminists alike. Antifeminists see feminists as colluding in the sexual revolution, however most feminists see that period as a man's revolution, with massive sexual exploitation of women's bodies. Both Purdue (antifeminist) and Spender (feminist) advocate celibacy as a potential life-style.

Relationships with other women varied among antifeminists. Some stated that they found men more interesting, while others had always had close women friends. But 'women's libbers' are attacked virulently as a threat to love and family, and to the identity of antifeminists as women and mothers. In comparison, feminists speak of the joy and really fulfilling experience of that first occasion when they 'made the simple but momentous discovery that I *liked* women' (Spender, p. 222).

Antifeminists argue that feminists devalue motherhood and family life, forcing women into the workforce. It is clear, however, that feminists value the *experience* as opposed to the *institution* of motherhood and that this provides them with a real dilemma: how to recreate family life so that it does fulfil the needs of people for 'security, commitment and continuity' (Curthoys, p. 224), without destroying a woman's self-identity in the process.

Abortion was obviously the most divisive issue. The orientation of antifeminists to the abortion debate takes the position of the unborn child as preordinate. The feminist debate centers on concern for the woman and her right to decide on abortion. Antifeminists misrepresent the 'pro-choice' view of feminists, as 'pro-abortion.' All antifeminists discussed this issue. Landolt points out that it divided the women's movement in Canada, and Purdue comments that 'this is the dividing line.' Both these antifeminists see women as conned by men on this issue, Landolt commenting: 'I believe that feminists have fallen into a male trap. They are attempting to adapt women to a wombless male society, instead of adapting society to meet the needs of women' (p. 225). Feminist Barbara Ehrenreich has elsewhere described the issue as double-edged, noting that freer abortion may further undercut 'male responsibility towards women and children' (1981: 99). Most of the feminist contributors did not discuss abortion, which may indicate that we are underestimating the importance of this debate. Landolt and Purdue would be strong feminist supporters, if it were not for the abortion issue.

The complexities of racial and cultural differences also emerged. The racism inherent within the women's movement itself, particularly in Australia, is reason enough for alienating black and migrant women from the movement, as Sykes and Fesl point out. Alternatively, Te Awekotuku placed male oppression of all women above white woman's collusion in black oppression. A similar issue emerges with respect to class. Feminists are aware of both these realities within the lives of women and the problems they pose for a united women's movement. The issues were not mentioned by antifeminists.

Within their statements, were there any elements which emerged to explain the differences in viewpoints between feminists and antifeminists, some of whom had very similar backgrounds?

One important difference was that for feminists the 'personal *is* political' in that a personal experience of discrimination often created an identification with the social group 'woman,' which was then seen as an oppressed class. If they had not themselves experienced discrimination, like Peggy Seeger they had made an effort to find out about the experiences of other women. She writes: 'I was lacking gut experience and I had to arrive at my awareness of most women's problems through observing, thinking about and listening to other women. . . . I discovered how other women lived. It was quite a shock!'

Antifeminists often cite Betty Friedan as a feminist who recanted, misrepresenting and misunderstanding her desire to grip the changing perspectives of feminism. But antifeminists too have a problem with one of their leaders, Anita Bryant, the fundamentalist preacher, singer, anti-gay and anti-liberationist leader, now divorced from her husband. Bryant says:

> 'The answers don't seem quite so simple now. . . . I guess I can better understand the gays' and the feminists' anger and frustration. . . . There are some valid reasons why militant feminists are doing what they're doing. . . . Having experienced a form of male chauvinism among Christians that was devastating, I can see how women are controlled in a very ungodly, un-Christ-like way . . . most men are insensitive to women's needs. We have been so conditioned and so taught.' (1980: 68).

This interview indicated the power of the *personal* experience of oppression. But for women who have been lucky, the personal-as-political may not be effective. Women need to understand their own experience, but also to validate, understand and empathize with other women's experiences which may be totally different to their own.

There is a difference in the average level of education between feminists and antifeminists in the book, though no strong deductions can be made from this. What can be said, though, is that as Dworkin indicates, women in the Right are often manipulated through ignorance of the facts. So non-sexist language can be trivialized and dismissed without understanding the way language constructs social reality; and rape can be seen as an individual act of violence, without understanding either the facts of its incidence or the relationship of it to the control of women as a group.

A further difference lies in the sense feminists and antifeminists have of personal power and self-esteem. If a woman's power base lies in her role as mother in the family, she needs to defend that position from threat. If she has other sources of power, for example in work, her identity is different. Self-esteem, self-identity, a source of personal control and of being important and needed in her role, are necessary to *all* women and they will defend the perceived source of these feelings. Ehrenreich has commented: 'It is almost as if the economic stresses of the seventies split women into two camps: those who went *out* to fight for some measure of economic security . . . and those who stayed at home to hold onto what they had' (1981: 99).

Finally, two experiences seem to have shaped the contributors' attitudes to the women's movement. The first is their initial experience of meeting with a feminist group, which either drew or repelled them. The second is their relationship with men. Antifeminists lay claim to 'loving husbands.' But feminists have experienced the character of man differently, seeing it as violent, abusive, or exploitative. These experiences lead women to reassess the *reality* of sharing a world with men, as opposed to the *vision* which is handed down from patriarchy.

Some surprising similarities between feminists and antifeminists also emerged. All had a supportive mother, or father, or both. They were often made to feel 'special' or were given the expectation that men and women *were* equal. They are all strong women with a sure sense of self. They believe they make an impact on the world. They will not be dictated to.

All the women are pro-family, pro-children, and pro-women, but differ in their definitions of these positions and in ways of achieving the related goals. They believe in choices for women but differ in the choices they think women will make. They all want the role and status of 'mother' redefined and upgraded. All believe in equal pay and equal opportunity.

Finally, all agree that 'women's' values are superior and should be cultivated. They loathe the dominance of violent, aggressive male values, and stress the life-force of women; their strong, caring, conservationist elements. But the danger from antifeminism cannot be underestimated. Mobilized, the strength and energy of women can be powerful. The ERA *was* successfully defeated. The hatred itself can be powerful. Dworkin effectively recalls her experience of fear when trying to discuss issues with Right-wing women and men who consistently labelled her as Jew or Lesbian and could then make her invisible. The rigid and narrow thinking of conservatives is dangerous when they take power. Jill Tweedie (1982) has also warned of the danger of women on the Right who 'provide men with excuses to turn deaf ears' and 'bring up children in the old destructive pattern.' They also allow that questioning of feminist men: 'If I don't care, why should you.'

These points cannot be overlooked. Nor can the use of fear and guilt in the antifeminist rhetoric which creates an insecurity and anxiety in some women, alienating them from the women's movement on the basis of false information.

There is a value in opposition to a social movement. It can strengthen solidarity within the movement. It may encourage a healthy and constructive self-criticism, which the women's movement can encompass. Dworkin points out that Right-wing women see women's position as it really is, but that their response is not sisterhood, but a 'self-protective sense of repulsion. The powerless are not quick to put faith in the powerless. The powerless need the powerful' (1983: 234). So antifeminist women opt for alliance and compliance with men against women who call the balance itself into question, seeing the alternative to accommodation within the system as a fruitless and doomed struggle to overturn male power.

Women's liberation is often deliberately misrepresented. It could be too that the movement has failed to get its message across clearly enough. Dialogue is essential. Antifeminists may work to undermine all the positive changes women have made. But if they continue to support antifeminist men, they may lose more than they bargained for, and find, like Anita Bryant, that they give men the ammunition they need to fire at *all* women—including homemakers. They may find that the education they do want for their daughters is no longer available for women, who are 'naturally' mothers and need no further education; that they are refused jobs because a lower qualified man needs one; or find that their divorced daughter is unable to obtain credit because we have gone back to the good old days when men supported women—except that their daughter's husband turns out *not* to be 'decent' and leaves her with three children to support, no money and no maintenance.

The one continuing link between feminists and antifeminists is the reality of our shared oppression. Hope lies in this reality of common struggle and the possibility that antifeminists may be challenged by their own internal conflicts. As Dworkin writes:

'This struggle alone has the power to transform women who are enemies against one another into allies fighting for individual and collective survival that is not based on self-loathing, fear and humiliation, but instead on self-determination, dignity, and authentic integrity' (p. 35).

REFERENCES

Arditti, R., Klein, R. Duelli and Minden, S. (eds), 1984. *Test Tube Women. What Future for Motherhood?* Routledge & Kegan Paul, London.
Bryant, A. 1980. In Jahr, C., Anita Bryant's startling reversal. *Ladies Home J.* 97(12), 62–68.
Cixous, H. 1980. The laugh of Medusa. In Marks, E. and Courtivron, I, de, (eds), *New French Feminisms. An Anthology*, pp. 245–264. University of Massachusetts Press, Amherst.
Dworkin, A. 1983. *Right-wing Women. The Politics of Domesticated Females.* The Women's Press, London.
Ehrenreich, B. 1981. The women's movements. Feminist and antifeminist. *Radical America* 15, 93–101.
Fairbairns, Z. 1979. *Benefits*. Virago, London.
Firestone, S. 1972. *The Dialectic of Sex. A Case for Feminist Revolution.* Paladin, London.
Rich, A. 1980. *On Lies, Secrets and Silence, Selected Prose, 1966–1978.* Virago, London.

Rowland, R. (ed), 1984. *Women Who Do and Women Who Don't Join the Women's Movement*. Routledge & Kegan Paul, London.

Schafly, P. 1977. *The Power of the Positive Woman*. Arlington House Press, New York.

Tweedie, J. Beating the Queen Bees. Article in the *Guardian*, reprinted in the *Age*, Melbourne, Australia. 'Accent' pages. 27 August 1982.

II

Feminist re-vision: the meaning of patriarchal theories and institutions from feminist perspectives

II

5

Rape as a Paradigm of Sexism in Society—Victimization and Its Discontents[1]

Pauline B. Bart

'It's cleavage to go with carnage at pro football games these days as skimpily clad cheerleaders cavort and prance to keep the fans' spirits up. As CBS sports producer Chuck Milton sees it, "The audience deserves a little sex with violence!" ' (*Newsweek*, November 7, 1977).

INTRODUCTION

For the past year Marlyn Grossman and I have been listening to over 100 women tell us about the violence in their lives. Originally I wanted to learn how women could avoid being raped when attacked. In order to find women who were nearly raped as well as a comparative group of rape victims I advertised, put up flyers, spoke anyplace people would let me, from tiny colleges to TV shows, as well as tried to get publicity in newspapers in the area, meeting with no success from the major newspapers since the study was not 'news.' I asked women who had been raped or nearly raped in the past 2 years to talk to me confidentially (they were given expenses and $25 since the study was funded by the Center for the Prevention and Control of Rape of the National Institute of Mental Health).

The women were asked about the situation surrounding the assault, about how they usually dealt with stress, about what skills they had (e.g., self-defense) and about how they were brought up, the latter to test the feminist hypothesis that being brought up to be a girl and then a lady, or what sociologists call female socialization, sets you up to be a rape victim rather

[1] This paper along with others which have been published in *Women's Studies Int. Quart.*, was presented at the Feminist Scholarship Conference, at the University of Illinois at Urbana-Champaign, in March 1978. We are grateful to the Feminist Scholarship Conference Committee for their permission to publish such papers.

than a woman who avoids the rape (all other things being equal). I chose this topic because women would always ask me what to do if attacked and I had no answer since at that time the data were contradictory. I am trying to find the answer by learning what factors, especially what strategies under what circumstances are associated with avoiding rape when attacked.

While listening to these stories I was overwhelmed by the amount of violence in women's lives—incest, child abuse, woman abuse, molestation—and with the intertwining of the prior violence with their response to the recent assault. Originally I thought there were two categories—(1) women who had been raped and (2) women who were attacked and avoided being raped. That analysis underestimated the variety and pervasiveness of violence. There were some women who had been both rape victims and rape avoiders within a 2-year period, and more if I extended the time; women who had been raped several times in their lives (one twice on the same day by two different men in different places), and women who had avoided being raped several times. Some women recalled or redefined prior incidents as rape in the course of recounting their current experiences. Some women, who had been raped and had learned from their prior experience not only the damage it had done to their lives but what not to do, managed to avoid being raped the next time someone tried to assault them. On the other hand, at least two women who avoided being raped were shortly thereafter raped, one by her boyfriend who was 'turned on' by the avoidance and the other by her husband (a wife-beater) who demanded his 'marital rights' when she, like most women who have had an assault experience, was not able to have sex.

While I have not yet systematically analyzed the interviews, I have been thinking and speaking and writing about rape (Bart, 1975a, 1975b, 1975c, 1976a, 1976b) and more recently woman abuse (Bart, 1978) as well as speaking about violence against women in general and the change in ideology from one blaming the victim to one stating 'women do it too' (Bart, 1978) (e.g., Steinmetz's (1978) alleged data on battered husbands) for the past 4 years and would like to set out some of my thoughts.

DIFFERENCES AND SIMILARITIES AMONG FORMS OF VIOLENCE AGAINST WOMEN

In this analysis I differentiate between rape by someone you know and rape by a stranger. The reason will be apparent below.

(1) Rape by someone you know, woman abuse and incest are violations of trust. Rape by a stranger is not. That is why I found (Bart, 1975a) that the more intimately you know your attacker, the more likely you are to have psychological problems after the rape. However, the treatment women receive from society's institutions after being raped generally has a radicalizing effect on women who believed in the system and for them rape by a

stranger can also cause a loss of trust, but in the society, not in men. One woman was raped while serving with one of the branches of the armed forces. When it became clear they had protected the rapist, she said, 'I didn't believe the . . . [branch of service] would do such a thing.' Another upwardly mobile young black woman and her family lost their faith in the system generally, and Mayor Daly, whom they admired, in particular, when rape charges against the two rapists were dismissed and she had no recourse. (While we may see these cases as progress, in fact, the loss of trust in the system caused severe existential depression.)

(2) Victims of woman abuse and incest are ecologically locked in their situation, at least temporarily, since they share the same residence. (Even if the relative does not live in the house he has easy access to it.) There is an ongoing relationship. This is not true for rape (except for systematic husband rape).

(3) Victims of all of these forms of violence have been blamed, but this is somewhat less likely for victims of stranger rape and most true for women who have been date-raped and for battered women who remain in their marriage.[2]

(4) In all of these situations the man has no respect for the needs of the other person and in some cases he assumes an identity of interest, e.g., the woman enjoys being raped, the father is giving the daughter necessary sex education.

(5) In both kinds of rape, in woman abuse and in incest, mental health professionals traditionally have been part of the problem, not the solution.[3] Their intrapsychic approach, or what I call 'It's what's inside that counts' (Bart, 1972) leads to blaming the victim, and in the case of woman abuse and incest, their commitment to the importance of the nuclear two-parent family emphasizes working things out rather than getting him out.

(6) Woman battering is a recurrent event. Incest is sometimes recurrent. Rape (by the same person) is not recurrent. (Husband rape may be an exception, but we have little information on this.)

(7) 'Depersonalization,' or splitting yourself off so that you think it is happening to someone else, not you, is a common response to these events. One rape victim told me she felt as if she were on the ceiling of the car watching the rape taking place on the car seat.

[2] There are no data supporting the pervasive myth that battered wives don't leave. It takes some women longer than others for reasons which we are well aware of. Since 'experts' primarily see battered women in the marriage where they are being abused, they make this assumption which leads to the conclusion that either nothing can be done for them or they must 'need' the battering. It is as if one visited a pneumonia ward every day, every day saw people with pneumonia, and said, 'People get over pneumonia.' Both battered women in my study had left and all my friends who were battered left.

[3] This tradition is changing, notably in the work of psychiatrist Elaine Hilberman on rape (1976) and battered women, and of Judith Herman, whose article with Lisa Hirschman on father-daughter incest (1977) is a feminist classic.

(8) While stranger rape functions as a form of social control over women not attached to men (whose presence, presumably, though not always in fact, would deter the rapist), 'date rape,' women abuse and incest are forms of social control over women attached to men.

(9) All of these events are under-reported to the authorities. Stranger rape is the most likely to be reported of all of these crimes. Thus, while all forms of violence against women (including those we have not discussed, such as hassling on the street) have many elements in common and stem from our situation living under patriarchy, there are differences among them which it is useful to recognize and understand so that we may fight them more effectively.

SEXISM, SOCIAL CLASS AND RAPE

We know that working-class women suffer because of their class and gender, but we also know that almost all women are underpaid, relegated to the female occupational ghetto where, unless they have someone with whom they can combine their incomes, they frequently fall below the poverty level, particularly if they head families. The relevance for rape is as follows. While all women are vulnerable to rape by known assailants, one can buy a certain amount of protection from street or apartment rape by strangers. Many of the women I interviewed were raped waiting for public transportation or walking from public transportation. Sometimes they had typical female jobs, such as nurse or waitress, which meant that they usually had to leave work at late hours. One of the women deliberately chose the night-shift so that she, a divorced mother (her husband had systematically beaten her) could spend time with her children during the day. If they could have afforded cars or cabs and had inside or secure parking, which is of course expensive, those particular rapes would have not occurred. Similarly if one can afford to live in an apartment with a doorman and/or an expensive security system that works, it is more difficult for rapists to enter. (When one of the women I spoke with told me she had been raped at gunpoint two houses down from where I live I truly understood what it meant to me to be able to afford locked parking and not have to search on the street for a space, having to walk by the very place she had been assaulted.) Similarly many women hitchhike because it is the only means of transportation they have. One victim had no money and didn't want to spend Christmas alone. She was hitchhiking to another city to be with some friends, assumed men driving vans were gentle hippies, was picked up, assaulted, her virginity was destroyed and she was dumped back on the road. Again, had she travel funds she could have avoided the rape. However, these kinds of rapes are not the majority of rapes and while some can buy some safety, as long as we live in a society where women are brutalized, women themselves constitute a class.

SEXISM AND DEFINITION OF RAPE

Definitions, notably legal definitions, reflect the belief system of the dominant groups in society. It is therefore not accidental that the *de facto* and *de jure* definitions of rape embody sexist beliefs, and that these definitions are changing because, in part, of the impact of the women's movement. The following are two examples of sexism in the definition of rape:

(1) Forcible intercourse between a husband and wife is not included in definitions of rape, a carryover of the concept of the wife as the husband's property.

This law is being modified in some states so that a man can be charged with raping a wife from whom he is legally separated. It is interesting to note that in an unpublished paper I read, the largest gender difference in defining what was rape was in the case of a man separated from his wife. It should also be noted that in fact, though not in law, it is extremely difficult for women who are prostitutes, cabdrivers and exotic dancers to have their charges of rape taken seriously. One male cabdriver, when hearing that I was a rape researcher told me a 'funny' story about a prostitute who had intercourse with several men, none of whom paid her, and then claimed to have been raped. I asked him how he would feel if I didn't pay for the cab ride, which he would not have given me were it not a commercial transaction. He thought a bit and then said, 'If that's rape then there's certainly a lot of rape around.' He's right.

(2) Rape is defined as penile vaginal penetration (although this definition is being changed in some states). Men think of rape as a sexual act and that is how they conceptualize sex. Moreover, this definition excludes the serious problem of males raping males, a dramatic example of rape as an expression of dominance.

SEXISM AND INDIVIDUAL RESPONSES TO RAPE

1. The Double Standard

The double standard is applied to rape in two senses. In the first sense the double standard refers to conventional sexual morality where men have sexual freedom while women who stray from the path of virginity prior to marriage and monogamy after marriage are 'bad.' It is difficult for such 'bad' woman to receive just treatment from the police and courts, and people are more likely to believe she 'got what she deserved' or 'was asking for it.' Thus, a study of college students showed that they responded more negatively to a vignette describing an assailant raping a virgin than to vignettes describing the rape of a divorcee or cocktail waitress (Hoffman and Dodd, 1975). This finding is similar to Elizabeth Pleck's (1978) research on court records where she discovered that in nineteenth-century wife-beating cases only husbands who beat 'virtuous' wives were found guilty. In the archetypal situation, the situation that everyone would agree was rape, the victim would be a 16-year-old virgin, raped by a black felon, while she was sitting in her parents' house, baby-sitting for her siblings, with all the windows closed and the door locked,[4] crocheting the flag while watching 'The Waltons' on television.

A second manifestation of the double standard in the case of rape is that more stringent requirements are applied to proving guilt in rape cases than in other felonies. Thus, for example, corroboration was required in cases to prove the rape took place, a requirement not necessary for other crimes. Judge Morris Ploscowe opposed changing this requirement in New York State 'because ladies lie.' But a reading of history does not lead one to the conclusion that truth telling is a sex-linked male gene. Rape victims alone among all victims of crime are required to fight back to prove that it was indeed a crime, furnishing another example of the double standard in the case of rape. Such a demand requires that a women transcend her traditional socialization which is to be 'nice,' trusting and compliant and not be a tomboy after 12, so that she usually does not have fighting skills, or even skills in physical contact sports, such as football. Non-traditional females who are more likely to have the skill to fight back are less likely to be treated justly by the societal institutions, while traditional females are, in this situation, supposed to behave non-traditionally, without the skills to do so.

2. The ideology of the rapist as mentally ill

One of the most common ideologies about rapists, and one that invalidates the feminist analysis of rape, is that men rape because they are mentally ill. Some of the women with whom I spoke gave that reason for the rape, although their major evidence for mental illness was 'Why else would he rape?' This circular reasoning psychologically protected the women because were they to believe men raped because they wanted to dominate women, that the dehumanization of women and misogyny inherent in rape are endemic in the society, that there are no data indicating that rapists are more crazy than anyone else, then women would have to confront the fact that they were always at risk of being raped as long as they lived in a sexist society.

In fact we know nothing about rapists. We know something about imprisoned rapists, but since so few rapists are convicted, fewer still convicted on charges of rape (i.e., they have not been plea-bargained) and fewer still in prison rather than on probation, by examining rapists in prison, as some researchers do, we can make inferences not to men who are rapists but to men who are losers. Even in the case of incest there is little data that the

---

[4] I mention this point because I have heard people say of a rape victim, 'Why did she have to have windows open?'

men are mentally ill. Herman and Hirschman (1977) note that incestuous fathers are neither psychotic nor intellectually defective. 'They are especially hostile toward women' and 'see the sex act as an act of aggression.' Clearly such beliefs characterize a large proportion of the male population. To call people holding such beliefs mentally ill makes the term meaningless since mental illness is a deviant status. If everyone is sick the term loses its analytic utility.

Psychiatric explanations of behavior have replaced religious explanations in our society. Psyche has replaced sin to account for behavior. But a feminist analysis must use a structural or institutional analysis of behavior rather than an individual one. If we are not suffering from private problems but from public issues, as we learned in our consciousness raising groups, then we have to discuss what the public issues are and why they lead to violence against women. To call rapists mentally ill is an individualistic explanation; to say that rape is the logical culmination of male sexual socialization and thus neither abnormal nor unexpected behavior is a feminist alternative interpretation.

3. The ideology of the imperative nature of male sexuality

Another ideology justifying incest and rape is the mistaken view that the demands of male sexuality are so imperative that if a man becomes aroused he has no choice but to assault the woman who has stimulated him or a substitute. Masturbation is not considered a more ethical or viable alternative. This belief can account for one incest researcher explaining incest by noting that the girls are unusually charming and attractive in their outward personalities (Herman and Hirschman, 1977). What's a poor man to do? Similarly the view that the rape victims bring it on themselves by being sexily dressed, and thus break through the thin veneer of control men have over their sexual drives leaving them with no choice but rape, assumes this view of male sexuality.

But no man ever died of an erection—though many women have.

In other areas of our life we are not allowed to take what we want, even if provoked, e.g., store windows are deliberately designed to make people want the products. Yet that does not legally justify breaking the glass and taking them. Only in the case of violence against women is doing what one wants in response to 'provocation' a justification. Without giving any credence to the provocative dress theory of rape by answering it I want to note that of all the women interviewed only one was 'scantily clad' since she was walking home from the beach in shorts. Most were wearing pants, and many were assaulted in the dead of Chicago winter dressed as if they were about to climb Mount Everest.

It is easy to understand why men hold these views of rape which narrow the definition so most rapes are not defined as such, particularly if the man is 'provoked.' Since male sexual aggression is endemic, if any sex act against a person's will is considered rape, the majority of men would be rapists. They could not only be accused of rape but found guilty. But if rapists are mentally ill, since most men consider themselves sane, they are not rapists. Viewing rape as normal in our society is threatening to men. I account for Judge Simonson's defeat in Madison by realizing that men voted against him because they were threatened by his definition of rape as normal male behavior. One male newscaster told me he felt insulted by Simonson's remarks about rape being a normal response. Contrast the outrage against Simonson with the low level of response to the judge in California who freed a rapist who had assaulted a hitchhiker. The latter judge kept the definition of rape narrow and thus was acting in the interest of men. The former broadened the definition of rape and so threatened men.

In addition, just as some women have rape fantasies (never to be confused with the actual desire to be raped, since one has power over a fantasy and the essence of rape is a feeling of powerlessness), men, I have been told by male clinicians, have fantasies of being rapists. This fact, combined with general male sexual aggressiveness, particularly in dating (Kanin, 1957, 1971) can explain why women who went to court told me that the states' attorneys and judges identified with the rapist rather than with them. This identification crossed both class and race lines.[5] While racism and class bias certainly are present in the judicial system, they operate more clearly when men of different classes and/or races are involved. When, however, the case is male vs female, particularly in instances of violence, identification along gender lines rather than along race or class lines seems to predominate, at least at this particular historical time.

It is more puzzling to understand why many women hold conventional ideologies about rape. Women jurors were never considered especially sympathetic to rape victims. One reason is as follows. To live with the knowledge that not only are all women vulnerable to rape, but that frequently they are raped by men they know (Bart, 1975a) is difficult. If, however, women believe in fact that only bad women can be raped and only crazy men who are strangers are rapists, then they can feel safe.

SEXISM AND THE INSTITUTIONAL RESPONSE TO RAPE

In this section I will briefly discuss the response to rape by the police, the hospitals and the courts and somewhat more extensively the 'helping' professions and criminology, the 'scientific study of crime.'

[5] See Marilyn French's *The Women's Room* (1978) for a fictionalized depiction of this phenomenon. See also *Chicago Sun Times,* Wednesday, May 3, 1978 for additional evidence (pp. 4, 16).

1. Police

Probably because most attention of feminists and then the media has been focused on the sexist treatment of rape victims by the police they have improved. Both the data I collected in 1975 and the women I have been speaking with throughout the year have relatively few horror stories about the police, some good stories, and have been delighted with the police women if they have been lucky enough to have one on duty when they called. There is no room in this paper for discussion about why and how this change came about.

2. Hospitals

Since sexist treatment of women by physicians has been a recurrent theme in the women's movement (e.g., Scully and Bart, 1973; Howell, 1974), and a radical analysis of the health care system points to the inordinate power that physicians have, it is to be expected that the hospital experience can feel like another rape. One physician asked a 17-year-old woman I spoke with who had been beaten and raped by two men 'were you really raped or are you just trying to make trouble for someone?' Increasingly hospitals have lay rape victim advocates to help demystify the process for the woman, and women who had such advocates reported good experiences to me. But the following facts must be overcome so that women, victimized by patriarchy in their rapes are not further victims if they seek or are brought to hospitals for medical attention.

Examination is by physicians, who, be they male or female, have internalized a male perspective in medical school (except for a small group of socially-concerned feminist and pro-feminist students). Furthermore the women see gynecology residents. We know (Scully and Bart, 1973; Scully 1977) that gynecological training is pervaded by paternalism at best and misogyny at worst; the ignorance of female personality and sexuality boggle the mind. Moreover they define the residency as a place to learn and define rape victims as people they can learn nothing from. Thus they do not enjoy having their time 'wasted' (Scully, 1977).

3. The Courts

The courts are a disaster area for rape victims, as they are for battered women (in the latter case when there are advocates, as in Chicago, battered women fare better). Women tell me they want to prosecute their rapist(s), or the man (men) who tried to rape them, out of concern for other women not out of vindictiveness, and so that their suffering will not be meaningless. Their pain will have some use if, through their efforts, other women are not raped at least by this rapist. Third-World women whom I have interviewed were incredulous when I presented to them the radical argument that Third-World men should not be prosecuted because the system was racist. Not only did they not care what happened to the rapist, they did care for their female kin whom they wanted to protect by having rapists locked up.

Not all women who want to prosecute are able to get through the various gate-keepers prior to the court appearance (e.g., states' attorneys must believe they have a chance of winning so as not to spoil their records). Moreover rape cases, like most cases, are frequently plea-bargained, but this plea bargain makes the victim feel invalidated. She thinks it means people don't think she was raped. But unless the rapist had a prior history of conviction for felony, particularly if he was out on parole, the chances of his being convicted and sent to prison were minuscule. Having a prior history of felony meant that men and male-dominated institutions judged him and found him guilty frequently of crimes against men. That now he raped or attempted to rape was consistent with his prior criminal behavior. But simply raping or attempting to rape a woman is not enough.

For example, in one case the woman interviewed was a Jewish legal secretary working for her father. She was raped in her home by two young black adolescents. Yet the white (by definition upper middle class) judge stated the infamous Hale's dictum, 'Rape is an accusation easily to be made and hard to be proved and harder to be defended by the party accused, tho' never so innocent.' He found the defendents innocent. Hale was a famous British jurist and that dictum is quoted by every legal writer on rape. Only recently, through the efforts of the women's movement, and probably the 'law and order' people who also want rapists convicted but for different reasons than we do, have Californian judges stopped routinely reading these instructions to their juries before the juries have to decide on the guilt of the accused.

4. Sexism and professions dealing with rape

Mental health professions. Traditionally schooled mental health professionals have a 'trained incapacity,' to use Veblen's term, to deal with female victims of male violence since their analysis is intrapsychic rather than institutional. As mentioned previously in this paper such an approach is conducive to blaming the victim. Not only does their intellectual armamentarium include female masochism and the intrapsychic approach but, in the case of family therapists, this armamentarium is augmented by family systems theory where it is assumed that each participant gets 'something' out of what is going on. They do not mean broken bones in the case of battered women, or sexual trauma in the case of incest victims. In the traditional analysis of father–daughter incest the mother is complicitous and the child is seductive. Only the father is assumed to have no free will.

Marolla and Scully (1978) have reviewed the psychodynamic literature on rapists and found four types of motive statements presented, sometimes combined. They are: (1) uncontrollable impulse; (2) mental illness or disease; (3) momentary loss of control precipitated by unusual circumstances; (4) victim precipitation; (5) no societal or institutional analysis or critique of rape was found.

Just as the psychiatric literature suggests that women and girls are responsible for incest it suggests that rape too is caused by women—the rapist's mother, his 'frigid' wife, and the provocative victim (Albin, 1977).

Criminology. Criminologists, like mental health professionals, are supposed to be experts on rape, because rape is a crime. Moreover their textbooks are used to train law enforcement personnel. Therefore Wisan's findings (1978) that current American criminology textbooks embody cultural myths and stereotypes, particularly 'she was asking for it' or 'victim precipitation' is both relevant and distressing. Other myths found in criminology textbooks are 'women want to be raped,' 'you cannot rape a woman' and 'rape is simply explained by sexual frustration.'

Victim precipitation, as used by Amir (1971) did not really mean 'she was asking for it.' It refers to a breakdown in communication where the man assumes the woman is interested in sex, because for example, she had a drink with him in a bar, while she believes she is simply engaging in friendly behavior. Men and women do live in different worlds and there are different meanings attributed to events, but to call such instances where rape results *victim* precipitation exemplifies a male perspective.

SEXISM AND ITS IMPLICATIONS FOR ONE WAY OF AVOIDING RAPE

In order for patriarchy to survive girls need to be brought up to believe that men, specifically men in their family and later their husbands, can be trusted and will take care of them. Conversely we are told women are not to be trusted. In order to win a caretaker of one's own, girls are told to be 'nice'—it is our stock in trade. Niceness not only refers to sexual behavior but to a whole way of dealing with men in a pleasant, unassertive, supportive manner. Girls who were not nice in this way came to a bad end.

But the Queen's Bench Foundation Study, *Rape, Prevention and Resistance* (1976) found that 'attempted rape victims were more than twice as likely to respond in a rude or unfriendly manner,' when they were approached by men who were planning to assault them. Moreover 'attempted rape victims were more likely than rape victims to be suspicious of their future assailants' and to trust these feelings even though they didn't know why they felt uneasy. These feelings may have arisen in the course of an apparently friendly conversation, since in over half the cases they report the attack was preceded by casual conversation. They trusted their feelings even though we have been taught that we as women are illogical, and our sense of how things are has been systematically devalued.

There are a number of examples of suspiciousness leading to rape avoidance in my own study. For example when a would-be rapist told one woman that he had a gun in his pocket and another was told he had a knife under the car seat both women said, 'Show me.' In both cases the men were bluffing and because the women knew there was no weapon they were able to use strategies to avoid the rape.

I therefore suggest that notable psychologist Erik Erikson's famous developmental stages be changed for women. He states that the successful outcome of the first stage is basic trust. I say that for women living in our society as its exists, the successful resolution is basic *mistrust*, at least if you don't want to be a rape victim. This perspective makes life difficult and unpleasant, but that is what we mean when we say women are oppressed.

THE ROLE OF THE WOMEN'S MOVEMENT IN FIGHTING RAPE: A SELECTIVE CHRONOLOGY

Since we must have hope in order to continue our struggle, and this paper has been a woeful litany, let me end with some landmarks in the role of the fight against rape by the Women's Movement.

1971: Radical Feminist Speakout on rape.
       Susan Griffin's *Rape, the all-American crime* published.
1972: Feminist Rape Crisis centers started.
1972: NOW National Task Force on Rape started.
1974: Process of revising rape laws having some success. Michigan law passed at the behest of and with the support of feminists. (It went into effect in 1975.)
1975: Brownmiller's *Against Our Will* published.
1976: Favorable outcomes of the Inez Garcia and Joann Little trials. Legitimization of rape a social problem. Mathias bill set up Center for the Prevention and Control of Rape as part of the National Institute of Mental Health to fund research. Struggle against the co-optation of the anti-rape movement and loss of the feminist analysis, e.g., the FAAR newsletter.

There is no *conclusion* to this paper because we must *continue* our struggle against violence against women.

REFERENCES

Albin, R. S. 1977. Psychological studies of rape. *Signs* 3 (2), 423–436.
Amir, M. 1971. *Patterns in Forcible Rape*. The University of Chicago Press, Chicago.

Bart, P. 1972. The myth of a value-free psychotherapy. In: Bell, W. and Mau, J. A. (eds), *The Sociology of the Future*, pp. 113–159. Russell Sage Foundation, New York.

Bart, P. 1975a. Rape doesn't end with a kiss, *Viva* 2 (9).

Bart, P. 1975b. Rape and the criminal justice system. Paper presented at The Society for the Study of Social Problems, San Francisco.

Bart, P. 1975c. Unalienating abortion, demystifying depression and restoring rape victims. Paper presented at the meetings of the American Psychiatric Association, Anaheim, California.

Bart, P. 1976a. Book review of Hilberman, E. *The Rape Victim*, American Psychiatric Association, Washington, DC, 1976. *Woman and Health* 1.

Bart, P. 1976b. Book review of Brodyaga, L, *et al., Rape and Its Victims*. A Report for Citizens, Health Faculties and Criminal Justice Agencies. National Institute of Law Enforcement and Criminal Justice, 1975. *Women and Health* 1 (5).

Bart, P. 1978. Victimization and its discontents or psychiatric ideologies of violence against women as a form of violence against women. Paper presented at the meetings of The American Psychiatric Association, Atlanta.

Brownmiller, S. 1975. *Against Our Will: Men, Women and Rape*. Simon & Schuster, New York.

French, M. 1977. *The Women's Room*. Jove (HBI) Book, New York.

Griffin, S. 1971. Rape, the all-American crime. *Ramparts* 10, 26–35.

Herman, J. and Hirschman, L. 1977. Father–daughter incest. *Signs* 2 (4), 735–757.

Hilberman, E. 1976. *The Rape Victim*. American Psychiatric Association, Washington, DC.

Hoffman, S. and Dodd, T. 1975. Effects of various victim characteristics on attribution of responsibility to an accused rapist. Paper presented at the 21st annual meeting of the Southeastern Psychological Association.

Howell, M. 1974. What medical schools teach about women. *New Engl. J. Med*. pp. 304–307.

Kanin, E. 1957. Male aggression in dating-courtship relation. *Am. J. Sociol*. 63, 197–204.

Kanin, E. 1971. Sexually aggressive college males. *J. College Student Personnel* 12, 107–110.

Marolla. J, and Scully, D. 1978. Rape and psychiatric vocabularies of motive. Paper presented at the meetings of the American Sociological Association.

Newsweek. 1977. 90, 19.

Pleck, E. 1978. Wife beating in America. Paper presented at the meetings of the American Studies Association, Boston.

Pleck, E., Pleck, J., Grossman, M. and Bart, P. 1977–1978. The battered data syndrome. *Victimology* 2 (3–4), 680–683.

Queen's Bench Foundation. 1976. *Rape Prevention and Resistance*. San Francisco.

Scully, D. and Bart, P. 1973. A funny thing happened on the way to the orifice: women in gynecology textbooks. *Am. J. Sociol*. 78 (4), 1045–1050.

Scully, D. 1977. Skill acquisition in obstetrical gynecology: social processes and implications for patient care. PhD dissertation. University of Illinois.

Steinmetz, S. 1977–1978. The battered husband syndrome. *Victimology* 2 (3–4), 499–502.

Wisan, G. 1978. The treatment of rape in criminology textbooks. Paper presented at the meetings of the American Sociological Association.

COMMENT: PAULINE BART

Rereading this decade-old article I was surprised at how the analysis held up and pleased that there has been progress in rape law reform. Thirty states [of the USA] have abolished or modified the marital rape exemption. The phrase 'against her will' has been modified in some states to say 'without her consent' and in Illinois the phrase has been eliminated (1984). Thus in Illinois, instead of the prosecution having to prove the victim did not consent, the defense has to prove 'by word or deed' that she did. The constitutionality of the law is currently being challenged, because the opponents say the terms 'force' and 'bodily harm' are vague and overbroad (Pennock, 1986)—they do not understand what force means in this context, thus providing evidence for the radical feminist contention that men can't distinguish between forced and consensual sex, or understand what constitutes harm to women.

Were I to write the article now, I would discuss pornography as pro-rape propaganda (see Bart, 1985, 1986), and refer to the work of Malamuth and Donnerstein (1984). They present a series of empirical articles demonstrating the harm of pornography, particularly the combination of sex and violence. Surely I would share my enthusiasm for the theory and practice of MacKinnon and Dworkin's conceptualization of pornography as sex discrimination and MacKinnon's latest book, Feminism Unmodified: Discourses on Law and Life *(1987).*

And, of course, I would include the findings of the research which furnished the basis for the above article, findings which have been presented in four articles and a book (1981, 1983; Bart and O'Brien, 1984; Bart and O'Brien, 1985). We found that active strategies were associated with avoiding or preventing rape when attacked, that talking by itself was ineffective, and that pleading was associated with being raped. Thus women who physically resisted, who yelled or screamed and who fled or tried to flee were more likely to avoid rape than those who didn't, contrary to the extant ideology that the best method of avoidance is the humanistic strategy of trying to get the rapist to see you as a human being, and that physical resistance will only result in serious injury (it is likely to result in minor injury, but lack of resistance is no guarantee of lack of serious injury in addition to the rape). In addition, the more different types of strategies the woman uses, the more likely she is to avoid rape, and women who avoided rape were much more likely to focus on not being raped, while those who were raped focused on not being killed or mutilated. The feminist analysis that traditional 'feminine' socialization was associated with victimization was supported. Women who, when they were children, played football, a contact sport; whose parents did not intervene when they physically fought with other children, or advise them not to fight back; whose image of the future did not include marriage and a family, were more likely to avoid rape. And women who, as adults had acquired competency skills such as knowing how to extinguish a grease fire, administer first aid, who had taken self-defense courses, and who exercised regularly were more likely to avoid rape when attacked.

In sum, both the traditional advice we were given to avoid rape and the traditional socialization we were given (if we were white and middle-class) does indeed set us up to be vulnerable to rape when attacked.

MacKinnon writes that if we do not see the bloody footprints tracking across our desks we are not writing about women (1987: 9). I have seen the bloody footprints.

REFERENCES TO COMMENT

Bart, Pauline. 1981. A study of Women Who Both Were Raped and Avoided Rape. *Journal of Social Issues*, **37**, 4, pp. 123–137.

'Why Men Rape'. In: *Western Sociology Review*, Special Issue on Micro Macro Linkages, **14**, 1, 1983, pp. 46–57.

'Through Women's Eyes: Defining Danger in the Wake of Sexual Assault.' Kim Lane Scheppele and Pauline B. Bart, *Journal of Social Issues*, **39**, 2, 1983, pp. 63–80.

'Stopping Rape: Effective Avoidance Theories,' with Patricia O'Brien. *Signs*, Autumn 1984, **10**, 1, pp. 83–101.

'Pornography: Institutionalizing Woman Hating and Eroticizing Dominance and Submission for Fun and Profit.' *Justice Quarterly*, **2**, 2, 1985. And rejoinder to Durham, March 1986.

'The Different Worlds of Women and Men: Attitudes Toward Pornography and Responses to 'Not a Love Story'—a Film About Pornography.' (with Linda Freeman and Peter Kimball). *Women's Studies International Forum*, **8**, 4, 1985, 307–322.

Stopping Rape: Successful Survival Strategies (with Patricia O'Brien). Pergamon Press, New York, 1985.

Illinois Criminal Sexual Assault of 1984, P.A. 83–1067 and 83–1117. Springfield, Ill., Illinois Coalition Against Sexual Assault.

MacKinnon, Catherine A., *Feminism Unmodified: Discourses on Law and Life*, Cambridge: Harvard University Press, 1987.

Malamuth, Neil M. and Donnerstein, Edward, (eds), Pornography and Sexual Aggression. Orlando, FL: Academic Press, 1984.

Pennock, Jr., Harold H. Brief and Argument for the Defendant-Appellee, Haywood Nos. 63082, 63539, 63540, 63541 in the Supreme Court of Illinois, 1986.

6

Androcentric Rhetoric in Sociobiology[1]

Sarah Lucia Hoagland

> The word, dominate, comes from the proto-Indo-European root,
> *dema*, meaning house or household. Words sharing the same root
> include madam, mademoiselle, madonna, danger, dungeon, despot.
> (*American heritage dictionary*)

As long ago as 1948, Herschberger exposed the androcentric nature of language scientists use in describing human and other animal behavior. Scientists persistently depict males as the norm while defining females in relation to them, naming females passive and inferior. Herschberger assures us, against 'expressed fears of poets,' that language retains its myth-making qualities (p. 73). Today, over 30 years later, the scientific appropriation of the power of naming remains in full force. Syntactic and semantic features of scientific language about wimmin and females in general force the unsuspecting reader to agree to stereotypic hypotheses which the scientist never openly defends.

The suasive use of language in science cannot be considered independently of its political context. Wimmin's attempts to gain equality in this democratic society have been met by official appeals to biology where the dogma of male supremacy appears on safe ground. It is no accident that just as the feminist demand for rights again achieves public acknowledgement, those in power divert ethical attention to biology, this time sociobiology. Here amid allegedly objective descriptions of animal behavior, male domination, including rape and infanticide (Brown, 1977: 32-39) becomes an ethical necessity for the preservation of the species.

The suasive use of language is particularly apparent in Wilson's (1975) book, *Sociobiology: The new synthesis*. Wilson states that 'males are dom-

[1] This paper was delivered at the panel, 'Language About Women' for the forum, 'Women and Language' at the annual meeting of the Modern Language Association, December 28, 1978, New York, NY. I am grateful to Julia Penelope (Stanley) and Susan Wolfe (Robbins) for their work on sexism in language and to Julia Penelope for her work on the passive.

70

inant over females' (p. 291; see also pp. 552, 568), and expects the reader to accept this as a universal or near-universal (p. 531) natural, and therefore moral, imperative. Yet nowhere does he defend such a claim; instead he embeds its bases in the semantics and syntax of the language he uses to describe animal behavior. Further, he depicts male aggression as the norm while characterizing female resistance as antisocial and non-adaptive, thereby rendering it invisible *qua* resistance. By his use of language, Wilson avoids defending a thesis of near-universal male domination and instills in the reader the impression that the thesis is a mere summation of the data.

Wilson distinguishes 'dominance aggression' from 'sexual aggression' and 'territorial aggression,' defining 'dominance aggression' as 'the assertion of one member of a group over another in acquiring access to a piece of food, a mate, a place to display, a sleeping site or any other requisite that adds to the genetic fitness of the dominant individual' (p. 257; see also pp. 11, 242 and 287). Since dominance results in access to mates, dominant males must dominate other males, not females. If males dominate females, according to Wilson's own definition, males must assert themselves over females to gain access to territory or food or other females. Yet nowhere does Wilson argue that this occurs as a near-universal phenomenon; nor does his data support such a hypothesis. One is left to wonder, thus, what exactly is the basis of Wilson's assumption of near-universal male domination over females.

In elaborating his claim that 'males are dominant over females,' Wilson states, 'It is typical for the rank ordering of the males to lie entirely above that of females' (p. 291). Wilson apparently means that in most societies males engage in dominance aggression and females do not, or females engage in dominance aggression with other females but not with males, and so do not fall within the male ranking. Yet how does this show that males dominate females, or even that males are dominant over females? Without the institutionalized male-supremist power difference of human societies, separate male and female spheres in and of themselves do not indicate dominance of the male sphere.

Wilson's linguistic androcentrism takes a variety of forms. For example, having pointed out that pike blenny males engage in territorial aggression while females come and go through any male's territory at will, he implies that pike blenny males thereby control females. (Pike blenny is a type of fish.) He states:

'Female pike blennies *are not challenged* by resident males. Very probably the *tolerance* toward them is the prelude to courtship during the breeding season' (p. 260).[2]

Thus pike blenny males must dominate female pike blennies not because they engage in dominance aggressive encounters with females and win, but rather because they do not engage in them. This bit of significant reasoning lies

---

[2] Throughout this chapter, all emphases are mine.

buried within the language of description and so removed from logical or factual challenge. Female pike blennies also do not challenge males, or all males, during breeding season; yet we find no statement about how females *tolerate* males.

By choosing the word 'tolerance,' Wilson embeds a justification of the thesis of male dominance in the language, and so is in a position to present the thesis as a statement of fact rather than an hypothesis in need of investigation and defense. Further, upon examination a hidden line of reasoning surfaces: If males engage in dominance aggressive encounters with other males, then dominance must be the standard; and by the law of excluded middle, females not engaging in them, or not engaging in them with males, must be submissive.

Another case of this form of semantic manipulation appears in Wilson's discussion of the *lion* pride. Until recently it was generally accepted by the scientific community that lions dominate lionesses. Yet sociobiologists substantiated the claim with nothing more than the language of description which originated from an androcentric perspective. For example, in *African genesis* Ardrey states:

> 'A lion pride is a hunting unit, and this would seem to be the sole reason for its existence. And it is the extraordinary dominance of the male lion, and little else, that welds the society together' (Ardrey, 1963: 101).

Reed refuted Ardrey's hypothesis in *Women's evolution from matriarchal clan to patriarchal family*:

> 'What Ardrey calls a 'lion pride' is actually a pack of lionesses who have *permitted* a male access to their group. On his own, the male lion hunts and kills his own food; but when he is attached to a group of females they are in charge of the hunt. As Ardrey puts it, 'The male lion rarely makes the kill. Such *entertainments* he leaves to the lionesses. His normal position in a hunting pride is in the center with the lionesses spread out on either flank considerably in advance.'
> If, as Ardrey says, the 'sole reason' for the lion pride is hunting and providing food, the male is not an indispensible member since he does neither. The females are the huntresses providing food for themselves and their cubs and even feeding the male they have permitted in their group. Contrary to Ardrey's opinion, the pride of lionesses is welded together not by the extraordinary dominance of the male, but by the maternal function of the females' (Reed, 1975: 55).

Nevertheless, Wilson chooses to make the following statement:

> 'The pride males *permit* the females to *lead* them from one place to another, and they *depend* on them to hunt and kill most of the prey. Once the animal is downed, the males move in and use their *superior* size to push the lionesses and cubs aside to eat their fill' (Wilson, 1975: 504).

Notice that the size of the lions is not *larger* but *superior*. More importantly, by using the word '*permit*' and not stating that the lions *follow* the female-centered, female-led pride, Wilson manages to incorporate some of Reeds' information from her refutation of Ardrey while linguistically retaining the general androcentric assumption that lions dominate lionesses. Nowhere does Wilson claim that lionesses *tolerate* lions, even though he admits that lionesses will unite to launch concerted attacks and drive a lion off (p. 504). Through the use of words like 'permit' and 'tolerate' Wilson embeds an hypothesis of male domination in such a way that the explicit claim appears to be a mere summation of fact, in no need of defense.

Wilson's linguistic male supremicism is even more prominent. By using the word 'harem' he imposes a semantic pattern upon various animal groupings to instill in the reader the general feeling that males are dominant over females. He defines 'sexual aggression' (as distinct from 'dominance aggression'), selecting the hamadryas baboon as his model:

> 'Males may threaten or attack females for the sole purpose of mating with them or forcing them into more prolonged sexual alliance. *Perhaps the ultimate development in higher vertebrates* is the behavior of male hamadryas baboons, who *recruit* young females to build a *harem* and continue to threaten and harass these *consorts* throughout their lives to prevent them from *straying*' (p. 242).

Wilson later mentions 'true harems' for which 'females are specifically recruited and defended' (p. 445); and twice in the book he distinguishes herds of females 'controlled' by a single 'dominant' male (i.e., a male who has driven other males off) from herds of females attended by males during breeding season (pp. 480, 468). However, he defines *'harem polygamy'* merely as 'simultaneous multiple matings' (p. 327; see also pp. 328-329), and he freely applies the term 'harem' when mentioning female-centered societies such as the mountain sheep (p. 36). The careful reader will discover bits of information on the mountain sheep scattered throughout the book to use in forming a composite: This society is female-centered (p. 36), a few males 'associate' with the female herd only during mating season (p. 438), and females 'inherit' home ranges from other females (p. 169). To term such groupings of females *harems* is nothing short of semantic exploitation for the purpose of proposing the hypothesis of near-universal male domination without openly defending it. By his definition of 'harem polygamy' and his use of the term 'harem' throughout the book, Wilson manages to include under the category 'harem-forming' those societies in which females and males have separate spheres and interact only during mating season, indeed, all societies in which females do not clearly dominate males.

Significantly, Wilson takes the behavior of the male hamadryas baboon as a model of ultimate development (of heterosex) in higher vertebrates (p. 242). He terms threatened and attacked females *consorts* who have been *recruited*; and if they escape, according to him they have *strayed*. Elsewhere in the book Wilson terms the initial stage of this male behavior *mothering*. He states:

> 'Kummer found that subadult males start herding females even before sexual activity begins. They try to kidnap and *mother* infants less than six months of age. Eventually they *adopt* juvenile females and use *threat* to *condition* them to stay close. Kummer

believes that the bond has evolved as a *transferred* form of the *mother–child relationship*'
(p. 514).

Thus a physically violent relationship between a subadult male and an infant
or juvenile female is, according to Wilson, based on the *mother*-child
relationship; and female infants, who upon growing up must be conditioned
by means of threats into remaining with a male, have been *adopted* and
mothered.

The behavior of the hamadryas baboon society does in fact offer a model
of male dominance of females. Yet Wilson never defends a claim that this
particular behavior is a near-universal phenomenon. He offers no evidence
for many of the societies he discusses that there are any dominance aggressive
or territorial aggressive or sexual aggressive encounters between male and
female. As a result the careful reader is led to the conclusion that in claiming
male dominance over females is a near-universal phenomenon, Wilson
associates sexual activity *per se* with dominance aggression—that he views
the heterosex act itself as an act of dominance aggression performed by males
against females. A hint appears in the opening lines of his chapter, 'Sex and
Society': 'Sex is an anti-social force in evolution. Bonds are formed between
individuals in spite of sex and not because of it' (p. 314).

Perhaps most indicative of this line of reasoning is his equation of the
phrase 'female *receptive* posture' with the phrase 'female *submissive* posture'
(see pp. 283, 153). Through this equation Wilson embeds the idea that by
merely engaging in sex, the male dominates the female: A female who has sex
with a male is, by that act, dominated by a male. Significantly, he depicts a
subordinate male as 'presenting himself in a *female receptive posture*' (p.
281) or elsewhere, 'in a *pseudofemale* posture to be mounted' (p. 181).
Wilson uses the label '*homosexual*' to characterize this activity (p. 281); and
he notes that one scientist compared to a *military salute* a 'homosexual
appeasement ceremony' in which the 'male [hamadryas baboon] receiving
the presentation mounts briefly in an *imitation* of copulation' (p. 230). The
linguistically embedded message is clear: Male penetration equals male
domination.

Wilson claims 'females are dominant over males' in a few societies (p. 291),
though he has difficulty accepting the idea: He offers a table of correlates of
dominance rank order of ungulates and primates. One of the categories he
lists is 'resource controlled.' When he lists males as dominant, he includes
such resources controlled as females, food, territory. However, when he lists
female ungulates and primates as dominant, only a question mark appears in
the 'resource controlled' column (p. 293). In light of his equation of 'female
receptive posture' and 'female submissive posture,' to engage in sex with a
male is itself to be dominated or controlled. No wonder Wilson is puzzled
about what *resource* dominant females *control*.

Describing the female hyena who dominates males, Wilson labels the
clitoris a pseudo-penis:

'A . . . mutually beneficial form of *trickery* is performed by the female hyena, who possesses an *extraordinarily realistic pseudopenis* that she uses as part of appeasement signaling' (p. 229).

Even though the female is larger than the male, she must, according to Wilson, resort to trickery to dominate the male. As to his label, '*pseudo-penis*,' Wilson enlighteningly explains:

> Sometimes a phenomenon allows only one reasonable explanation. The *pseudopenis* of the female hyena is a unique structure used conspicuously as part of the greeting ceremonies of these dangerously aggressive animals. Wolfgang Wickler has suggested that the organ evolved as a *mimic* of the *true* male penis to *permit* females to participate in the *conciliatory communication* within packs, which is *based* principally on penile displays. Druck (1972) has stated flatly that 'it is impossible to think of any other purpose for this special female feature than for use in the meeting ceremony'; and he is probably right' (p. 29; see also p. 181).

Note also, while Wilson claims the female hyena dominates, he characterizes her as engaged in *conciliatory communication,* not in *dominance aggression.* Further, her behavior is *based on* behavior of the subordinate male.

Other instances of androcentric semantics abound. When describing an experiment with female hamadryas and anubis baboons, Wilson terms the refusal of the female anubis to tolerate the attacks of a male hamadryas an *adjustment failure*:

> 'Kummer has described an experiment that illustrates how dramatically one feature of social behavior can change if sufficient stress is exerted. When a hamadryas female is placed in a group of anubis baboons, she quickly alters her social responses from the hamadryas forms to those of her new associates. Within half an hour she starts fleeing from attacking males like an anubis female rather than moving toward them. The reverse experiment is even more suggestive. An anubis female inserted into a hamadryas troop learns within one hour to approach the attacking male, thus conforming to the harem system that characterizes the species as opposed to her own. The adaption is *imperfect*, however. After learning the behavior perfectly, the majority of anubis females escape the herding male and stay away for good. This *inability to make a total adjustment* might be sufficient by itself to explain why the anubis troop at the Awash Falls *failed* to shift to a hamadryas organization even when surrounded by hamadryas societies in an unaltered environment' (p. 518).

Further, Wilson implies that the active repulsion of males by females during food shortage is *anti-social* (p. 36). Yet when male hamadryas baboons injure females over which they are fighting, or bull elephant seals trample pups to death while 'flopping about their spectacular territorial battles,' Wilson discusses *evolutionary compromise* (p. 132). And infanticide by males is casually discussed as a *social mechanism* (p. 321).

Throughout the chapter on sex and society, Wilson characterizes females through institutionalized forms of human male domination. He freely refers to *marriage, divorce* (p. 331), *cuckoldry, adultery* and *promiscuity* (p. 327). He characterizes female behavior as *coy* (p. 320).[3] And he uses the terms,

---

[3] Wilson uses all these terms despite his argument elsewhere against 'religionists' who claim that sex should be reserved for reproduction: he admonishes them to recognize as incorrect the assumption that 'in reproduction man [*sic*] is essentially like other animals' (p. 554).

'the *courting sex*, and 'the *courted sex*' or 'the *passive sex*' (see, e.g., p. 320). While he states that the *courted sex* is ordinarily female thus implying that males are sometimes the *passive sex*, nevertheless his terminology evokes a passive/active dualism whereby in virtue of heterosexual activity alone, Wilson implies one sex is dominant over another.

To complete his male-identification of females, Wilson uses the phrase, '*spinster* hypothesis' to characterize a situation in which 'an animal that has little chance of succeeding on its own chooses instead to *serve* a close relative' (p. 290). Further, he characterizes females who bond with other females who have offspring, *maiden aunts* (pp. 311, 343). Had he used the term '*lesbian*,' he would have implied that there are females who choose not to bond with males. As it is, he leaves the reader impressed with the idea that all females are heterosexual and that females who do not have a male could not get one, further semantically embedding the hypothesis that males are dominant over, control, females.

Not surprisingly, therefore, Wilson selects as 'most satisfying' a table of evolutionary arrangements of primate societies based on the degree of male involvement, on the degree to which males are tolerated in these societies (p. 525, also p. 468). The more males 'are tolerated' in a given society, the higher it falls on this particular evolutionary scale. Further, while Wilson defines a troop as 'the basic social grouping of adult females and their dependant or semi-dependant offspring,' he nevertheless identifies the grades of evolutionary levels in male terms: '*unimale troop*,' '*age-graded male troop*,' 'and *multimale troop*.' In view of Wilson's semantic coercion, one may forgive the reader who neglects to ask, 'Tolerated by whom?' We are expected to understand that males tolerate males (p. 522). Yet among the species listed are the Colobus in which females are more powerful than males (p. 522), and the Lemur and Propithecus (p. 524) as well as the vervet and Sykes' monkey (p. 291) in which the females 'are dominant over' the males. Again, one must ask, who tolerates whom, and under what conditions?

Semantic exploitation also appears in Wilson's syntax. He employs, of course, the usual pseudo-generics. He uses '*man*' throughout the book as if the term designated a species. He refers to the male of a species by the species' name: a *cichlid fish* and its *mate* (p. 200), the courtship of the *goldeneye duck* (referring only to the male [p. 200]), or *chimpanzees* 'lead troop *mates* to food' (p. 199). And he uses a pseudo-generic in order to give the impression that males control a predominantly female activity; for example, he talks of the *lion* hunt (p. 54).

Most interesting is Wilson's choice in using the active or the passive voice to describe sexual behavior, for it contributes to the impression that males dominate females by virtue of engaging in heterosex. On occasion Wilson uses the passive to bury the male agent:

'Females are *recruited* and *defended* . . .' (p. 445).

Or:

> '. . . chimpanzee mothers *are attacked* far less often and with less intensity when they carry infants on their backs than when the infants are carried in a ventral, less visible position' (p. 352).

Or:

> '*Reproductive dominance* can result in the *insemination* of . . . females . . .' (p. 329).

Or again:

> 'As Darwin himself noted in 1871, even the naked skin of the woman *is used* as a sexual releaser' (p. 554).

In the third case, we also find a nominalized passive which buries the agent even further, making it more difficult to properly access the claim of dominance.

When using the active voice to describe female sexual behavior Wilson couches the action in significant contexts. For example he states:

> 'In intrasexual selection, which is based on aggressive exclusion among members of the courting sex, the matter is settled in a . . . direct way. A member of the *passive* sex simply *chooses* the winner or, to put the matter more realistically, it *chooses* from among a group of winners . . .' (p. 320).

When discussing 'reproductive success,' i.e., the number of copulations observed per number of individuals (male or female), Wilson states, females 'that *mated* only once or twice *received* more than sufficient sperm' (p. 325). And when discussing female birds *choosing* a courting male, Wilson argues that it is to the advantage of the female to join a *harem* (p. 328). By using the phrase '*passive sex*,' by referring to *harems*, and by characterizing females as *receiving* sperm, Wilson contextually undermines the effects of the active voice.

Very often he portrays biology as the agent in female activity. For example, the *pseudopenis* of the female hyena *permits* her to participate in *conciliatory communication* within the packs (p. 29). In at least one case, Wilson makes biology the agent in female sexuality in order to give the impression that males control female sexuality. In discussing a thesis that females select males on the basis of breeding time, Wilson announces proof that:

> '. . . females will tend to *evolve to breed* at the time most fit males are active' (p. 320).

Further, male behavior can activate female biology:

> '. . . the bowing of a male ring dove in the initial states of courtship . . . *activates* centers in the brain of the female dove that in turn induce secretion of pituitary gonadotropins. The gonadotropins induce growth of the ovaries and the release of estrogen which readies the female for sexual and nest-building behavior' (p. 199).

Wilson describes male sexual activity, on the other hand, most often without reference either to females or to biology. In describing the courtship of the goldeneye duck, he makes no reference to females or to the female estrus cycle as catalysts (p. 200). And describing automimicry, he states that 'males *possess* colored rumps only in those species in which the female sexual skin *is transformed* during estrus' (p. 230). In other words, what males *possess, happens* to females.

When Wilson does involve biology in male sexual behavior he nevertheless initially uses the active voice and excludes the female as agent or partial agent. Instead, part of her anatomy becomes object:

> '. . . the male silkworm moths *start searching* for the females when they *are immersed* in as few as 14,000 molecules of bombykol per cubic centimeter of air. . . . Tightly bound by this extreme signal specificity, the male *performs* as little more than a sexual guided missile, *programmed* to home on an increasing gradient of bombykol centered in the tip of the female's abdomen—the principal goal of the adult male's life' (p. 182).

When he depicts the female as agent, he uses the passive voice and focuses on the male:

> 'But only the males whose territories overlap the mating center *are accepted* by the females' (p. 332).

Most often, when discussing sexual behavior, Wilson designates the male as sexual agent. For example:

> 'Males of the *Pheidole sitarches* form conspicuous mating swarms into which the virgin queens fly *to be mated*' (p. 324).

Or:

> 'As many as 400 males spread out over a lek area of a hectare or more, and a comparable number of females visit for short intervals *to be mated*' (p. 332).

Or again:

> 'Each of the three displaying cocks occupies a small territory at the center of the lek. The less showy hens crowd in from all directions *to be mated* by these favored few' (p. 333).

Or:

> 'Receptive females wander through the networks as part of nursery herds and *are mated* by those territorial males able to detain them' (p. 332).

Although Wilson uses the passive voice in designating the male as agent, his point is clearly to give the impression that the male is in control. In these contexts the male remains stationary, waiting for the female. Had Wilson used the active voice, he would have had to designate the female as agent or depict the male as waiting on the female.

In general, Wilson uses the active and passive voices to underwrite claims of dominance on the one hand, and submission on the other:

> 'Dominant male rhesus monkeys *raise* their tails and heads and *display* their testicles by *lowering them*' (p. 181).

Whereas:

> 'Subordinates present themselves in a pseudofemale posture *to be mounted*' (p. 181).

Scientists often describe female sexual behavior in the passive voice, creating the impression that whatever occurs, *happens* to us. One attempting to justify such a characterization on the grounds that females are controlled by hormones and go through cycles has been tricked by androcentric rhetoric scientists use in description. Males are subject to just as much hormonal control (p. 320) and go through cycles also. Even when this information is mentioned, male scholars typically bury and ignore it. Through Wilson's suasive use of language, both syntactic and semantic, the reader is left with the impression, but with no substantial argument, that females are subjected to biology or to males while males control their biology and females.

Androcentrism in the language of sociobiology and other social sciences abounds. Of course, androcentrism appears at other levels of scientific endeavor, in particular at the level of explanation and theory.[4] But significant manipulation emerges from the language scientists use which makes their androcentric assumptions virtually inaccessible: By engaging in dialogue with them, one has already accepted a particular perspective and set of stereotypes, sexist as well as racist and heterosexist. By the very act of our naming, scientists and other male elite determined the boundaries of female behavior. Under the existing female stereotype, only certain descriptions of our behavior count; and the limits of description in turn determine the boundaries of possible explanation and theory.

REFERENCES

Ardrey, Robert. 1963. *African genesis*. Dell, New York.
Brown, Rid. 1977. The monkeys who kill their young. *Mother Jones*, 2 (1), 32–39.
Herschberger, Ruth. 1948. *Adam's rib*. Harper & Row, New York.
Reed, Evelyn. 1975. *Women's evolution: From matriarchal clan to patriarchal family*. Pathfinder Press, New York.
Wilson, E. O. 1975. *Sociobiology: The new synthesis*. Harvard University Press, Cambridge, Mass.

[4] See, e.g., Andrée Conrad. 1979. Intractable ambiguities: love, death and other birth defects as seen by sociobiology. *Book Forum*, 4 (4), 602-614 (a review of E. O. Wilson, *On human nature*; Mary Midgley, *Beast and man: The roots of human nature*; and Arthur L. Caplan (ed.), *The Sociobiology debate: Readings on ethical and scientific issues*).

7

Men, Women and Sexuality: A Feminist Critique of the Sociology of Deviance[1]

Sue Rodmell

INTRODUCTION

The study of deviance has become one of the most popular sub-disciplines in sociology during the last 10 to 15 years, especially among the radical-chic. An unflagging interest in dope smokers, alcoholics, homosexuals, delinquent gangs, transvestites and transsexuals has brought to the fore an awareness of the activities of a number of 'marginal groups,' particularly in America, but also in other Westernized societies. Researchers into deviance are, in Gouldner's words

> 'at home in the world of hip, drug addicts, jazz musicians, cab drivers, prostitutes, night people, drifters, grifters, and skidders: the "cool world" ' (Gouldner, 1974).

Two pronounced features of the sociology of deviance are firstly, a concern with various forms of sexual conduct, and secondly, the adoption of a sympathetic identification with the world view of the deviant in question. The study of deviant behavior or deviant states-of-being lends itself easily to the description and analysis of sexual conduct, such that in everyday parlance the term 'deviant' is often taken to be synonymous with 'sexual deviant.' The sympathetic stance of the researcher with the world view of the deviant is in part a reaction to earlier criminological analyses in which criminals and deviants were seen as pathologically abnormal in a normal, consensual world. This empathizing perspective remains as a response to what is held to be the harsh moralizing of law enforcement agencies in their treatment of deviant individuals and groups. But it is more than this. Sociologists of

---

[1] I should like to thank Sheila Allen and Carol Smart for their helpful comments on an earlier draft of this chapter.

deviance aim to articulate the views of groups or individuals whose access to institutionalized power structures is restricted. Deviants, and particularly sexual deviants, are thus provided with an authoritative outlet through which their voices may be heard. The authenticity of their life-styles is affirmed and validated through sociological recognition (Gouldner, 1974).

This is, of course, an admirable form of political practice, in accordance with a critical approach to the structural inequalities suffered by the powerless in any given social system. We should be concerned, therefore (but not surprised), that many scholars of deviance fail to situate their analyses within a broader framework of socio-sexual power structures in male-dominated societies. This failure has already been succinctly criticized with regard to female criminality (Heidensohn, 1968; Rosenblum, 1975; Smart, 1976). In the discussion that follows I shall focus on one specific aspect of socio-sexual power relations, that is, on *male sexual violence towards women*, and the treatment of these relations within the sociology of deviance.[2] I have been necessarily selective in my criticisms, but the works quoted are not atypical of the general tenor of analysis. I begin by considering the conceptualizations of deviance and crime put forward by sociologists of deviance, which in themselves lead to misconceived notions about the dynamics of male–female sexual relations.

DEVIANCE AND CRIME

Many sociologists of deviance make a basic assumption concerning the conceptualization of deviance and crime, an assumption which leads them to misinterpret the nature of sexual power relations between men and women. The most common definition of deviance is that of behavior which contravenes the dominant social or cultural mores of a given society. Crime, on the other hand, is usually defined as behavior which breaks the criminal law of a society. Most sociologists are quick to point out that not all deviance is crime (for example, mental illness, alcoholism, most male homosexuality). It is taken as given, however, that most crime, and especially 'serious crime' is also deviant. That is, *because* crime is a violation of the law it is *also* a contravention of cultural mores. We find, in fact, that the terms 'crime' and 'deviance' are often used indiscriminately by writers in their discussions of crime, though not in their discussions of non-criminal deviance. 'Serious crime' typically refers to murder, rape, robbery, burglary and assault. These are conceptualized as deviant acts in so far as they all meet with condemnation from the general population as well as from the judiciary and agents of social control.

This would appear to be a grossly over-simplified view of the matter. As

---

[2] I have not included in this discussion any analysis of the treatment of male-to-male sexual offences in the sociology of deviance.

feminists have pointed out, there are many indications that in practice sexual crimes against women do not meet with universal or even consistent condemnation (Brownmiller, 1975; Griffin, 1971; Reynolds, 1974). We cannot assume, although many deviancy theorists do, that because rape is purported to be a crime 'second only to murder' in its seriousness, it will be perceived as such by the population as a whole or by the agencies of law enforcement. I shall discuss this in more detail below, but I want to make the point here that even in works which *do* recognize a conceptual distinction between deviance and crime, this does not extend to the arena of male sexual violence.

An American sociologist recently noted that certain forms of sexual conduct are no longer deviant. These are

> 'the minor, taken-for-granted acts that meet with considerable acceptance by both the perpetrators and the general populace' (Sagarin, 1975).

Such behavior as non-marital sex or oral-genital heterosex, which remain crimes in some American states, are not deviant because

> 'they meet with little negative reaction, or would meet with little if discovered . . . *adult consensual* sexual acts, when they are in contravention of the law, might well be considered crimes without deviance' (my emphasis).

For Sagarin, the possibility of non-deviant crime hinges around the issues of consent between adults. Neither 'consent' nor 'adulthood' can be seen as unproblematic, however. In Britain at the present time, for instance, it is a crime for a male to have sexual intercourse with a female under 16 years, but there has been pressure for some time from a number of sources to lower the age of consent for females—in other words, to define adolescent girls as 'adults' for the purposes of consensual heterosex, since this type of sexual conduct should not be seen as deviant.[3] It is not my intention to expand on this particular debate here, but merely to point out that the issue of what constitutes consent to heterosex is open to conflicting definitions.[4]

Because of his stress on adult consensuality, Sagarin falls into the same trap as those deviancy scholars who fail to correctly conceptualize deviance and crime in the first place. He too assumes that there are some sexual acts which are universally condemned. Rape, he suggests, is a crime which 'virtually everyone agrees is evil,' a 'heinous offence' which is intrinsically bad.[5] However, as Weis and Borges have noted, it is only within a very narrowly defined frame of reference, based on the perceived *legitimacy of the victim*, that rape is condemned (Weis and Borges, 1973). It is precisely on the

---

[3] For example, *The Times* of February 8, 1978 reported the recommendation of modest sentencing for males convicted of having sexual intercourse with 'willing mature girls of under 16.'

[4] The Criminal Law Revision Committee is currently reviewing the law on the age of consent to sexual intercourse in Britain.

[5] In British legal terminology such offences are '*mala in se*,' that is, acts which are wrong in themselves. Other, less serious offences are '*mala prohibita*'—acts which the law prohibits but which are not intrinsically wrong.

issue of consent to heterosex by women that their legitimacy as rape victims hinges in English law. The view of the general populace towards rape in an American study shows a similarly ambivalent stance. When asked to rank crimes according to their perceived seriousness, respondents placed forcible rape of a stranger in 13th position, behind selling heroin, hijacking an aeroplane and the planned killing of a policeman (the latter being ranked most serious) (Rossi *et al.*, 1974). From the point of view of the rapist, Judy Gilley has shown that 'rape is a crime which *does* pay.' She points out that

> 'only 56 per cent of reports of rape lead to arrest, only 62 per cent of arrests lead to a prosecution, and only 36 per cent of prosecutions lead to a conviction. The conviction rate for actual rapes is therefore 0.9 per cent' (Gilley, 1974).

When we recall that the offense of rape has long been recognized as a notoriously under-reported crime in the first place—estimates of the ratio of reported to unreported rapes vary from 1:7 (Ennis, 1967) to 1:10 (Griffin, 1971)—then it is hard to understand why researchers persist in claiming that rape should be categorized with other non-sexual crimes such as murder, assault or robbery.

The inappropriateness of this simplified categorization can be seen in Sagarin's suggestion that these 'predatory acts' are not only condemned by the general public but also by the perpetrators themselves:

> 'The person committing the act does not feel self-righteous about his action; he believes it to be wrong, does not defend it, would not wish to be victimized in a similar manner by another and *demands protection ... against others* who would commit the very act he has performed' (Sagarin, 1975; my emphasis).

This statement is clearly nonsensical when applied to heterosexual sex offenders. It is precisely because such conduct cannot be collapsed into an overall conception of 'predatory acts' that Sagarin's argument becomes illogical. This does not mean, of course, that male sexual crimes against women are not predatory acts. They should be seen, however, as qualitatively different from other non-sexual offences, since they are *one-directional, sex-specific* acts. Whilst a robber or burglar may well seek protection against being robbed or burgled, a rapist has no need to seek protection against rape. The heterosexual sex offender is safe in the knowledge that the crime he commits will not be perpetrated on himself, that he will not be 'victimized in a similar manner.' This view of the rapist as being no different from any other non-sexual offender is in total contrast to the view of the rape victim who is perceived to have precipitated the event, at least in part (Amir, 1971), and who is put through a status degradation ceremony (Garfinkel, 1967) when she acts as a witness for the prosecution in a rape trial (Burgess and Holstrom, 1975). Sagarin is by no means unique among deviancy theorists in uncritically accepting the prevailing sexist definition of male sexual crimes in this way. Plummer, a British sociologist of sexual deviance, makes exactly the same error in his discussion. Making the point that the notion of deviance is relative to the culture of a given society at a given time, Plummer warns of the dangers of going too far, of sliding into a position of extreme relativity, in which

'it is possible to argue that anything is deviant and anything goes. If I choose to call homicide and rape 'normal' whilst tagging routine conversation and sleeping 'deviant' then this is my relativistic right. But it clearly leads to nonsense' (Plummer, 1975).

Yes, it does lead to nonsense, given the examples selected by Plummer. No one is likely to label routine conversation or sleeping 'deviant' but why choose rape, of all the possibilities available, to illustrate the inappropriateness of the 'normal' label? There are many instances in which rape is seen as just that; not only in the case of the conquering army taking its rewards (Brownmiller, 1975) but also in the case of the sexual assault of wife by husband (Maidment, 1978), and in the day-to-day relationships between men and women in male-dominated societies. As the authors of the Rape Crisis Centre Annual Report have noted:

'In a society where man is seen as the initiator and woman the consentor, aggressive and passive, predator and prey, wolf and chick, then rape is not abnormal. Obviously some rapists are clearly disturbed but they make up 2-2.5% of convicted rapists. Rape is the logical and extreme end of the spectrum of male/female relationships' (RCRP, 1977).

The point I am making is that through an inadequate conceptualization of the distinction between deviance and crime, many deviancy theorists habitually reduce male sexual crimes against women into an overall category which includes non-sexual offences like murder and assault. A more satisfactory specification would note that whilst there are acts and states-of-being which can be referred to as non-criminal deviance, there are also certain acts which should be seen as *non-deviant criminality*. In societies structured by male supremacist ideologies, male sexual crimes against women will not be treated in practice as deviant unless they contain elements which can be confidently condemned as savage and barbaric—that is, as pathologically abnormal forms of conduct. I noted earlier that the stance of empathy with the position of the deviant which characterizes the sociology of deviance arose partly in response to the pathological label imposed by legal and criminological theories and practices. I argue here that this reaction has had the result of effectively reducing the qualitative difference between sexual and non-sexual offenses and thus of negating the very real effects of male sexual crimes on women.

An awareness of this difference draws attention to the inadequacy of Plummer's statement that:

'You cannot steal, murder, rape, be blind, deaf or mentally ill without being aware that you are violating some publicly held norms (even if you adhere to the belief that they are not deviant statuses)' (Plummer, 1975).

Plummer here collapses both voluntary and involuntary deviance (for example, stealing and murdering with being deaf or blind) into over-all norm violation, but for the purposes of this paper it is his ignoring of the very effective mechanisms employed by those who *do* adhere to the belief that their acts are not deviant, with which I am concerned. These 'techniques of neutralization' (Sykes and Matza, 1957) involve such devices as the denial of injury or the denial of the victim. As Stevi Jackson has noted, these techniques are derived by the offender from widely accepted cultural norms (Jackson, 1978), and they are, moreover, taken by magistrates in considering pleas for mitigation (Taylor, 1972).

In the next section I should like to consider the implications of this failure to specify the difference between non-criminal deviance and non-deviant criminality for an analysis of male sexual crimes against women.

VICTIMS AS DEVIANTS: DEVIANTS AS VICTIMS

The perception of heterosexual crimes against women as the logical outcome of the socio-sexual structuring of male-dominated societies does not mean that 'deviancy' is not involved. I should like to suggest at this point that heterosexual crimes against women are particularly suited for the process of transferring the deviant label *from the offender to the victim*. This process takes place at various stages in the degradation ceremony, beginning with the initial contact with family, friends, the police, through the courts to the reponse of the media. It is often difficult to apply the deviant label to the sex offender since he is behaving in a socially typical masculine manner—being assertive, aggressive, with an eye for the main chance—yet it is important to present and perpetuate the view that sex offences are socially undesirable forms of behavior. This is necessary in order for the agencies of law enforcement to be seen to be doing their job of controlling the lower orders. There are more opportunities for the maintenance of the sex offense as socially undesirable in the presentation of the female victim as deviating from culturally prescribed norms of femininity, than there are in seeking to present the sex offender as the deviant. By the mere fact of *becoming a victim* she must be suspected of deviance.

This process of transferring the deviant label from the offender to the victim is the concern of the agencies of social control and its implications for women are the concern of feminism, since it centers around the operation of the 'double standard of morality' (Smart and Smart, 1978).

It has not, however, been the concern of the sociologists of deviance. I should like to briefly consider some of the reasons why many sociologists of deviance have not focused their attention on the ways in which victims of male sexual crimes become labeled as deviants. As I noted earlier, the sociology of deviance seeks to validate the authenticity of deviant life-styles. One of its basic premises is that in order to understand the phenomenon of deviance, it is necessary to 'place ourselves in the position of the actor, to empathize with him, to see the world as he does . . . [to see the deviant] . . . as a person responding in a recognizably purposive manner to an abnormal situation, the abnormality of that situation being only truly appreciable by a process of empathizing with the deviant.'

This process of empathizing, outlined by Taylor (1971), involves a perception of the deviant as, in Becker's words, 'more sinned against than sinning' (Becker, 1967). The 'actor,' once identified through the labeling procedure of social control agencies, is seen by sociologists of deviance as the 'underdog,' as the victim. There is, therefore, no other victim than the person labeled deviant through the social control process. It would be reasonable to assume, therefore, that sociologists of deviance would show interest in female victims of the judicial system in the same way as they focus on other powerless individuals and groups. But this is not the case.

Marcia Millman has already drawn attention to the invisibility of the victim within the sociology of deviance (Millman, 1975). She argues that it is important to look

'not only at the experiences of the 'deviant' . . . but also those of the victims, family members and innocent bystanders who have curiously vanished from sociological view.'

On the occasions when the actual victims of deviance enter into the analysis, they typically enter at the familiar level, in studies which focus on how wives, mothers or children manage to live with the deviance of a (usually male) family member. Even this is rare, as Millman indicates. In a collection of 52 readings on deviance, only three were devoted to patterns of accommodation to deviance within the family (Millman, 1975).

It appears that many sociologists of deviance are primarily interested only in the relationship between the labelers (the agencies of social control, bureaucrats and 'moral entrepreneurs') and the immediate and direct recipient of the label, the latter being overwhelmingly male. There is a clear awareness of the existence of institutionalized power structures at this level, but not on the level of male power over women through the exhibition of sexual crimes. Gouldner has pointed out that the sociology of deviance fails to recognize that 'everyone who is a subordinate *vis-à-vis* his superior is also a superior in relation to some third party' (Gouldner, 1974). It is precisely this third party who is ignored with the adoption of a stance in which the focus of concern is with the male deviant. It is only possible to empathize with the heterosexual sex offender, to 'place ourselves in his position,' if one is able to, and prepared to, ignore the third party. To do this, furthermore, one must be unlikely to be placed in the position of *being* that third party, the female victim of sexual crimes. Within the world view of the male sociologist of deviance, the actual victim of male sexual offenses does not enter into the analysis.

The invisibility of women, as victims in the case of deviancy theory, is characteristic of sociology as a whole, as many feminists have been pointing out for some time (Bart, 1971; Millman, 1975; Smith, 1974). The examples drawn from the sociology of deviance merely strengthen the view that sociology remains centrally concerned with male activity and male reasons for their activity. In a recent paper, Jalna Hanmer and Diana Barker reiterate the point that 'men only pay real attention to, and treat as significant, what has been said by other men as a social category' (Hanmer and Leonard, 1980). Women feature less frequently in sociological analysis, and then typically in relation to men (as the wife, mother, daughter, employee, etc.). The sociology of deviance reflects this. As Cynthia Epstein has stated

> 'even the radicals' bias, which favors the most modish underdog, is found to be in curious alliance with the bias of the profession's establishment on the woman question' (Epstein, 1974).

Thus, I argue that the sociology of deviance, in spite of its apparently radical perspective, remains male-oriented and male-defined. Many writers continue to perpetuate a sexist view of male/female relations which are unacceptable to feminism. From a feminist viewpoint there is clearly something amiss with the following statement made by an American sociologist regarding the social control of sexuality:

> 'A male might be sexually attracted to a fat female . . . dating an extremely fat girl violates normative expectations; such an offender runs the risk of derision and laughter, scorn and gossip—all powerful techniques of social control' (Henslin, 1978).

This may well be perfectly true. But the writer is obviously only concerned with the effects of scorn and gossip on the male 'offender.' The female's experiences in this regard are not of interest. She becomes *invisible* to the writer although it is her very *visibility* which prompted the example in the first place. Henslin is not concerned with the reasons why dating fat women induces comment, nor why it is less likely that the reverse would occur. That men can achieve a certain status regardless of their size and shape, whilst the status of women is ascribed in precisely those terms, does not merit a mention. Similarly, with regard to social control by age and peer group, Henslin suggests that:

> 'If a highschool student dates someone much younger than herself, she will receive negative reaction from peers, and a sanctioning system is likely to be put into effect' (Henslin, 1978).

The casual inclusion of the female pronoun is easily missed, yet to use the male pronoun would make the example far less meaningful. The question the author does not raise is why are women expected to relate to older men and not vice versa? Again, there is no consideration of differential access to status, power and authority between men and women. It is not that these statements are inaccurate. On the contrary. My criticism is that embodied within such statements are certain assumptions regarding the nature of heterosexual relations and socio-sexual control. These assumptions are never fully articulated, largely, I suspect, because they are not consciously realized by the writer.

The inadequacies discussed above—the failure to make clear the distinction between non-criminal deviance and non-deviant criminality, and the failure to specify the power structures on which sexual relationships are predicated—are facilitated by the narrowly defined parameters of the sociology of deviance within Western scholarship. It is to this inadequacy that I now want to turn.

DEVIANCY THEORY AND ETHNOCENTRISM

I have argued that many sociologists of deviance are preoccupied with the activities and experiences of male deviants, and consequently fail to take account of the trauma suffered by the female victims of sexual criminality. I want to suggest, further, that these theorists express an ethnocentric view of the world of Western heterosexuality in which the sexual dynamic between men and women is believed to be more restrained, more egalitarian and more civilized than that of 'other cultures,' It is not that sociologists of Western deviance are not interested in sexual conduct in other societies. Many writers use evidence from anthropological research to draw comparisons between one society and another (usually their own). In doing so, however, there is a tendency to project an objectively detached fascination for the bizarre practices of exotic peoples—a fascination reminiscent of early studies by anthropologists such as Malinowski or Frazer. The conclusion most usually drawn from the comparison is that such institutionalized methods of sociosexual control have no place in more 'advanced' cultures, with the possible exception of the lower orders operating within the 'sub-culture of violence' (Wolfgang and Ferracuti, 1967).

One of the most frequently cited societies in which male violence is exhibited is the Yanomamo—'the fierce people' (Chagnon, 1968).[6] Henslin comments that 'from the Yanomamo perspective, *not* to participate in wife-beating and gang-rape is the deviant act' (Henslin, 1978). Both men and women, he argues, hold to the normative expectation of male violence.

'The husband, his friends, his relatives and *even* his wife expect that a good husband beats his wife. A wife is *even* disappointed if she is not beaten, for she views bloody beatings as a sign of affection' (Henslin, 1978; my emphasis).

The methodological problems involved in gathering and analyzing anthropological data of this type, where male and female respondents may well be inhabiting 'autonomous but overlapping cognitive worlds' have been recognized by feminist writers and are well documented by Paula Webster (1978). Henslin fails to raise these issues, but proceeds to compare Yanomamo

[6] The title of Napoleon Chagnon's work is a misnomer. The men are fierce; the women are treated fiercely.

methods of social control with the relationships formed between men and women in American society. Yanomamo practices, he concludes, are

'so totally contrasting with our own cultural assumptions of normalcy that we have no equivalent comparative base . . . [and] . . . our perspectives have little match.'

Whilst there are aspects of Yanomamo relationships which may be seen as extreme manifestations of the 'complex of male supremacy' (Harris, 1975), there is no justification for arguing that Western heterosexual power structures are totally contrasting with these. Only last month (May 1980), *The Observer* newspaper reported the findings of a study carried out by the Department of Experimental Psychology at Oxford University, in which the researchers claimed that women

'admire men who are physically dominating, and they see aggression as a manifestation of manliness . . . they see their men as contemporary James Dean or Marlon Brando figures—rebels with spirit and anger. The men's anger is seen as an indication of their undying love. As long as they care enough to hit you, everything is all right' (*The Observer*, 1980).

There is no space here to enter into the debate on the accuracy of such observations. My point is that Henslin's claim that 'our perspectives have little match' could merely be the expression of naïvety, which is nevertheless surprising, coming from a scholar of the sociology of sexuality. As Carol Erlich pointed out some years ago, in her critique of Kenkel's (1966) claim that 'the double standard finds some approval among females.'

'This is a curiously naive notion for a social scientist to hold, for women would not be the first subordinate group in history to internalize attitudes which confirm their subordinate status' (Erlich, 1971).

Henslin's view could, on the other hand, be the display of an arrogant ethnocentrism which effectively says 'it doesn't happen here': male violence to women is reprehensible—something on which 'civilized' societies have no need to rely. But as Jalna Hanmer has pointed out

'the use of force and its threat, even though highly masked, is of sufficient importance in our own western industrialized society to be recognized as a major component in the social control of women by men' (Hanmer, 1978).

The inadequacy of Henslin's analysis is ironically illuminated by his own comment on the possibility of dangers arising if and when

'those working in the field of the sociology of sex fail to gain a larger perspective on what they are studying . . . [when] . . . they fail to see relationships of cultural patterns because they themselves are so tightly embedded in their own culture that those things they take for granted conceal these interconnections' (Henslin, 1978).

These interconnections, in this case, between male methods of control across societies, have not been made precisely because of the ethnocentric limitations embodied within much analysis of heterosexual power structures. Henslin falls into exactly the trap of which he warns. Male sexual violence is recognized as an institutionalized power structure only in 'fierce' societies.

Rarely, if ever, is it admitted that male supremacist attitudes and practices permeate the entire socio-sexual formation of both industrial and non-industrial societies.

It appears, then, that scholars are unwilling to recognize the existence of coercive heterosexuality as a form of social control of women by men in Western culture. They are more than ready to concede that an entire range of unusual, bizarre sexual practices do indeed occur throughout the West—we can match anything that primitive people get up to—but these practices only exist *within the context of mutual, consensual 'interaction'*[7] between the sexes. Citing Buckner (1971), Erich Goode suggests that we consider

> 'some of the fantastic ways in which men ("and women"—Goode) gain sexual gratification: homosexuality, fetishism, necrophilia, paedophilia, masturbation, oral intercourse, anal intercourse, oral-genital and oral-anal intercourse, bestiality, heterosexuality, voyeurism, exhibitionism, cluster-fucks[?], masochism, sadism, to name only the more direct methods' (Goode, 1978).

Apart from the fact that Goode attempts to integrate women into the analysis in a totally inappropriate fashion (how many of these activities do women actually engage in?), we have a view of modern 'interaction' which constitutes a veritable orgy of sex. In Western societies a view is put forward in which *power becomes subsumed within mutual consensuality*.

I have tried to indicate that many sociologists of deviance fail to account for the expression of male sexual violence as a form of social control in Western society. What is needed, in my view, is a redefinition of heterosexual structures which locates male sexual criminality within an analysis of power mechanisms through which men seek to maintain control over women. The narrow parameters which define the sociology of deviance prevent writers from acknowledging the interconnections between their own cultural practices and those of other social groups. This redefinition of heterosexual structures, in which many feminist researchers are engaged, places the experiences of women in the center of the analysis. It is not good enough merely to insert 'and women' at various points in the analysis, as so many male writers (and some women writers) do. What is required, as Hanmer and Leonard argue, is a different paradigm:

> 'one which pushes men to the side, giving them only half the stage, and which stresses that what passes for sociology . . . is really culture from men's point of view. This will not only be good for women, it will be good for sociology' (Hanmer and Leonard, 1980).

A NOTE ON LANGUAGE

One final point needs to be made about the use of language. Feminists have been pointing out for some considerable time that women are defined out of

---

[7] 'Interaction' is defined in *Collins English Dictionary* as: a mutual or reciprocal action or influence. The validity of the interactionist approach to the analysis of sexual power structures is, in my view, seriously limited by the focus on mutual reciprocity.

existence in works which habitually refer to both sexes as 'men'. Whilst I fully agree with this, I feel there is the danger of a 'genderless' language being used to *deny* the differences between men and women, particularly within the context of sexual practices and attitudes. Male sexuality and female sexuality are experientially distinct and cannot be properly defined and analyzed by reference to 'individuals' or 'humans' of indeterminate sex.[8] Several recent works, in an attempt to overcome the use of sexist language, either refer to 'men and women' as synonymous entities, or present the world as being populated by 'people.' Numerous claims are made about the nature of 'human sexuality.' Thoughout this paper I have referred to men when I mean men, and to women when I mean women. Critics were quick to point out that Kinsey's research on the sexuality of the 'human male' and the 'human female' in fact referred to North American white men and women in the mid-twentieth century. It is equally important to be aware of the problematic nature of a superficial linguistic shift from 'men' to 'individuals.'

REFERENCES

Amir, Menachem. 1971. *Patterns of Forcible Rape*. University of Chicago Press, Chicago.
Bart, Pauline. 1971. Sexism and social science: from the gilded cage to the iron cage, or, the perils of Pauline. *J. Marriage and the Family* 33, 734–745.
Becker, Howard S. 1967 Whose side are we on? *Social Problems* 14, 239–247.
Brownmiller, Susan. 1975. *Against Our Will: Men, Women and Rape*. Simon & Schuster, New York.
Buckner, H. Taylor. 1971. *Deviance, Reality and Change*. Random House, New York.
Burgess, Ann Wolbert and Holstrom, Lynda Lytle. 1975. Rape: the victim goes on trial. In: Drapkin, Israel and Viano, Emilio C. (eds), *Victimology: a New Focus*, pp. 31–48. Lexington, Mass.
Chagnon, Napoleon. 1968. *Yanomamo: the Fierce People*. Holt, Rinehart & Winston, New York.
Ennis, Philip H. 1967. Crimes, victims and the police. *Trans-Action* 4, 36–44.
Epstein, Cynthia F. 1974. A different angle of vision: notes on the selective eye of sociology. *Social Science Q.* 55 (3), 645–656.
Erlich, Carol. 1971. The male sociologist's burden: the place of women in marriage and the family texts. *J. Marriage and the Family* 33, 421–430.
Garfinkel, Harold. 1967. *Studies in Ethnomethodology*. Prentice-Hall, Englewood Cliffs.
Gilley, Judy. June 27, 1974. How to help the raped. *New Society*. 756–758.
Goode, Erich. 1978. *Deviant Behavior: an Interactionist Approach*. Prentice–Hall, Englewood Cliffs.
Gouldner, Alvin. 1974. *For Sociology*. Penguin, England.
Griffin, Susan. 1971. Rape: the all-American crime. *Ramparts* 10 (3), 26–35.
Hanmer, Jalna. 1978. Violence and the social control of women. In: Littlejohn, Gary, Smart, Barry, Wakeford, John and Yuval-Davis, Nira (eds), *Power and the State*, pp. 217–238. Croom-Helm, London.
Hanmer, Jalna and Leonard, Diana. 1980. Men and culture: the sociological intelligentsia and the maintenance of male domination: or, Superman meets the Invisible Woman. British Sociological Association Annual Conference Paper.

[8] For a view which argues that the sex of the subject being studied is irrelevant in the sociology of deviance, see Paul Rock's review (Rock, 1977) of Carol Smart's book. *Women, Crime and Criminology* (Smart, 1976).

Harris, Marvin. 1975. *Cows, Pigs, Wars and Witches: the Riddles of Culture.* Fontana/Collins, Glasgow.
Heidensohn, Frances. 1968. The deviance of women: a critique and an enquiry. *Br. J. Social.* **19** (2), 160 175.
Henslin, James M. 1978. Towards the sociology of sex. In: Henslin, James M. and Sagarin, Edward (eds), *The Sociology of Sex*, pp. 1–26. Schocken Books, New York.
Jackson, Stevi. 1978. The social content of rape: sexual scripts and motivation. *Women's Stud. Int. Q.* **1**, 27–38.
Kenkel, William F. 1966. *The Family in Perspective.* Appleton-Century-Crofts, New York.
Maidment, Susan. 1978. Rape between spouses: a case for reform. *Family Law* **8** (3), 87–90.
Millman, Marcia. 1975. She did it all for love: a feminist view of the sociology of deviance. In: Millman, Marcia and Moss Kanter, Rosabeth (eds), *Another Voice: Feminist Perspectives on Social Life and Social Science*, pp. 251–279. Anchor Books, New York.
Plummer, Kenneth. 1975. *Sexual Stigma.* Routledge & Kegan Paul, London.
Rape Crisis Research Project. 1977. *Rape Crisis Centre Annual Report.* RCRP, London.
Reynolds, Janice. 1974. Rape as social control. *Telos* **15**, 62–67.
Rock, Paul. 1977. Review Symposium. *Br. J. Criminology* **17**, 392–395.
Rosenblum, Karen E. 1975. Female deviance and the female sex-role: a preliminary investigation. *Br. J. Sociol.* **26**, 169–185.
Rossi, Peter H., Waite, Emily, Bose, Christine and Berk, Richard. 1974. The seriousness of crime: normative structure and individual difference. *Am. sociol. Rev.* **39**, 224–237.
Sagarin, Edward. 1975. *Deviants and Deviance: an introduction to the study of Disvalued People and Behavior.* Praeger, New York.
Smart, Carol. 1976. *Women, Crime and Criminology.* Routledge & Kegan Paul, London.
Smart, Carol and Smart, Barry (eds), 1978. *Women, Sexuality and Social Control.* Routledge & Kegan Paul, London.
Smith, Dorothy. 1974. Women's perspective as a radical critique of sociology. *Sociological Inquiry* **44** (1), 7–13.
Sykes, Gresham M. and Matza, David. 1957. Techniques of neutralization: a theory of delinquency. *Am. sociol. Rev.* **22**, 667–670.
Taylor, Laurie. 1971. *Deviance and Society.* Michael Joseph, London.
Taylor, Laurie. 1972. The significance and interpretation of replies to motivational questions: the case of sex offenders. *Sociology* **6**, 23–39.
Webster, Paula. 1978. The politics of rape in primitive society. *Heresies: a feminist publication on Art and Politics* **6**, 16–22.
Weis, Kurt and Borges, Sandra S. 1973. Victimology and rape: the case of the legitimate victim. *Issues in Criminology* **8** (2), 71–115.
Wolfgang, Marvin and Ferracuti, Franco F. 1967. *The Subculture of Violence.* Tavistock, London.

8

A Feminist Analysis of the New Right

Sheila Ruth

For some years now, Americans have seen unfolding in our midst a bizarre phenomenon—new, yet not new, faintly ridiculous, yet chilling. It is called variously the New Right, the Radical Religious Right, the New Conservatism, the 'Moral Majority,' or other similar names, and while it is composed of many independent groups, it has a unity which can be articulated and has been effectively mobilized for action

First ignored, the movement started to earn attention when it began accomplishing certain of its goals: the removal of liberal senators from Congress, the stopping of the Equal Rights Amendment, the censorship of liberal ideas in the media and education, the introduction of 'pro-family' legislation, and, to a large extent, the election of Ronald Reagan. Now one cannot fail to mark the insanities of electronic preachers who exhort the faithful to go forth and 're-moralize America' while awaiting with joyous anticipation the Glory, the rapture, delivered as promised by the good offices of the next and final holocaust. What was once a 'harmless' social and spiritual preoccupation of a minor segment of the ignorant and poor has become a consciously, overtly political movement of a much larger, economically pinched and hostile middle class, a movement of major proportion and consequence.

Finally, after a quiet gestation, the push and thunder of the current movement has elicited some organized responses. Daily one receives in the mail pamphlets, letters, and pleas for funds from such counter organizations as Common Cause, the American Civil Liberties Union, Planned Parenthood, the National Organization for Women, Norman Lear, Public Citizen, or the National Abortion Rights Action League, to name just a few. They warn of 'the most serious challenge to the constitution, American Democracy, and freedom of thought that we have ever witnessed in our times.' They are right.

The danger, to some extent at least, has been recognized. Its source, I think, has not.

In many ways the 'New' Right is a puzzling construction. A peculiar amalgam of fundamentalist Christianity and authoritarian politics, it holds a series of values and goals which upon first examination seem entirely inhospitable to one another.

The New Right favors 'Americanism,' patriotism, and the 'American Way,' yet it seeks to alter some of the most fundamental principles of American government—separation of church and state, the guarantees of the First Amendment, the political party system.

> 'We've already taken control of the conservative movement. And conservatives have taken control of the Republican Party. The remaining thing is to see if we can take control of the country.'
> (Richard Viguerie, key fundraiser and strategist for the Religious New Right)

> 'Groups like ours are potentially very dangerous to the political process . . . a group like ours could lie through its teeth and the candidate it helps stays clean.'
> (Terry Dolan, Chairman National Political Action Committee)

> 'We're radicals working to overturn the present structure in this country . . . we're talking about Christianizing America.'
> (Paul Weyrich, Director Committee for the Survival of a Free Congress[1])

The New Right is 'pro-life,' but not anti-death. It means to save 'unborn babies,' but militaristic, it shrugs off the murder of persons born—it favors a 'tough' American foreign policy and opposes gun control legislation. It is pro-Israel, but anti-semitic. It professes the Christianity of Jesus the Lamb, but values wealth and power. It stands for 'families,' but opposes AFDC (Aid for Families of Dependent Children), shelters for battered wives and mothers, and child abuse legislation. It denounces violence and prepares for all out war. On the hillside of Illinois, in a training camp in Missouri, on the fields of Florida, guerrilla-type warriors make ready for Armageddon.[2]

Certainly some of this apparent paradox is borne simply of the New Right's very canny use of rhetoric. *Pro-life* is a far more persuasive, more popular term than *anti-choice*, although the latter more accurately describes the spirit of the drive. Likewise, it is more commodious, more practical to replace the term *aggression* with *strong defense, anti-constitutional* with *grass roots, military ally* with *Israel*, or *patriarchal* and *anti-individual* with *pro-family*. When one replaces the rhetorical term with the accurate term in the themes above, meanings clarify, and a great deal of paradoxical confusion is swept away.

Yet among the values and principles of the New Right peculiar combinations of ideas not attributable to rhetoric still remain. Fundamentalist,

---

[1] All three quoted in 'Are We All God's People?' a pamphlet of People for the American Way, project of Citizens for Constitutional Concerns, P.O. Box 19500, Washington, DC 20036.
[2] 'Headquarters for Armageddon is nestled in Illinois countryside,' *St Louis Globe Democrat*, 7/7/81, p. 1.

Jesus-centered Christianity, the religion of peace, love, and turn-the-other-cheek, finds itself in lock step with the Hawks of War. Priests, generals, and power-politicians on one stage sing in unison not about the give-what-you-have-and-follow-me God, but of Horatio Alger and go-get-em capitalism. Ultimately the entire case sits demurely, albeit gingerly, hip to hip with Phyllis Schlafly and the down with women crowd.

Christian principles of peace and simplicity—American chauvinism and laissez-faire economics; the New Testament of charity and love—bigotry, oppression, and hatred of women. These are not rhetorical paradoxes. These are contradictions in thought and spirit so deep and obvious as to be ludicrous, yet for a great number of not stupid people they stand in carefree proximity. How is this to be explained?

This phenomenon of comfortable contradiction is understandable only if one recognizes that the beliefs and principles described above do not stand as independent ideas, each examined and adopted, by whatever logic, on its own merits. Instead, these doctrines are externalizations, practical, contemporary applications of a more basic, primal system of beliefs and attitudes which precede them emotionally and logically. Within the context of that underlying turn of mind, the apparent inconsistencies of the beliefs are resolved. The turn of mind referred to here is Fascism.

Once articulated, New Right themes should recall a familiar schema. It is not difficult to discern that the New Right is not new at all, but an old warrior in new uniform. Crisply defined, cut to the bones, the body reveals a familiar skeleton: ultra-nationalism, militarism, racism, sexism, authoritarian discipline, a mystical principle of mission, a call for absolute devotion—it is the shape of fascism,[3] American style.

Fascism is not merely a political ideology. It is essentially a world-view, a way of seeing the self, people, and events, an ordering of reality. It is a set of presuppositions, beliefs, perceptions, and values, a consciousness, and from this is derived the political philosophy and its movement.

The term *fascism* derives from the Italian term *fascio*, which means a group, cluster or bundle; this concept reveals fascism's central principle—that the primary unit of social reality is the group or community, and that individuals have value only as members or participants in that group. The needs and interests of individuals are subordinate to and served by the state, which has a life and interest separate from, and superior to, that of its citizens.

Fascist organizations and states are marked by a series of sharply discernable characteristics: extreme nationalism and chauvinism; militarism; regimentation and an obsession with order and unanimity. In support of order one finds suppression of dissent, typically achieved through a strong propa-

---

[3] I use the term *fascism* here in the generic sense, as a recurring political phenomenon, not to refer to any particular instance of it, such as Italian fascism or Nazism.

ganda program, including censorship of the media and training of the young in carefully controlled educational and familial systems. As rationale, there exists some overriding ideology or mystical principle, answerable only to itself, serving as justification for all remaining values or acts, for example, a new order; Aryan destiny; the end of history and the dissolution of the state; or now salvation, the return of the Savior and God's kingdom on Earth, or even 'restoring America to its original greatness.' Generally one expects to find an authoritarian, hierarchical government and a totalitarian environment, that is, a public community which has total power over, or complete intrusion into, personal life.

In 1961, Zbigniew Brzezinski together with Carl J. Friedrick described what they believed to be the six essential characteristics of the totalitarian dictatorship:

'1. an official ideology, consisting of an official body of doctrine covering all vital aspects of man's existence to which everyone living in that society is supposed to adhere, at least passively; this ideology is characteristically focused and projected toward a perfect final state of mankind, that is to say, it contains a chiliastic claim, based upon a radical rejection of the existing society and conquest of the world for the new one;

2. a single mass party led typically by one man, the 'dictator,' and consisting of a relatively small percentage of the total population (up to 10 per cent) of men and women, a hard core of them passionately and unquestioningly dedicated to the ideology and prepared to assist in every way in promoting its general acceptance;

3. a system of terroristic police control, supporting but also supervising the party for its leaders, and characteristically directed not only against demonstrable 'enemies' of the regime, but against arbitrarily selected classes of the population; the terror of the secret police systematically exploiting modern science, and more especially scientific psychology;

4. a technologically conditioned near-complete monopoly of control, in the hands of the party and its subservient cadres, of all means of effective mass communication, such as the press, radio, motion pictures;

5. a similarly technologically conditioned near-complete monopoly of control (in the same hands) of all means of effective armed combat;

6. a central control and direction of the entire economy through the bureaucratic co-ordination of its formerly independent corporate entities, typically including most other associations and group activities.'
(Friedrick and Brzezinski, 1961: 9-10).

It does not take much ingenuity to apply these characteristics to today's Right—doctrine, conveniently embodied in one simple (favorably interpreted) Good Book, wide and effective use of mass communication media, carefully orchestrated demonstrations and strategies for censorship and thought control, preoccupation with military 'defense,' and social order, and dedicated followers ready to do 'His will.' Even the tone is familiar. Deirdre English describes her experience at an anti-abortion convention in Florida:

'Could anyone, even on the fringes of Disneyland, be prepared to encounter prolife nuns pushing baby carriages in the midst of a prochoice rally, while men held crosses up to the demonstrating feminists as if warding off witches? Inside the convention were hundreds of apparently happy housewives, the women organizers of a powerful antiwoman movement. I had not anticipated the extent of their organization: the panorama of booths, the cornucopia of glossy brochures, the books, the videotapes, the movies, the tape cassettes, the computer printouts, the stacks of organizers' workbooks. I did not know how frightening it would be to find myself in an immense auditorium filled with people who bowed their heads at one point and prayed the Lord would 'send the enemy to the pit of destruction,' a congregation that enthusiastically applauded indirect references to vandalism and arson at abortion clinics. (Since 1975, there have been seven arson attacks in the U.S. on abortion clinics.)' (English, 1981: 16).

A recent fund-request letter from the Moral Majority's Jerry Falwell began 'Is our grand old flag going down the drain? . . . The answer . . . is "Yes!"' Terrible things are happening in America, perpetrated by 'amoral liberals': homosexual teachers have 'invaded' the classroom, 'smut' is everywhere, abortion—MURDER!—is legal, America's military might is fading, and Russia waits in breathless anticipation.[4]

One is asked finally to help Falwell fight 'the cancers that are destroying the moral fiber of our nation' by sending money and returning a 'petition on moral issues' which will be tabulated and forwarded to Congress:

TO THE
CONGRESS OF THE UNITED STATES OF AMERICA

The Undersigned Hereby Petitions Congress
To Pass Laws In Support of My Moral Opinions
Listed Below

1. Are you in favour of your tax dollar being used to support abortion on demand?
   YES   NO
2. Do you believe that smut pedlers should be protected by the courts and the Congress, so they can openly sell pornographic materials to your children?
   YES   NO
3. Should school systems that receive federal funds be forced to hire known practicing and soliciting homosexual teachers?
   YES   NO
4. Do you agree that voluntary prayer should be banned from the public schools?
   YES   NO
5. Do you agree with the liberals who say we should not increase our military strength up to the level of the Russians before continuing the Salt Treaty process?
   YES   NO

Your signature above

The New Right defines itself; the picture sharpens and the issues emerge. Military and economic concerns are melded together incongruously with fears of 'smut' and commitment to public prayer.

[4] Moral Majority, Inc., National Capitol Office, P.O. Box 190, Forest, BA 24551 (undated).
[5] Congressional Petition on Moral Issues,' Moral Majority, Inc., 499 South Capitol Street, Suite 101, Washington, DC 20003.
[6] By Frances Hill. Obtainable from Pro-Family Forum, P.O. Box 14701, Forth Worth, TX 76117. Lottie Beth Hobbs, National President.

Finally, the ultimate horror is named. In an incredible pamphlet entitled *Is Humanism Molesting Your Child*?[6] 'Secular Humanism' is uncovered as the sly demon of the public school system. Using a technique developed under Lenin and Stalin by Pavlov (*sic*), a technique called 'Values Clarification', clever psychologists, presumably 'liberal,' set out to change a child's conscience, personality and values until the child believes 'that he has the right to develop HIS OWN personal values, free from parental influence and authority, free from religious influences. It can further convince the child that there are NO ABSOLUTES, NO RIGHT, NO WRONG.' The culprit is none other than the familiar 7-step method of values analysis most educators learn as part of their teacher training.

But the prime monster is Humanism, the 'Faith' of the atheists, that denies God, the Bible, Creation, heterosexual superiority, absolutes, patriotism, free enterprise, and, oh yes, the right to control the thoughts of the young.

As educators, we might be appalled by such an inverted perspective and yet feel little more than cynical amusement. After all, such ignorance is not new. One might contend, indeed, that too much attention is spent, even here, on such small scraps of madness. This might be so were it not that these publications are not anomalies but instead representative and well supported. For a great number of highly manipulative and activist people, not to mention powerful people, they are frighteningly persuasive. And they are revealing. Inadvertently, perhaps, the true foe of the New Right is exposed— freedom. How simple.

Free thought, open analysis, deliberation and choice are transformed into enemies. What then is friend? Simply put: unfreedom, authoritarianism.

Closer to the core underlying fascism breathes this particular consciousness, a configuration of psychic traits and variables analyzed and defined in the 50s by a monumental work, *The Authoritarian Personality* (Adorno *et al.*, 1950). There have been challenges to the design and interpretation of the research, yet few have rejected the basic thesis of the work, that there is an identifiable personality syndrome, authoritarianism, which underlies certain forms of behavior and perception central to fascism. Authors Adorno *et al.* provide us with a broadly drawn portrait of the traits more or less central to authoritarian consciousness:

> 'a. *Conventionalism*. Rigid adherence to conventionalism, middle class values.
>
> b. *Authoritarian submission*. Submissive, uncritical attitude toward idealized moral authorities of the ingroup.
>
> c. *Authoritarian aggression*. Tendency to be on the lookout for and to condemn, reject, and punish people who violate conventional values.
>
> d. *Anti-intraception*. Opposition to the subjective, the imaginative, the tenderminded.
>
> e. *Superstition and stereotype*. The belief in mystical determinants of the individual's fate; the disposition to think in rigid categories.

f. *Power and 'toughness.'* Preoccupation with the dominance–submission, strong–weak, leader–follower dimension; identification with power figures; overemphasis upon the conventionalized attributes of the ego; exaggerated assertion of strength and toughness.

g. *Destructiveness and cynicism.* Generalized hostility, vilification of the human.

h. *Projectivity.* The disposition to believe that wild and dangerous things go on in the world; the projection outwards of unconscious emotional impulses.

i. *Sex.* Exaggerated concern with sexual 'goings-on.'

(*ibid.*, p. 288).

Additionally we may expect categorized, unanalytic thinking, sharply defined in-group/out-group orientation, belief in the submission to the supernatural and the inevitability of cataclysmic events, rigid categories of good and evil, a readiness to accept the essential incomprehensibility of 'many important things,' the glorification, even mystification of authority, hence conformity, discipline, and interestingly, even rigid family structures. Later, further research widened the concept to apply not only to a specific ideology, fascism, but to a way of thinking, dogmatism, a tenacity of belief even in the face of contrary evidence, an outlook of pessimism, fear and power, and party-line thinking (Rokeach and Fruchter, 1960).[7] Finally we have a cohesive image: the authoritarian individual is a

'basically weak and dependent person who has sacrificed his capacity for genuine experience of self and other so as to maintain a precarious sense of order and safety that is psychologically necessary for him. In the type case, the authoritarian confronts with a facade of spurious strength a world in which rigidly stereotyped categories are substituted for the affectionate and individualized experience of which he is incapable. Such a person is estranged from inner values and lacks self-awareness. His judgements are governed by a punitive conventional moralism, reflecting external standards towards which he remains insecure since he has failed to make them really his own. His relations with others depend on considerations of power, success, and adjustment, in which people figure as means rather than as ends, and achievement is valued competitively rather than for its own sake. In his world, the good, the powerful, and the ingroup merge to stand in fundamental opposition to the immoral, the weak, the outgroup. For all that he seeks to align himself with the former, his underlying feelings of weakness and self-contempt commit him to a constant and embittered struggle to prove to himself and others that he really belongs to the strong and good, and that his ego-alien impulses, which he represses, belong to the weak and bad.' (Kirscht and Dillehay, 1967: vi-vii).

In this context, the letter, pamphlets, worries and fears all make sense. The seemingly disparate and unrelated pieces of the puzzle actually fit. There is a way of looking at the world, rigid and puckered, which eschews all joy except the joy of subordination and the rush of self-abnegation, which fears the

[7] Quoted in Kirscht and Dillehay (1967: 11).

imperatives and processes of concrete existence, which closes off the feelings and narrows relationship, which flees the uncertainties of lived experience, of physical existence and personal responsibility, opting instead for a time and space of spurious certainty: all is known, sure, and clear—covered by the rules in The Book. The hard questions of ethics, morality, theology, now even politics, are answered. One need not fear any danger, not the folly of people nor the wrath of nature. 'Yea though I walk through the valley of the shadow . . .' All one need do is submit to the order and the power that maintains it, sacrifice the spontaneous and the unbound, do one's duty. Become as The Other One.

It is helpful to place The New Right into its proper contexts, fascism and authoritarianism. Within these models we are able to make some sense of the dissonant image of shining, God-intoxicated faces paradoxically calling for the strengthening of our nuclear capabilities. We begin to understand, to know what to expect and how to predict. Yet there still remains a final puzzlement, an unintelligibility. If fascism is the hidden face of The New Right, and authoritarianism is the ground of fascism, what is the ground of authoritarianism? What, beside private pathologies, accounts for a people, a whole gathering of beings, giving itself over to a 'pinched and puckered' rigidity? What undergirds and gives unity to the entire life and thought system exemplified by The Right?

Clues are to be found in what might appear the most unlikely quarter, unlikely, that is, for those unaccustomed to feminist analysis. Earlier it was pointed out that misogyny and opposition to feminism was a classic trait of authoritarianism and fascistic ideologies. Historically, in Rome, Germany, Italy and elsewhere, fascism and/or authoritarianism have always included in their programs the subordination of women, of the female principle and the suppression of feminist movements. Why, we should ask?

Why would militarism, submissive–aggressive psychologies, competitive economics, and hostility to freedom and difference stand in such close and equal partnership with hostility to women?

Misogyny in fascism is no accident. In fact, it is the key to its meaning. Were political analysts not typically busy looking elsewhere, they, with feminists, would see:

> Fascism, fully revealed, is the extreme, exquisite expression of masculism, of patriarchy, and thus the natural enemy of feminism, its quintessential opposite.

Fascism, authoritarianism, the New Right are three facets of the same reality—unchecked Patriarchy. The Right's age old quarrel with women is not incidental or petty; it is combat to the death.

Feminists understand masculism to be the guiding principle of partiarchy; we have put names to it. On its most obvious level it is the lived expression of the Martial ideals—a lust for power and control over others and self;

absorption by the abstract and unfelt, by duties, principles and behaviors legitimated only by rationalistic argument; the mystification of The Flight in all its aspects—war, competition, contention; a passion for order, the soldier's order; a belief in hierarchy, in the rights of the strong over the weak, in God over men, in men over nature and women, in winners over losers.

More profundly, masculism is an orgasm of rigidity. It rejects and diminishes anything relaxed, gentle, and easy, spontaneous or wild. That is why it disdains feelings and experience—they cannot be ordered, nailed down and controlled, regimented or legislated. That is why it fears sex and sensuality. Nothing is more liberating than the free expression of sensuality, because it puts the lie to the worship of control. It was no accident that the motto of the 60s was 'make love, not war.' When one goes beyond patriarchy's mere genital rubbing to the making of sensual love, the truth of it renders the pettiness of war visible.

As Sigmund Freud theorized in *Civilization and its Discontents* (1930), the free experiencing of sensual sex threatens order by challenging sublimation, the abstracting of human energy. Ultimately, that is why masculism must crush the feminine and women. For masculists, women are not only the occasion of sex, but the living, breathing symbol of sensuality, of live experience, the counter of their order. Free women, feminists, understand this, and so we must be stopped dead.

And yet another 'why?'. Why the order? What is it that is so scary; what protection is so precariously maintained that so much effort must be expended in its care?

In *Gyn/Ecology* (1979) Mary Daly characterizes patriarchy as *necrophilic*, death-loving and death-oriented. Its signs are everywhere. In its bombs and wars, its rape of nature and women, its quest for increasingly effective violence, and its growing desensitization to pain, even in its religion that pursues death after life as a solution to life, patriarchy obviously romances death. And yet, to fully understand the phenomenon we must introduce a paradox: masculists are seduced by death because they fear it so. The key to the masculist embrace of death is the denial of it which is locked within.

One fears death essentially for the fact of non-being. It is not the dying but the not-being that is so dissociating to human emotion and consciousness. It frightens. It threatens our sense of meaning. What is the point of life that merely begins, carries on, and ends? It has often been suggested, and it seems reasonable to suppose, that the dilemma of meaning looms even larger for men than for women, larger for 'civilized' or martial men than for 'primitive' men. Alienated by nature from the sharp sense of participation in the life-cycle experienced by women through the process of pregnancy-birth-nursing, alienated by their own rules from experiencing the concrete, day to day life-reality of feeding, cleaning, and keeping, martial men struggle ceaselessly with existential meaninglessness.[8] Estranged from the cycle, on the periphery of Nature, where are they? How are they to explain themselves and legitimate their existence if they merely 'are'? If meaning is not in simple, mortal being, it must be sought elsewhere, in Total Being, in Being big enough to conquer limit for us, to conquer smallness, powerlessness and finitude. For martial males to have meaning, power over the unpalatable, over death and limit must be regained, even if only through identification with a Maybe-Being bigger than self. To work, to yield meaning, to be big enough to conquer death, the identification with Being/Power/God must be very close, as close almost as identity. And its opposite, limit and nature, must be wholly negated. Mortality, death, can and must be denied.

And yet, how can death be denied? It is visible everywhere. Creatures finish. Their bodies decline and finally putrefy before our eyes. The body, yes. But for human beings, creatures just beneath angels, provided they dwell apart from nature, the being within, the real being, the one that counts, does not die. One is safe so long as one is not-body, but spirit, 'in this world, but not of it,' 'Man that is born of woman is of few days, and full of trouble. He comes forth like a flower and withers' (Job 14: 1 and 2.) '. . . if you live according to the flesh you will die, but if by the spirit you put to death the deeds of the body, you will live' (Romans 8:13).

One need not die, one need only keep to the undying realm. One need only eschew the mortal, the physical—Nature and all that she is—sensing, feeling, experiencing, and its signs—pleasure, sensuality, sexuality. One need only reject life to have it forever.

From this construction follows the dualism so crucial to masculism—the realm of spirit, God, and eternal life, and the realm of Earth, the Devil, and death. From it follows the entire, laboriously contrived superstructure—of fear and the carrot of redemption, of sin and salvation, of obedience, self-denial, and duty in the name of a better, more desirable life to be. From it follows the hostility, the bravado and the show of disregard for the living of life, for the Earth, for Nature and for her carrier, Woman.

But here is a precarious construction, paper and wind, flimsy at best, easily toppled. It crumbles at the slightest jostle. One must therefore protect and defend it with endless vigilance. The denial must be perfect, pure; there must be absolute constriction and puckering. Dissent of any kind must be crushed. And so women must be controlled, our bodies and life processes demeaned and hidden, for without saying a word we express dissent. We embody it. That is why the socialization of women must be even more total, more completely suppressing than men's: God forbid that Nature escape!

---

[*] Even George Gilder, rabid anti-feminist, admits to this in *Sexual Suicide*, Ch. 1 (Bantam Books, New York, 1975). On the other side, the idea appears in various forms in such divergent thinkers as Dorothy Dinnerstein, H. R. Hays, Monique Wittig, Susan Griffin, or of course Mary Daly.

For individuals in the grasp of such a consciousness, feminism and Women's Movement represent the ultimate horror—not only the loss of privilege for the warriors of God, which it is, but threat to the edifice of salvation, not simply the salvation advertised in The Book, but psychic salvation. For the opposition, at least, feminism is the triumph of Nature, of life, and so of death. Of course, it must be stopped.

All of us must come to terms with death, and spiritual alienation is a universal threat. For those unable to negotiate the uncertainties and unintelligibilities of lived existence, the absolutes of authoritarianism provide an attractive resolution, a safe harbor.

In this context authoritarianism is understandable, and fascism, its spawn, makes perfect sense—life and meaning, even some ersatz joy, regained in the eternal community, emotion and feeling regained in a safe, allowable fashion, in commitment to the Cause, Being which lives forever. Ultimately, death-life is perfectly embraced in War, the final paroxysmal orgasm of death-sex.

Round the circle we have come. Here are our problem themes re-iterated: militarism and death, competition, hatred and bigotry, pinched morality, abhorrence of sexuality, misogyny. The 'New' Right.

To understand the connection of these three, patriarchy, fascism, and the New Right, is of inestimable value. It affords us an explanatory context within which to comprehend the consciousness and to predict goals, strategies, and events. It enables us to cut through the fog of God-loving rhetoric to the demonic intent beneath. It reveals the character of the battle—why Falwell and Company are determined to stop us, and why we must not stop. It reinforces our will to act.

REFERENCES

Adorno, T. W., Frenkel-Brunswik, Else, Levinson, Daniel J. and Newitt Sanford, R.. 1950. *The Authoritarian Personality*. Harper & Row, New York

Crawford, Alan. 1980. *Thunder on the Right: 'The New Right' and the Politics of Resentment*. Pantheon, New York

Eisenstein, Zillah R. 1982. The sexual politics of The New Right: understanding the 'crisis of liberalism' for the 1980s. *Signs* 7 (3): 567–588.

English, Deidre. 1981. The War against choice. *Mother Jones* 6 (2): 16–21.

Falwell, Jerry. 1980. *Listen, America!* Doubleday, New York.

Freud, Sigmund. 1930. *Civilization and its Discontents*. Hogarth Press, London.

Friedrick, Carl J. and Brzezinski, Zbigniew K. 1961. *Totalitarian Dictatorship and Autocracy*. Frederick Praeger, New York.

Greene, Nathanael, (ed.), 1963. *Fascism: An Anthology*. Thomas Y. Crowell Company, New York.

Gregor, A. James. 1974. *Interpretations of Fascism*. General Learning Press, New Jersey.

Hoffer, Eric. 1951. *The True Believer*. Harper & Row, New York.

Kirscht, John P. and Dillehay, Ronald C. 1967. *Dimensions of Authoritarianism: A Review of Research and Theory*. University of Kentucky Press, Lexington, Ky.

Kitchen, Martin. 1977. *Fascism*. Laurence Verry, Connecticut.
Lang, Kurt and Lang, Gladys Engel. 1960. Decisions for Christ: Billy Graham in New York City. In Maurice R. Stein, Author J. Vidich and David Manning White, eds, *Identity and Anxiety: Survival of the Person in Mass Society*. Free Press of Glencoe, Illinois.
Martin, James G. 1964. *The Tolerant Personality*. Wayne State University Press, Detroit.
Rokeach, M. and Fruchter, B. 1960. *The Open and Closed Mind*. Basic Books, New York.
Steinem, Gloria. Watch on the Right. *Ms. Magazine*, monthly feature.
Viguerie Richard A. 1980. *The New Right: We're Ready to Lead*. Viguerie Co., Falls Church, Va.
Weber, Max. 1958. *The Protestant Ethic and the Spirit of Capitalism*. Trans. Talcott Persons. Charles Scribner's Sons, New York.

COMMENT: SHEILA RUTH

Since 1983 the New Right has grown stronger and more successful. In the United States they have placed judges on the Supreme Court, stalled affirmative action and reproductive freedoms, and befouled the educational environment with book burnings and bannings and organizations like 'Accuracy in Academia,' a watchdog group guarding against 'secular humanism' in the university. Serious damage has been done to First Amendment rights, the right to privacy, and the right to sexual freedom. Funding has been diverted from pro-female agencies to 'pro-family' agencies and from social programs to the military. Fundamentalist groups in the Middle East, in Rome, and in South Africa have been equally active.

The strategy and rhetoric of the New Right has evolved in step with its success. Now we know what secular humanism is: On March 4, 1987 in Montgomery, Alabama, a decision was handed down on Smith v. Board of School Commissioners of Mobile County. *The plaintiffs argued that a series of books should be removed from the public school because they contained 'religious' material, i.e., secular humanism. Judge W. B. Hand found for the parents. Following are some of the objectionable 'secular humanistic' quotations which were included in the appendix of Judge Hand's decision.*[9] *(Later the decision was overturned.)*

> *We can direct our own lives instead of letting others do the directing for us. Each of us can become the kind of person we want to be.* (Caring, Deciding, and Growing)

> *Once you are familiar with the many aspects of your personality, you will be able to answer the important questions, 'Who am I?' and 'How do I deal with who I am?'* (Contemporary Living)

> *Thus it is important to care for yourself. You are the most important person in your life.* (Today's Teen)

[9] Quoted by Susan Blank, 'Why 12 Parents Went to Court ...' in Civil Liberties #360, Spring, 1987, p. 5.

Freedom is still the villain. So is self-affirmation. Any orientation to life that suggests that we as individuals and as a human community can and should take charge of our own affairs out of love for self is anathema.

A response to this insanity is being formulated in my new work, Feminist Spirit: A Pagan Testimony.

9

The 'Men-Problem' in Women's Studies: The Expert, the Ignoramus and the Poor Dear

Renate D. Klein[1]

'There was a leaden silence in the room and it felt cold. Faces aimlessly staring at the wall, fingers purposelessly scribbling along, minds looking blank . . . the 15 women scattered apart in the room avoided looking at each other. Then one woman spoke up but her words lingered dispassionately in the air where they were met by another equally sober and distant voice. A third voice joined in—an angry voice—and the atmosphere became tense. The next few seconds—uneasy. Women exchanging hostile looks and words, nervous shuffling of papers and moving of chairs, embarrassed coughing . . . But soon, the lifeless, low-energy and draining silence had returned. Then, one by one, the women drifted away. Finally the rest of the group decided on a lukewarm statement which evaporated without consequence.'

It was the question of whether men should be teaching on a Women's Studies (WS) course that led to the depressing scene described above—a modern version of the old, old script called 'men-dividing women'—which took place among the participants of a WS course in Britain, and it is this topic—the 'Men-Problem' in WS—that I want to examine. Part of me feels ambivalent about giving space to men, especially in connection with WS, for I have come to believe strongly during the last 2 years of my involvement in WS in the USA and the UK[2] that WS *must* remain a space for women. *In my view there is no room for men in WS, none whatsoever.* However, I think it is difficult to escape the fact that men's interest in WS, in one form or another, is increasing[3] and ironically, the laws designed to protect women's space—

---

[1] Renate D Klein is a Swiss biologist currently engaged in research on the theory and practice of Women's Studies in the UK and the USA.

[2] This chapter is based on observations during the research for my PhD on the theory and practice in WS in higher education in the USA and the UK.

that there should be 'no discrimination on grounds of sex,' can be used by men to gain entry to WS courses. Moreover, the women themselves involved in WS are often divided on the issue of men's participation and it is this division which concerns me.

For some women, men in WS can be seen as a useful alliance in our quest for social change from within education. Yet others suspect—and I share their views—that the increasing participation of men in WS will fundamentally alter its basic concepts. That is, WS could change its direction from aiming to provide women with the space to legitimately pursue a self-enhancing positive feminist education, and move towards a supposedly 'balanced curriculum'[4] for both sexes; already this is occurring and has been referred to as 'gender studies' (Stimpson, pers. comm.). Desirable as this supposed harmony might be in theory, the persisting power inequalities between men and women require the skeptic to ask: 'Balance on whose terms and for whose benefit?' Men who recognize women's oppression and who apparently feel an urge to help in ending it, will—even with the best of intentions—almost inevitably embark on this work from their own experiences and perspectives *as members of the dominant group*. They remain men regardless of the divisions among them and despite the fact that in many respects they may have also experienced some form of oppression—for it is indisputable that while all men may share features of a common reality there are also divisions within the small, white Western elite enjoying power which is not commensurate with their numbers. Nevertheless, they 'look at the world through male eyes' (Stanley, 1982: 193), and cannot but refer to their own reality. Seen in this light, it is feasible for men to equate WS with the study of women or oppression—in general—and many of them may come to WS to do precisely that—to study 'women' and 'gender' from *their* male-centered, 'outsider' point of view, as specific *objects* of oppressive practices.

The presence of men in WS, for me, is an impossibility: a contradiction in terms, but one that demonstrates rather illuminatingly that the days of the patriarchal ideology of 'man-is-the-norm' (Acker, 1980) and 'the measure of significance' (Lerner, 1979) are not of the past, and that male-centered thinking continues to thrive—despite the challenges and even among 'self-styled male feminists'[5] (Leonard, 1982: 158). The issue is not that (some) men are oppressed too; the issue is why on earth men claim entry, and assume a

---

[3] In the USA, part of the WS movement is presently on its road to 'integration into mainstream education' and conferences/publications on this issue list a growing number of male participants. The amount of research by men on 'feminism' or 'women' is increasing worldwide from Ivan Illich to that notoriously well-known man in the UK (I will not give him the benefit of being named) who is writing a book on the British women's liberation movement although I know of no feminist who gave him her time or information.

[4] 'Balanced curriculum' is a term currently widely used in the USA in the move towards integration of WS into mainstream education. For an in-depth discussion of the autonomy/integration trends in WS, see Bowles and Duelli Klein (1983).

right to participate in WS in the name of support and commitment when it is the only small space within male-centered education that women have created for women's use.

It seems to me that even under the guise of being 'non-sexist' and 'feminist,' men in WS do *not* need to depart from their male-centered perspective. And indeed why should they voluntarily abandon that confirmation which they have experienced as a result of being reared as males in a male-centered world? They cannot but be 'detached' from feminist research —for in this case *they* are the 'others.' Ironically, this 'detachment'—both the cause *and* consequence of patriarchal power structures—may give men's 'feminist' engagement a real edge over women's feminist work: they may not get personally involved in their research to the same passionate degree as female students/teachers/researchers, and the product of their 'research "on" women' invariably reflects this detachment. So in its apparent 'impartiality' (which I regard as a product of men's socialization and certainly not their biology) they are constrained from grasping in full the complexity, nuance, and reality of female experience with the result that their work is more likely to be praised as 'objective' and 'rigorous,' to be simply, clearly and convincingly presented and even to be preferred to a woman's work, where the struggle to do justice to the intricate fabric of women's experiences encourages assessments such as 'subjective,' incoherent, and even 'implausible.'

By such means do men continue to assume central significance and continue to arbitrate on the rules and practices. As Scarlet Friedman says, 'Any feminist theory which does not include men's interest as pivotal, and which is not offered to men's "wider" and "more objective" sociological gaze, is obviously invalid' (1982: viii).

John Schilb's (1982) discussion of 'ethics involved in a man's teaching of WS' for mixed and women-only classes helps to demonstrate the point. It is not surprising that this man writes from his male experience and perspective but the accompanying illustration of his article is somewhat disturbing: it consists of a drawing of a man with huge feet on a table, while reading *Ms-Magazine*. Is a more crude example of the significance of male dominance possible? For me this supposed 'extension' of his case *is* the 'Men-Problem in WS,' and it is the problem of the perpetuation of male power and control over women!

But why *do* men want to participate in WS?[6] Obviously I cannot speak for men and so it is difficult if not impossible for me to answer this question

[5] 'Can men be feminists?' is one of these questions which stimulates some people to write long papers whilst others yawn. Pleading guilty to both responses, my answer here is a simple 'no: at best, men can be feminist *supporters*.' For more sophisticated analyses see the papers by Elizabeth Sarah, Diana Leonard, Jan Bradshaw and Liz Stanley in *On The Problem of Men* (Friedman and Sarah, (eds), (1982) and Freeman's and Jones' article 'For women only?' (1980).

—and yet I have not seen many articles from men which address this crucial issue. But there are a few possible explanations which can be given for their participation.

I have often heard from 'open-minded,' 'liberal' or 'progressive' men that they are bored with their 'conventional' research and that they well recognize that much of what goes on in their disciplines is alienating and has little significance outside the circles of the initiated few. The new feminist scholarship, therefore, seems like a stimulating and interesting new area of research. There is no doubt that the new questions asked, the new material unearthed, the new theories emerging from feminist research can provide an intellectual feast. Some men, it seems, want to have their share in this: they want to become involved in both the production and distribution of the new knowledge.

In addition, there has been the commercial viability of feminism and it is not too cynical to suggest that being an 'avant-garde' male 'feminist' might even be advantageous for many a male career. In the market place there are many rationales which will support the 'authoritative' man rather than the 'unreliable' woman—and men can benefit accordingly from this. Furthermore, it cannot be overlooked that in many a WS program the course is enriched by the presence of interesting, articulate, enthusiastic and energetic women and it is sometimes suggested by men who profess to be liberated that such women are indeed just as bright—or even brighter—than men and constitute a stimulus! All good reasons it seems—for men. But what about women? How do we deal with men in WS?

There are many ways in which men have been able to 'penetrate' (*sic*) WS with a considerable degree of success, and sadly, it seems one of the results of their increased presence is often a correlative division among women who invariably find that they are obliged to compete with each other in the presence of the still authoritative and powerful sex. A documentation of the dynamics of men's appropriation of WS not only has application to men's appropriation of resources in the wider society but also helps—through the process of unmasking 'how they do it'—to reduce the effectiveness of some of the power plays which are used. Seen in this light, an investigation of the presence of males in WS has considerable value for women who are concerned with the elimination of all forms of oppression and the means by

---

[6] Only a year ago I devoted a large part of a paper on WS to the question 'Why Women's Studies?' (Duelli Klein, 1983), arguing that the very fact that some people ask this question exposes the largely unconscious and internalized male-centeredness of our society. If today I am discussing men's intrusion into WS this seems to be another example of a 'no-win' situation for women: men either dismiss our legitimacy to have a feminist perspective in education, or, should we, against their will, have succeeded in creating our own sphere, they can't let us have it either. Out of curiosity, or fear, or a mixture of both and more, they try to impose their norms, and, as Dale Spender has said (1982a), use what suits their needs, *lose* what doesn't fit—in short are about to change WS into another version of Men's Studies.

which oppression can be structured and sustained. It is in the interest of promoting a constructive debate among women that this has been written and thus—albeit 'on men'—it is *for* women.[7]

THE MEN IN WS ...

During my observations of men in WS, I have witnessed the operation of three distinct 'styles.' Of course, such a broad categorization runs the risk of over-simplification yet it can be helpful to begin with basic categories before moving to an elaboration. It seems possible to capture the attitudes and behaviors of men quite adequately by dividing them into three groups of 'intruders'—those of 'expert,' 'ignoramus' and 'poor dear.' (Such categorization, of course, is not confined to the realm of WS.) Moreover, these three main styles of behavior cut across men as 'teachers,' 'researchers,' 'administrators' and 'students' in WS—and they also cut across national boundaries and cultural identities.

'*Experts*' in WS come in a variety of guises and seem to be particularly prevalent. They are the matter-of-fact types who state that, of course, women are oppressed ('but don't forget so are many other people, right?') but thanks to their male 'mastery' of a particular area of knowledge, they do not see any reason why *men* could not be the conveyors of 'objective facts and figures' to enlighten women about our oppression. The study of budgerigars or the study of women—what is the difference?[8] This type of expert is usually a recognized authority in his field, a brilliant speaker, generally confident in himself and his ability, convinced of the rightness of his 'truth' and well versed in the particular esoteric jargon of exclusivity that makes his disciples few, but as special as himself. He has done his homework and knows (superficially) of the major feminist texts and gives some well-known feminists (patronising) credit for their 'interesting' work. But he delights most in analyses of the contributions of 'great men' to feminism—from Plato to Foucault. What he fails to understand is that although this research might be necessary for *men* (often to boost their 'feminist' egos), it is a *male-centered* approach to knowledge which is not appropriate for WS because the

[7] My warm thanks go to Róisin Battel, Sigrid Brauner, Jane Cholmeley, Felicity Henwood, Joy Howard, Catherine Moorhouse, Joan Ryan, Elizabeth Sarah, Dale Spender, Liz Stanley, Sue Wise and Christine Zmroczek who took the time to comment extensively on earlier drafts of this paper; some of them disagreed with my views and will undoubtedly continue to do so. Their remarks changed my paper from an ironic polemic spontaneous recording of my experience of men in WS dividing women, to a much more serious piece, as they have made me acutely aware that indeed women's responses to the 'men-problem' in WS are of great concern and worry to many women.
[8] I have actually witnessed all the incidents described in this paper. It is lack of space *and* an unwillingness to make certain men more visible than others that prevents me from naming particular individuals.

focus of interest is still the 'greatness' of men.[9] When we have the lives and ideas of the millions of our forgotten fore*mothers* to explore and use for creating strategies for the future, the *positive* contributions of men should not be at the center of our work: WS isn't about vindicating men! But the 'expert of experts' doesn't agree—and why should he undermine his and other men's self-made emporium of 'greatness'?

Other 'experts' in WS are men who fit into Robyn Rowland's lovely phrase 'The Fairytale Brigade.' In her own words she says (1982: 490).

> 'These are usually men who for some strange reason are attracted to the ideas of involvement in women's studies. They tell you fairytales. They offer you many marvellous visions of how they can help you, which they never back up and which never come true. They want to "help" you to design and run the course, but in discussions they aim to manipulate and control, and do not understand the basis of feminism.'

In contrast to the type of expert described above, these men say that women are great, that feminism is great, that WS is great, that previous knowledge was inadequate and one-sided because male centered, and therefore is in need of change. They fail to notice that by delivering brilliant 'expert' speeches on women's greatness, they construct themselves—once again!—as authorities 'on women'. They do not understand that their help may rightly be rejected. Often 'hurt' by more or less subtle hints from women to listen, rather than impose their 'expertise,' experts of the 'fairytale brigade'-type may retreat into sulking and/or wallowing in feelings of misgivings and anger at 'militant narrow-minded separatist feminists' and deplore that we give away that marvellous opportunity of forgoing their precious, 'non-biased' contribution to our WS class.

Equally male-orientated as the above described 'expert of experts,' is the male teacher who fails to understand that his place to talk about women might not be in a WS class but rather, if feminist insights are really of such vital importance to him, to incorporate feminist bodies of knowledge into his regular teaching, in whatever field this might be.

Yet another sub-group of 'experts' comprises those men who are quite willing to acknowledge that their point of view is not the same as a woman's, and that indeed they, as a consequence of their socialized maleness, might choose a different focus from a woman's. However, in the name of academic freedom (and because they need a job) their teaching/doing research in WS may be seen as quite reasonable and justifiable. Furthermore, they argue, couldn't it be beneficial for women to hear 'now and again' a male point of view? Wouldn't this be helpful in keeping our anger and 'bitching at men' to a sensible, intelligent and constructive perspective? In other words, what they are 'offering' us is to 'save' us from practising 'reverse sexism' and to protect

---

[9] Such research is of course different from feminist research which seems to expose 'how (great) men oppress/exploit women': the underlying assumption of this very paper. I am grateful to Liz Stanley for suggesting to me that I explicitly state this difference.

us from the error of 'stereotyping men.' Another example of the unquestioned power of being an authority and seeing the world through the lens of
the group in power.

It so happens that in terms of appearance and values that are adhered to,
'experts' of all types quite often fit the image of what has been called 'the
bearded feminist' (Spender, pers. comm.): open-minded, sensitive, of lef-
tish-progressive dynamism, and all this combined with an openly displayed
contempt of sexist, brutish macho men, they are horror-stricken and dis-
gusted by any suggestion that they—as men—could be rapists too. Having
discovered that men are allowed to have emotions and cry, many women both
in- and outside WS have had to stop such men's in-depth 'expert' elabo-
rations on 'men-can-be-human-beings-too': this may be an interesting possibility and constitute evidence which we certainly welcome in the world, but in
my view it is not the desired focus of our WS classes! 'Bearded feminists' of
the 'expert' type are full of appreciation for the excitement of WS and
feminist research, and can openly praise their women students (and female
colleagues) as ever so bright, interesting, hard-working, thought-provoking
and 'stimulating'. . . . The subtle (and not so subtle) sexual harassment
associated with ostensible praise and well-meant statements could be the
focus of yet another paper on 'How Men Do It.' When it comes to showing
'respect' for feminist *processes* (called 'political astuteness' by another name)
some of these most enlightened 'experts' will actually stay away from WS
classes on especially 'sensitive' topics such as male violence against women,
and in particular rape, battering, incest. Very often, these men are homosexual and/or working class and know oppression themselves. This gives them
(or so they believe) an edge over the average middle-class heterosexual male
who dominates in institutions of higher education. But it is not enough. It is
still *male power* which is an issue and which is being utilized, albeit a different
version of male power.

The 'subtleties' of knowing when and where to be quiet, to leave, or not to
show up at all, is a strategy alien to the '*ignoramus*'—the next category of
men in WS who can be dealt with briefly. (Although speaking from personal
experience, 'ignoramuses' are more frequent in WS—and not only as
students!—than common women-sense would have us believe.) They inform
us quite frankly that they don't have a clue what WS (and feminism) is all
about, and would we please tell them. Here the analogy of racism to sexism
comes to mind: who would dare attend a Black Studies class or conference
admitting openly that they didn't have a clue what racism was all about, and
would black people please tell them? As more women and men seem finally to
be attempting to make a more serious effort to understand the mechanisms of
internalized racism and how to fight it—crucially, that it is we ourselves who
have to make the effort to unlearn our racism—the same amount of
consideration is rarely given to internalized and overt sexism. This can be

taken as another example of the deep-seated contempt and low esteem that men—regardless of whether or not they experience oppression themselves —have for women.

Returning to the 'ignoramuses' in WS it can be said that in the event that they find a patient feminist who gives her time to explain what we are about and, moreover, given that the men are able to *listen* to her (an assumption which more often that not remains unsubstantiated), the response to the woman's explanations will almost invariably be: 'what we really need *too* are men's studies'—then they proceed to talk about the danger of reverse sexism and discrimination against men . . . although of course (of course!) women have a point, we'd better be careful not to lose the support of liberated men (*his* type that is) by being overly militant, or even separatist . . . Don't we know that such an attitude could be perceived as 'man-hating'? While such ignorant male students in WS usually don't last long (even nurturing women—thank goodness—can be rude), in the unfortunate cases where they have come to be teachers in WS, 'ignoramuses' may display their total ignorance of the essence of feminism by (a) reading women-only material in class, (b) openly favoring one woman over the others and (c) making comments such as (and this is a 'real' quote!) 'Gosh, I'm really glad you seem to think too that this Mary Daly is a strange weirdo.' But because of the power position such a teacher may occupy, it can be almost impossible to remove him.

'Ignoramuses' are also well represented among high-ranking figures in institutions of higher education who of course don't think that (a) WS is a study in its own right (or—God forbid—an autonomous 'academic discipline'!); (b) don't have the faintest idea about the depth and breadth and sheer volume of feminist research; (c) often reject suggestions for doing some home-work on WS along the lines of 'What do you think *my* time is for?' or, 'Surely it can't be so complex that you can't tell me?,' or 'If WS *is* so complex that you can't tell me, then there must be something wrong with it/you;' and (d) or it may be that they cannot even *hear* what we are about, because of their biases against feminism, and ideas about women, which place a feminist conceptualization of education outside their range of acceptable theories and practices.

Frustrating to deal with as 'ignoramuses' might be, especially when 'to be or not to be'—the continued existence of a WS course—is dependent on the goodwill of such a specimen, the 'ignoramus' is nonetheless often more easily dealt with than the final 'type'—the 'poor dear.' 'Poor dears' also come in a variety of guises (and often their behaviors overlap with those of the 'experts'). A man of this 'type' confides in you how really deeply awful it is to be a member of the dominant group. 'Women,' he may say sadly—looking an image of sheer misery—'are my only hope, and it is to you I look (hence my interest in WS). Although, of course, I know I shall always be a man (curse, curse), will you please help me to understand my worst sins and excesses in oppressing women?' Again the analogy to racism comes to mind: why can't he see that he himself must change his attitudes, rather than making demands on women and impinging on our time and space? For what I have seen happening more than once is that so desperate is the poor soul in expressing his need for female 'advice,' that once he finds compassionate listeners among the women of a WS class he can quickly assume a dominant position by ensuring that he is the center of attention. He may take all the physical and verbal space, define the topic (*his* oppression by being an oppressor) and thus by copying the usual pattern of men relating to women (Spender, 1980) in fact continues to oppress women by doing the talking, and using us as a sounding board for his problems. This is not to suggest that he doesn't have problems—very real problems indeed—but they are problems which he had better deal with together with other men.

Another man of the 'poor dear' type may be silent (this category is especially diverse). Sitting shyly in a corner, gazing admiringly, or perhaps desperately at these strong articulate women, he is dying to get a smile and be included in the discussions. This is almost certain to happen because one or several women simply cannot bear the weight of his unhappiness reflected in his wounded 'deer' eyes and emphasized by his silence. She (or they) will rescue him by making an encouraging comment—'ego-massaging' by another term (Spender, 1982a)—and there is a strong likelihood that this man too will end up being the focus of attention because encouraged by such signs of support, he either finds his voice and turns into the 'poor dear'-variety described before, or through his continuing silence is able to press our female 'guilt-button' so that we are uneasy until we have succeeded in putting him at ease . . . Rare is the woman who tells a man to 'get lost' (to use a mild expression) . . . and clear off women's space.

AND WOMEN'S RESPONSES

How do women respond to men in WS? Wouldn't it be wonderful if we could just treat men as a 'non-problem' and either not admit them into our WS classes or, if their presence is outside our control, not let them intrude an inch on our interactions and work? Although I think that this is what most women aim for, it is my contention that not only do men often succeed in intruding, but also set up divisions among women. One of the reasons this happens is, I think, because—fortunately—WS isn't a monolithic enterprise which is run by and for one 'brand' of feminists. Women who call themselves what Freeman and Jones (1980) have described as 'liberal feminists' see WS as a reformist strategy to achieve egalitarian positions for women and men without challenging the fundamental male-centeredness of our society. Some of them might welcome men in WS, arguing that 'there is nothing women can afford not to know' and that if men offer us this knowledge 'their services should be gratefully employed, and efforts at counter-sexist education redoubled for them and their students' (Russell, 1982). Women of the 'radical-revolutionary' type—the other side of the feminist spectrum—disagree vehemently with this perspective and argue that knowledge is always connected with the way it is transmitted. These ideological differences then set the scene for conflict among WS practitioners. However, in my experience, although any woman rarely changes her particular ideological position, the participants of a WS course in which there is a 'men-problem' out of respect for each other may in fact arrive at a joint understanding and as one group of students states, 'men teaching in WS is a theoretical impossibility.' But 'theory' doesn't necessarily match 'practice'—despite our attempts to practice what we preach! Firstly, there are the institutional constraints; it is indeed legally impossible for teachers and students to keep out men who insist on teaching/studying WS within formal education. But there are more complex issues than this open manifestation of ongoing patriarchal control over women. (And even more important ones than the occasional pragmatic argument that the participation of a particularly 'brilliant/famous' man might enhance the status of WS, and/or without his expertise a certain course could not be offered as the 'female expert' could not be found.) One of the most difficult issues to deal with is the behavior and personalities of *individual* men. They make our theories falter and conflict with our practice, and it is to this thorny question I shall now turn.

DON'T SPEAK IT—LIVE IT[10]

The discussion about whether men should be teaching WS described at the beginning of this paper was particularly difficult and painful because it took place *after* one man had taught on the WS course for a full year. Man *A* was of the 'enlightened-bearded-feminist-expert-I-am-oppressed-too-type' and he had succeeded in avoiding open confrontations with or among the women on the course. Discussions about the 'soft' variety of his manipulation surfaced periodically and the male-centered nature of his knowledge was attacked by some students but no one took action to stop him from teaching. A new group of students and a new teacher (man *B*) who made some crucial mistakes that demonstrated his ignorance of feminist processes, had to enter the scene to trigger the fundamental discussion not about *a particular* man, but about *all* men and their role in WS. In theory, the participants on the course agreed on the incompatibility of WS and men. However, some women defended *B*'s 'expertise' and others *A*'s sensitivity, expertise and support. In

---

[10] These are my friend and landlady, Mona Howard's, words and reflect the intensity of our many feminist conversations over the past 2 years on a million topics, for which I owe her more than thanks.

fact they said *A* had been more 'feminist' in handling content *and* process than one of the women who taught on the course. Other participants vehemently protested and the resulting split on this issue was never resolved and may have been one of the factors responsible for the lack of cohesion and 'sisterhood' within this specific group of students—a sad example of men's contribution to the divisions among women.[11]

As the women who were against men in WS in principle argued—and I share their view—the question is not whether men in WS are 'good' or 'bad,' or 'better' or 'worse' than any of the female teachers, but that, as one student put it, 'they are part of the problem, whereas any woman is part of the solution.' While one might take issue with the idealist nature of this statement—we all know women who are ghastly, unsisterly and anti-feminist 'social males'—we may be more at ease with the contention that 'every woman's situation is part of men's problems,' be they the actions of the Margaret Thatchers of this world or those of radical feminist separatists! Indeed it was the understanding that something is wrong with *men* and the society they have organized—not women—which was a catalyst a decade ago for the contemporary Women's Movement, and later WS. WS began as a feminist teaching/learning concept in which it was not only the content that we altered but equally, or even more crucially, the *process*. WS was created as an educational concept based on the presence of women convenors of courses, students/teachers, makers and distributors of knowledge—in short as those who make all the decisions, are in 'power' and have 'control': not to 'dominate' others but to empower women ourselves.

In practice we often don't live up to our theories. Many of us still feel the need to use our 'expertise' to compete with (and try to control) other women, disguising our insecurities by using scientific jargon with resultant intimidation and alienation instead of sharing the different kinds of 'expertise' and knowledge we have. Undoubtedly, it is hard to shed all the layers of conformity to an androcentric educational system—in whatever country but especially in Britain—that those of us who have 'made it' far enough to be teachers/students on a postgraduate WS course, were obliged to acquire in the interest of sheer 'academic' survival. But it is precisely these inconsistencies and contradictions between our feminist theories and our practice that could be pursued in the WS classroom . . . in the absence of men.

While unfortunately there is a general reluctance among women to discuss these dynamics and our different views about and attitudes towards them, if *men* are present we feel even less free to talk about 'us.' This, I think, has also to do with our deeply entrenched equation of 'authority' and 'male

---

[11] Both men continued to teach on the course. It was the students who had to make the 'sacrifice:' those who could not bear to have a male lecturer on female and male homosexuality and criminology took another option. Some of them felt very cheated because they could not get information on these two important areas for feminist theory and practice.

expert.' We still take men too seriously and we are still dependent on male approval.[12] I quote the following condescending comment made after a student's presentation: 'I daresay the problem is a bit more complicated than the way you've just presented it.' Such a comment is shattering enough when it comes from a female 'expert'—but devastating when it comes from a man. In the particular instance the woman who was treated in this manner remained silent for the rest of the seminar. The years of deference to men as the experts take their toll. It was not until she was with other women—and free from the interference of men—that she abandoned her position of withdrawal and became angry about the anti-educational power play that had been used against her. But in the classroom the other women had also remained silent. Patriarchy had ruled and other students continued the discussion on the teacher's terms, brilliantly displaying their 'grasp of the material' on ideologically 'safe' grounds. The speculative, but innovative and inspiring, questions that the student had raised in her presentation were never pursued and a chance for creative thinking and brain-storming was missed. Undoubtedly a non-feminist female teacher could have behaved equally condescendingly, but perhaps a dialogue about power relationships between students and teachers might have started, and it could have been 'part of the solution' which is working *for* women and a future *without* power relationships.

As feminists we get most of our emotional, intellectual and often sensual/ sexual support and stimulation from women. We can even construct a paradoxical situation where we have low expectations of men but in turn tend to be overly critical of women and rarely give each other enough credit for what we do. In fact, at times 'trashing' and being trashed by women is so bad and bitter that the 'nice,' unthreatening and sensitive guy who doesn't dare to openly say 'you're wrong' (and if he does we'll simply scoff at him) may be less of a problem. In fact, what we 'expect,' that is, take for granted and don't validate enough from a woman, may come as a total surprise from a considerate 'expert/poor dear' man. Tired of fighting 24 hours a day we may welcome his support, but the likelihood is high that we are too polite and gentle, too understanding and nurturing, and most of all far *too* impressed by the *one* 'good' and/or supportive idea he had. All of a sudden, we find ourselves again being controlled by his alleged need to give up control! Thus, in- and outside WS, women do it again: we take care of men's problems along with our own!

While it is each woman's individual choice how much energy and time she wants to spend with 'nice and considerate men' in her private life, *in WS*, it

---

[12] Unfortunately, many of us are still dependent on male approval. The remark of a feminist friend of mine, when giving me her latest paper, that all the men who read it thought it was extremely good, stands for many others. Why mention the men rather than the women who thought her paper was brilliant?

seems to me we have more important things to do than use our energy and time for men. Feminists have been saying for a long time that women need to be autonomous and have to have our separate spheres. For many academic feminists this demand was not being met by academia and they left. They felt at a loss to accommodate the many contradictions emerging from complying with the conflicting demands of patriarchal institutions and feminist principles. But what I've been arguing throughout this paper is that by making it clear that WS is *only for women* (rather than 'for women only;' after all, we are 51 per cent of the world's population), we claim a tiny bit of autonomous space *within* the educational institutions which supposedly exist to serve the interest of *all* people, and to the maintenance of which women as taxpayers and service workers of all kinds (including faculty wives) contribute significantly.

WS is what we make it to be. Women have a lot to learn about, for and within ourselves. WS as a 'man-free' space is only a beginning. If other women wish to focus their energies on working with men towards *Gender Studies* or to integrate feminist scholarship into the other disciplines, that is their choice. But they should state clearly that both are no substitute for autonomous WS.

We should stop letting men interfere with our theories and practice of women-to-women work, life, loves and friendships. We should stop allowing men to continue to impose their values on what *we* do and to define the terms by giving them access to our spheres of knowledgemaking. As with racism, where it isn't black people who have to take the initiative to end white racism, it is not women who have to take the initiative to end male sexism! Undoubtedly it is hard for men to give up power and privilege, especially when it is in the form of the largely unquestioned assumption that they *are* at the center of attention. Indeed sometimes giving up power is beyond one's control. The 'nice,' 'considerate' man we know from inside the WS classroom, out on the street becomes just an ordinary member of the 'group men': because we live in a man's world he automatically profits (in varying degrees) from male privilege in its many forms. As Liz Stanley has put it pointedly, it is *phallocentrism* that rules; in this respect there are no different 'kinds' of men; 'Gay Men and Straight Men are all Men' (1982: 210). This difference in society's perceptions of 'him' and 'us' will invariably influence our power relationships in WS—in my view an 'egalitarian' relationship between women and men is *not* possible and won't be as long as patriarchy persists.

The power dynamics between me and the *woman* with whom I may fundamentally disagree in the WS classroom, from its start are entirely different. Out on the street (at least in our own cultures) we share being perceived as *women* and consequently are under male control. We are subjected to sexual harassment in all its forms. True, it is much worse for young or old, black, Asian, disabled, out-of-work women than for privileged middle-class white WS practitioners. But *these* are precisely the issues—the differences and problems among women—which we could concentrate on in our work in WS—and not 'men'!

Attacks on women-only WS as being 'separatist' (meaning 'unjust' and discriminating against men) are in my view easy to counter with a few simple questions: who defines what is separatism and who profits? Who is it that is separate? 'In effect sexist society *is* a *separatist* society' says Liz Stanley (1982: 212): malecentredness arbitrarily posits itself as the norm. Men are at least as 'separatist' as are autonomous women! Thinking of Margaret Mead's observation (1950) that whatever the activity, when *men* do it, it is termed 'legitimate' and accorded significance, men's participation in WS might indeed 'help us' to become 'legitimate.' A dubious 'offer,' however, which we would do well to decline with thanks! It is the *de-politicization* of feminism that is at stake and this is no small loss to fear!

I believe very strongly that the only way for men to 'participate' in WS is to respect our circles and be supportive OUTSIDE WS. This may include using their 'old-boys' connections to push our demands for financial support. But I wish they would stop demanding to participate, or wanting to 'understand' and 'share' feminism, feminists and WS.

As we know this claim meets with enormous resistance. It has been my aim to show, that as women, we ourselves have yet a lot of behaviors and attitudes to unlearn and shed. I hope very much that whether men come in the guise of the 'expert,' the 'ignoramus' or the 'poor dear' the 'Men-Problem' in WS does not succeed in dividing women. To go on claiming our only-women spaces where we try to come to terms with our differences and build on our similarities—in short live with our contradictions—promises high rewards: not only is WS a wonderful opportunity for women to work together for a feminist future, but, as Sue Wise has said (pers. comm.): 'The sound of women laughing together is the sound of revolution'! Autonomous WS has a lot of potential for women and we should work toward making it flexible enough to fit the different needs of different women. And last but not least, besides all this 'work' we should also enjoy our time together with other women: 'there is much to be said for laughing now rather than repenting later' (Spender, 1982b: 14).

REFERENCES

Acker, Sandra. 1980. Women, the other academics. *Br. J. Sociology Education* 1 (1): 81–91.

Bowles, Gloria and Duelli Klein, Renate. 1983. The autonomy/integration debate in WS. In Bowles, Gloria and Duelli Klein, Renate, (eds), *Theories of Women's Studies*, pp. 1–26. Routledge & Kegan Paul, London and Boston.

Bradshaw, Jan. 1982. Now what are they up to? Men in the 'Men's Movement'! In Friedman, Scarlet and Sarah, Elizabeth, (eds), *On the Problem of Men*, pp. 174–189. The Women's Press, London.

Duelli Klein, Renate. 1983. Women's Studies: an intellectual necessity. Forthcoming publication of the Society for Research in Higher Education, edited by Sandra Acker/David Warren Piper.

Freeman, Helen and Jones, Alison. 1980. For women only? *Women's Studies Int. Q.* **3 (4)**: 429–440.

Friedman, Scarlet. 1982. Report from Gender and Sociological Theory Conference September 13–14. *Feminist Forum* **5** (6): viii.

Friedman, Scarlet and Sarah, Elizabeth, (eds), 1982. *On the Problem of Men*. The Women's Press, London.

Leonard, Diana. 1982. Male feminists and divided women. In Friedman, Scarlet and Sarah, Elizabeth, (eds), *On the Problem of Men*. The Women's Press, London.

Lerner, Gerda. 1979. Placing women in history. 1975. In Lerner, Gerda, (ed), *The Majority Finds Its Past*, pp. 145–159. Oxford University Press, Oxford.

Mead, Margaret. 1950. 1971. *Male and Female*. Penguin, Harmondsworth, Middlesex.

Rowland, Robyn. 1982. Women's Studies courses: pragmatic and political issues concerning their establishment and design. *Women's Studies Int. Forum* **5** (5): 487–496.

Russell, Joan. 1982. The theory and development of feminism. Unpubl. MA dissertation in Women's Studies, Kent University at Canterbury.

Schilb, John. 1982. Men's Studies and Women's Studies. *Change* **14** (3): 38–41.

Spender, Dale. 1980. *Man Made Language*. Routledge & Kegan Paul, London.

Spender, Dale. 1982a. *Women of Ideas and What Men Have Done to them. From Aphra Behn to Adrienne Rich*. Routledge & Kegan Paul, London.

Spender, Dale. 1982b. Re-inventing the wheel. *The Leveller*, September 1982: 12–14.

Stanley, Liz. 1982. 'Male Needs': the problems and problems of working with gay men. In Friedman, Scarlet and Sarah, Elizabeth, (eds), *On the Problem of Men*, pp. 190–213. The Women's Press, London.

COMMENT: RENATE D. KLEIN.

In 1988 the 'men problem' in Women's Studies is even more urgent than in 1982 when I wrote the original article out of a sense of personal urgency. The USA, in particular, has experienced a substantive increase in so-called 'Gender Studies' with a glut of books by men on Women's Studies and the supposedly new field of 'Men's Studies'! Once more in history, it seems to me, men take over—and thereby change—the creation and distribution of knowledge begun by and for women whose clear aim it was to end women's oppression. Dale Spender's Women of Ideas and What Men Have Done to Them *(1982) revisited in the late 1980s?*

'Experts,' 'ignoramuses' and 'poor dears' have settled in alarming numbers in Women's Studies programs. I believe the question I raised about men's desire to interfere with women's places and women's needs to have their/our own legitimate space in academe needs a great deal of serious discussion by feminists. If this does not happen, I fear that Women's Studies will be further colonized, co-opted and lastly, may be phased out altogether.

10

The Reproductive Brothel[1]

Genoveffa Corea

Newspapers assure us that such new reproductive technologies as embryo transfer, *in-vitro* fertilization and artificial insemination of breeder women (usually known as 'surrogate mothers') are merely 'therapies' kindly physicians provide for infertile women. Of course there is more to it than that. Through the years, with widespread use of technologies, social institutions will be restructured to reflect a new reality—tightened male control over female reproductive processes. We do not know exactly how this new reality will be expressed, but as sociologist Jalna Hanmer has observed, 'we do know that in a system characterized by power imbalance, the greater the assymetry, the greater the potential abuse of the less powerful group' (Hanmer, 1984: 444–445).

  Andrea Dworkin has described one possible expression of the new reality: the reproductive brothel (Dworkin, 1983). Current male control over woman's reproduction, she points out, is sloppy. It is the farming model applied to motherhood. This is, according to Dworkin, one of two models which describes how women are socially controlled and sexually used. Under the farming model, men plant women with their seed and then harvest the crop of babies. This is inefficient. There are too many uncontrollable elements: the woman might be infertile; she might produce a bad crop one year—a defective child; there is room for her to exert her will against the man's—to secretly insert a diaphragm to avoid a pregnancy or, if she wants a child, to 'forget' her pill; she can find some time to organize with other women and foment rebellion; each woman lives with an individual man providing her with some room for a personal relationship. Women are not all penned together, controlled, used as reproduction commodities and nothing more.

[1] An extended discussion of this topic—in the broad context of reproductive technology—is to be found in the forthcoming book by Genoveffa Corea, entitled *The Mother Machine*. Harper & Row, New York.

Under the second, brothel model, women are collected together and held, unable to come and go freely. Sold as sexual commodities to men, the women are interchangeable. They are not seen as human beings with individuality and spiritual worth. The women, Dworking writes, sell parts of their bodies 'and they also sell acts—what they say and what they do' (p. 177). This brothel model, which reduces a woman to what she sells, is efficient. The women do not get out. They are controlled with force, degradation, drugs. (For documentation, see Barry, 1979).

With the new reproductive technologies, Dworkin observes, men will be able to apply the brothel model to reproduction: 'Women can sell reproductive capacities the same way old-time prostitutes sold sexual ones . . .' (p. 182). While sexual prostitutes sell vagina, rectum and mouth, reproductive prostitutes will sell other body parts: wombs, ovaries, eggs.

Of couse social institutions might be restructured in a less horrifying way. But the fact that women are hated in a male-supremacist culture makes it foolish to dismiss Dworkin's vision as unthinkable.

A model for the institution Dworkin envisions already exists. Many farm animals live in what are essentially reproductive brothels. On such a farm, the animal is seen as having no individuality, no spiritual worth. She is penned in under prison-like conditions. Reproductive engineers use parts of her body. They can artificially inseminate a 'superior' cow with the sperm of a 'superior' bull, remove the embryos from her body and transfer them into 'inferior' cows who will gestate the calves. Through this procedure, they can transform so-called valuable cows 'from once-a-year calf producers to machines that can produce embryos every two months . . .' (Brotman, 1983: 108). They can even transfer embryos of one species into female 'hatcheries' of another species. For example, in 1981, a Holstein dairy cow at the Bronx Zoo in New York gave birth to a gaur, a member of a wild endangered species.

Reproductive engineers have these techniques available to them in applying the brothel model to animal reproduction.

Artificial insemination: The fresh or frozen sperm of a 'superior' male animal can be placed into a 'gun,' the gun inserted into a rod and the rod inserted into a female animal for insemination.

Superovulation: Normally animals release (ovulate) only one egg a month. Reproductive engineers want many eggs 'for efficient operation' (Murray, 1978: 292). Increased efficiency is possible because of the 1927 discovery that hormones produced by the pituitary gland affect the ovaries. It occurred to men that they could inject such hormones into a female and force the growth and ovulation of eggs from an abnormally large number of follicles—the small sacs which enclose the eggs. This is superovulation. Hormones can and experimentally have been used to force the immature ovaries of even newborn animals to produce eggs. Superovulation of very young and very old females can extend the period of their egg-production and hence, of their usefulness to brothel management.

Estrus synchronization: In order to transfer embryos, the reproductive cycles of 'donor' and recepient cows must be in accord so that when the donor ovulates and her uterus prepares itself for the implantation of a fertilized egg, the uterus of the recipient cow is also prepared to receive an egg. This can be done naturally or hormonally.

Ova recovery: After superovulating and inseminating the females, the fertilized eggs must be retrieved. Early collection techniques involved killing the females and cutting into their oviducts. 'Slaughter of donor animals augments the consistency of [egg] recovery,' researchers reported (Avery and Graham, 1962: 220). Later they tried to recover the eggs surgically but frequently the females were left 'problem breeders,' or even sterile due to surgical damage (Elsden, 1978). So men moved on to non-surgical methods. Using a two-way flow catheter, they flushed fluids into the uterus and collected those fluids, along with the eggs, in a receptacle. This is the method frequently used today.

Embryo evaluation: After recovery, men inspect the embryos under dissection miscroscopy, eliminating those considered unfit for transfer and ranking the acceptable ones according to quality.

Twinning: Dr. S. M. Willadsen has devised a method for dividing the embryo in half, producing identical twins—two animals from just one fertilized egg. An official of the International Embryo Transfer Society told me that the advantage of twinning is 'that you double—reliably, easily, fast, cheaply—the number of embryos a valuable donor produces.' Three sets of females can be used to produce the twins: the egg donors; the primary recipients in whose bodies the divided embryos are cultured; and the secondary recipients in whose bodies the embryos come to term. The animals need not be of the same species. Cows, pigs and sheep were used in various phases of one experiment on twinning (Willadsen, 1981).

Embryo transfer: Sometimes reproductive engineers transfer the embryo from the donor recepient non-surgically, inserting a catheter through the cervix to deposit the embryo in the uterus. More often, they transfer surgically because the resulting pregnancy rates (50 to 70 per cent) are better.

Cesarean section: When the pregnant cows approach full-term, veterinarians often perform cesarean sections on them 'since the calves are usually large and the recipients are generally heifers of smaller breeds' (Seidel, 1975).

One pioneer in reproductive technology estimates that techniques for maturing and fertilizing eggs in the laboratory (*in-vitro* fertilization), twinning embryos and determining their sex will have commerical application before 1986 (Seidel, 1981: 324).

How does a female live on such a brothel-farm? The words of L. J. Taylor, export development manager for the Wall's Meat Company Ltd, give some indication: 'The breeding sow should be thought of, and treated as, a valuable piece of machinery whose function is to pump out baby pigs like a sausage machine.' Peter Singer and Jim Mason (Singer, 1975; Mason and Singer, 1980: 35), who quote these words, have described the life of the sow-machine on a factory farm. It consists of pregnancy, birth, watching her babies taken from her to be fattened for market, and then, endlessly, a repetition of the cycle: pregnancy, birth, loss of babies, insemination.

The sow is almost continually pregnant or nursing throughout her adult life. For at least ten months of every year, she is unable to walk around. After weaning, she has at most only a few days of comparative freedom before she is placed in a pen to be, once again, serviced by a boar. When she is pregnant, she is placed in a 'gestation' building. Her stall is often little bigger than she is herself—two feet wide and six feet long. She may also be tethered by a collar around her neck. She is able to stand up and lie down but does not have enough room to turn around or to exercise at all. Except at feeding time, she lives in darkness. The lights are turned off to reduce the stress and excitement in the confinement system.

About a week before the birth, farmers move her to the 'farrowing' building where she may also be closely confined in order 'to keep her in a position only to eat, drink, and keep her teats exposed to the young pigs' (Mason and Singer, 1980: 11). In Britain and in other countries, she may be placed in the 'iron maiden,' a frame which prevents free movement.

As I have mentioned, many animals in a reproductive brothel, considered genetically unworthy, serve as breeders for the embryos of superior animals. This distinction between the genetically worthy and unworthy is likely to increase. Writing of one scheme to obtain large-scale genetic improvement in a herd, Dr Peter Elsden of the Animal Reproduction Laboratory at Colorado State University noted that the top 10–20 per cent of the herd could be superovulated and used to produce many embryos while the bottom 90–80 per cent of the cows could be used as recipients for those embryos. 'Therefore, the lower two-thirds of the herd is being culled in regard to their own progeny, while the top one-third of the herd is producing four times as many progeny as normal since the average number of calves per superovulation treatment is four,' he wrote.

It is easy to dismiss the fate of animals as one entirely different from that of women. However, I do not believe women and animals inhabit such vastly different categories in a male supremacist world. Over centuries in many patriarchal lands, women and animals shared a common legal status. We were chattel, or moveable, animate property. Men owned slaves, cattle, concubines, beasts of burden, wives—all chattel. To this date, some laws in the United States retain common law concepts about ownership, possession and control of marital property which reflect the notion that women are economic chattel. Women's status as sex and reproduction chattel remains in law and in practice today in the United States, as Dworkin observes. Even now, a man's 'marital right' to rape his wife is recognized in at least 37 states (Shulman, 1980).

Farmers now use female animals as breeders; numerous male commentators have discussed or predicted the creation of a class of professional women breeders (Davis, 1937; Westoff, 1978; Scott, 1981; Scott, 1981; Francoeur, 1970; Kieffer, 1979; Packard, 1979). This would be unthinkable were women acknowledged to have the same right to bodily integrity enjoyed by men.

With the development of the surrogate motherhood industry beginning in 1977, references to professional breeders are on the increase. (The surrogate industry is one which rents women's bodies for reproductive purposes. The woman is inseminated with the customer's sperm. She then gestates the resulting baby, births it, and, for a modest fee, turns it over to the customer.) Lawyers, physicians, legislators and ethicists write of 'institutionalizing' surrogate motherhood, of the state regulating the women, of some agency certifying and licensing the mothers (Francoeur, 1970: 106; Keane and Breo, 1981: 233-267). Professional breeding could become commonplace, attorney Russell Scott writes, if 'healthy young host mothers' were offered not only a payment, but social security, educational facilities and other signs of public approval as well (Scott, 1981: 218). 'There are certainly enough women available to form a caste of childbearers, especially if the pay was right,' observes one bioethicist. He refers to an unemployed nurse who offered to bear a child for a California couple so she could take herself and her young daughter off welfare (Kieffer, 1979: 73).

Social commentator Vance Packard suggests that surrogacy would provide young women with an undemanding career. 'It would help if the hired mother was of an easygoing nature and enjoyed pregnancy and TV-watching,' he wrote. The women would no doubt be free to take on a physically undemanding extra job. (He suggests ticket selling at a movie theater.) If the 'mercenary mother' were to gestate an embryo conceived with another woman's egg, the job should not require much of the surrogate 'in the way of education, family background, good looks, or even skin color. If the woman is simply to be an incubator, the price would certainly be lower than if she contributed half the baby's heredity.' In south Texas, he wrote, 'pleasant, conscientious Mexican-American girls' might leap at a fee of $5000 for bearing a child and girls (sic) south of the border might leap at half that fee. 'If lawyers can arrange Mexican divorces for Americans,' wrote Packard, 'they surely can arrange Mexican gestations' (Packard, 1979: 268-269).

Fees paid to 'host mothers' would probably vary with the country, as several commentators have suggested. Mexican women would do it for less. When it becomes possible to transfer human embryos routinely from one woman to another (and it has already been done experimentally), then the way opens up to use Third World women to gestate babies for wealthier Westerners.

The president of a U.S. foundation which helps arrange surrogate pregnancies told me: 'If we could cross international lines, then $1000 is a significant sum of money, whereas here (in the U.S.), it's just a week or a month's wages.' Asked what countries he had in mind, he replied: 'Central America would be fine.' It is 'inevitable' that the United States go to other parts of the world and 'rely on their support' in providing surrogate mothers, he thinks. Comparing the United States to the city and Central America to the country, he pointed out that 'the cities are always supported by the country.'

A Third World surrogate mother would not even need to be healthy. 'The mother could have a health problem which could be quite serious,' he said. 'However if her diet is good and other aspects of her life are o.k., she could become a viable mother for genuine embryo transfer.'

His foundation issues a quarterly directory containing pictures of North American women willing to serve as breeders. One photograph displays Number 36, 'Gabriel,' an attractive woman wearing a blouse with a low neckline. An entry describing each available woman appears in the Spring 1982 Directory. An example:

> Martha F., *Address*: Escondido, Ca. *Pregnant*: No. *Status*: Divorced. *Employer*: County
> . . . *Birth date*: 6.11.48. *Height*: 5' 2". *Weight*: 110. *Hair*: Blond. *Racial Origins*:
> Caucasian. *Children*: Kammy, Age 14 and Crissy, Age 10. *Medical*: Normal delivery both
> children . . . no surgery or other problems. Medical release and detailed medical history
> completed. *Could begin*: Immediately. *Insurance*: Greater San Diego. *Expenses Antici-
> pated*: $20,000. *Photographs*: Available. *Contact*: By mail forwarding. *Comments*: My
> oldest child is a mentally gifted child. (Interested in planned or surrogate mothering.)

Sometimes the reproductive prostitute is or was a sexual prostitute as well. In Britain a childless couple hired a 19-year-old prostitute for $5500 to bear a baby for them conceived through artificial insemination with the husband's sperm. The couple entered London's Bow Street Magistrate's Court, surveyed the women who paraded to pay their regular fines, and chose one. That woman would not bear them a child but agreed, for a finder's fee of $925, to locate a prostitute who would, and did (Scott, 1981).

Setting up stables of surrogate mothers would be establishing a primitive form of the reproductive brothel. The assembly line approach would be used, but only to a minor degree. ('Some of the surrogates are pregnant, some are being inseminated, some are waiting to be selected,' an attorney who operates a surrogacy business told me in 1982. 'About four or five are waiting to get final reports in from the physician.') With improvements in technology, a brothel employing much more sophisticated assembly line techniques and providing greater control over women becomes possible.

As I envision it, most women in a reproductive brothel would be defined as 'non-valuable' and sterilized and, in this way, their progeny culled. This 'vision' came to me after repeatedly seeing reproductive engineers link their new technologies—*in-vitro* fertilization, embryo transfer, egg banks—with sterilization (Muller, 1961; Fletcher, 1974, 1976; Seed and Seed, 1978; Djerassi, 1979; Edwards, 1979). They invariably suggest that the sterilization will benefit those operated upon. Women could be sterilized knowing that if they later want a child, they can have one through use of the new technologies. In this way, women would be able to avoid modern steroidal contraception.

In the United States, women of color probably would be labeled 'non-valuable,' sterilized and used as breeders for the embryos of 'valuable' women. The white women judged genetically superior and selected as egg donors would be turned into machines for producing embryos. Through superovulation, 'valuable' females as young as two years and some as old as 50 or 60 could be induced to produce eggs.

Reproductive engineers would engage in three major activities in the brothel: (1) getting eggs, (2) manipulating them, (3) transferring embryos.

GETTING EGGS

There are a number of ways engineers might recover or, as they term it, 'capture' eggs from women. They could flush them out of women using the technique developed by Drs Richard and Randolph Seed with the medical team at the Harbor-UCLA Medical Center. (The Seed brothers worked on egg flushing and embryo transfer for six years in cows before moving on to women. They had their first human success in 1983 when they established pregnancies through embryo transfer in two women in Torrance, California.) However, the Seeds' flushing procedure would probably not yield the necessary quantity of eggs. It is also unlikely that engineers would use two techniques employed experimentally in animals: placing tubular instruments inside the women's reproductive tracts and keeping them there permanently so eggs would pass into the instruments and out of the bodies; and relocating women's ovaries to make it easier to get at the eggs. These techniques had been 'found wanting' in animals and abandoned (Betteridge, 1981: 8).

Eggs are far more likely to be obtained by extracting them directly from the ovaries, a procedure which requires control over the female cycle. In *Farm Journal* in 1976, Earl Ainsworth, identifying the factor which prevented farmers from treating sows totally as machines, wrote: 'Estrus control will open the doors to factory hog production. Control of female cycles is the missing link to the assembly-line approach.' (Mason and Singer, 1980: 19). The 'missing link' to the assembly-line, brothel approach to human reproduction is being forged in *in-vitro* fertilization clinics around the world where teams are working intensely to control the cycles of women.

In the brothel, on the appropriate days of their cycles, women would line up for Pergonal shots which will stimulate their ovaries. Engineers would superovulate only the top 10–20 per cent of the female population in the brothel. Then, after following the development of the eggs through ultrasound and blood tests, they would operate on the women to extract the eggs. Perhaps they would allow the women to heal from the operation every other month so that women would only be subjected to surgery six times per year.

To obtain eggs, engineers could also do what they now do with certain cows. When the championship cow Sabine 2A died in 1982 during a cesarean section, embryologists from the firm Genetic Engineering Inc. removed her ovaries, obtained 36 eggs from them, and froze the eggs. During her lifetime, Sabine's embryos had been fetching $10,000 or more on the embryo transfer market and when the eggs from the dead Sabine are thawed and fertilized in *in-vitro*, they may fetch the same (Brotman, 1983). In the reproductive brothel, as a valuable woman dies, engineers could operate on her, remove her ovaries and salvage eggs from those ovaries, perhaps by using enzymes to eat away the connective tissue and release hundreds of thousands of eggs. They could then freeze the eggs for future *in-vitro* fertilization and transfer into a 'non-valuable' female. A woman could be used for reproduction long after she is dead.

Not only could dead women be used in reproductive brothels. So could women who were never born. A female embryo could be developed just to the point where an ovary emerges and then the ovary could be cultured so that engineers could get eggs from it. The full woman would never be allowed to develop. Just her ovary.

Partial ectogenesis—culturing organ rudiments from their earliest appearance to a mature state—is already well established as a technique used in certain biological studies. If various fragmented procedures reported by different scientists could be brought together and, in combination, used in one species, mature organs might soon be produced externally from a fertilized egg, embryologist Dr Clifford Grobstein has predicted. One of the organs men have extensively investigated is the ovary. By maturing the ovary externally, Grobstein wrote, a supply of eggs for *in-vitro* fertilization could be provided without surgical intervention in a woman's body (Grobstein, 1981: 48).

MANIPULATING EGGS

Once the eggs have been recovered, reproductive engineers along the assembly line could manipulate them in a number of ways:

- Twin the embryos, producing two humans out of one embryo.
- Use the eggs of 'non-valuable' women for clones, destroying the egg nuclei with lasers and injecting the nuclei of valuable men.

- Remove the female genetic component from the egg and inject two sperm into the egg, producing a child with two fathers and no mother.
- Genetically engineer the embryo for various qualities. If ever partial or total ectogenesis were applied to humans, it would be 'no more than a game for the "manfarming biologist" to change the subject's sex, the color of its eyes, the general proportions of body and limbs, and perhaps the facial features,' wrote biologist Jean Rostand, over-confidently (Rostand, 1959: 84).
- Fertilize the eggs in the laboratory using a culture media concocted from bits and pieces of women. 'We made our culture fluids resemble the female reproductive tract by adding very small pieces of human uterus or Fallopian tube,' wrote *in-vitro* fertilization pioneers Patrick Steptoe and R. G. Edwards (Edwards and Steptoe, 1980: 54). Another reproductive engineer used 'minced fragments of [women's] fallopian tubal mucosa' (Shettles, 1955).
- Select the sex of the embryo by fertilizing the egg with either gynosperm (female-engendering) or androsperm (male-engendering). Researchers are hard at work now trying to separate these two types of sperm. Should they fail, there is another way to predetermine the child's sex. Engineers could snip a few cells of the fertilized egg to check its gender. Most female embryos could simply be discarded. The brothel administration would decide how many would be needed.

TRANSFERRING EMBRYOS

Once the embryo has been manufactured, reproductive engineers would have several options.

They could freeze the embryo in the bank for later use. Or they could immediately transfer the embryo into a woman in the lower 80-90 per cent of the female population. These would be the breeders, the women who had been called 'surrogate mothers' in the early stage of reproduction revolution when engineers had been conscious of the need for good public relations.

The transferred embryo might gestate in the breeder for the entire nine-month pregnancy. When delivering time approached, the breeder would find no cosy 'birthing rooms' in the brothel but rather an assembly line. The descriptions women gave of the obstetrical experiences in American hospitals in the 1950s are likely to be as apt for the brothel of the future: 'They give you drugs, whether you want them or not, strap you down like an animal' (p. 44). 'Women are herded like sheep through an obstetrical assembly line, are drugged and strapped on tables while their babies are forceps-delivered' (p. 45). 'I felt exactly like a trapped animal' (Schultz, 1958, 1959).

Alternatively, engineers could transfer the embryo into a breeder, allow it to gestate for a certain number of months, and then remove the fetus by cesarean section at whatever point at which their incubators could take over.

(Today that point is 21 weeks gestation). In the incubator, they would perform surgery on the fetus, innoculate it or undertake whatever alterations they deemed desirable.

The breeder into whom an embryo is placed need not be alive. This possibility is suggested by several recent cases in which the bodies of the brain-dead pregnant women were kept functioning until the fetus had developed enough to be delivered. In one case, a 27-year-old woman suffered a fatal seizure when she was 22-weeks pregnant. Her husband and other family members wanted the woman's body kept in operation until the fetus became viable. Physicians put her on a life-support system. Their most difficult medical challenges during the nine weeks they maintained the dead woman, were keeping control of the woman's many failing body functions and combating infection, they report. The woman developed diabetes insipidus and Addison's disease and, periodically, a blood infection throughout the body. Doctors did blood studies on the dead woman every two hours. They performed a cesarean section on her more than two months after she had been declared dead, extracted a healthy baby and then removed the life-support apparatus. She stopped breathing. Relatives reportedly expressed 'a great deal of pleasure' at the birth (*Star-Ledger*, 1983).

'The experience left me with real confidence that this can be done without any great difficulties. . . . In the future, I'll suggest to family members that the option is there,' Dr Russell K. Laros Jr of the department of obstetrics, gynecology and reproductive sciences at the University of California School of Medicine in San Francisco, said (OGN, 1983: 2).

(Immediately over the Newark *Star-Ledger's* account of the birth—'Brain Dead Woman Gives Birth'—appeared a photograph of smiling parents holding their infants, the nation's first test-tube twins.)

Perhaps in the distant future, few women, dead or alive, will be required. If reproductive engineers have developed an artificial womb, they might place the cultured embryo directly into The Mother Machine.

The reproductive brothel is one possible institution within which men might control women, or various groups of women, in the future. Other scenarios involving use of the new technologies are also conceivable. Women need to grapple with this issue. Jalna Hanmer has urgently called for: (1) a series of meetings within feminist movements around the world on what action to take, (2) an international feminist network to monitor developments in these new reproductive technologies and (3) an International Tribunal on Medical Crimes Against Women. I add my voice, urgently, to hers.

REFERENCES

Avery, T. L. and Graham, E. F. 1962. Investigations associated with the transplanting of bovine ova: III Recovery and fertilization. *J. Reprod. Fertil.* 212–217.

Barry, Kathleen. 1979. *Female Sexual Slavery*. Prentice-Hall, Englewood Cliffs, New Jersey.
Betteridge, K. J. 1981. An historical look at embryo transfer. *J. Reprod. Fertil.* **62**: 1–13.
Brotman, Harris. May 15, 1983. Engineering the birth of cattle. *New York Times Magazine*.
Davis, Kingsley. 1937. Reproductive institutions and the pressure for population. *The Sociological Review*.
Djerassi, Carl. 1979. *The Politics of Contraception*. W.W. Norton, New York, London.
Dworkin, Andrea. 1983. *Right-Wing Women*. Pedigree Books, New York.
Edwards, R. G. January 5, 1979. Letter to U.S. Ethics Advisory Board in *Appendix: HEW Support of Research Involving Human In Vitro Fertilization and Embryo Transfer*. May 4, 1979. U.S. Government Printing Office, Washington. D.C.
Edwards, R. G. and Steptoe, Patrick. 1980. *A Matter of Life*. William Morrow, New York.
Elsden, Peter. February 10, 1978. Advances in embryo transfer techniques. *Holstein Friesian World*.
Fletcher, Joseph. 1974. *The Ethics of Genetic Control: Ending Reproductive Roulette*. Anchor Press/Doubleday, Garden City, New York.
Fletcher, Joseph. 1976. Ethical aspects of genetic controls. In Shannon, Thomas A. (ed.), *Bioethics*, Paulist Press, New York/Ramsey, New Jersey.
Francoeur, Robert T. 1970. *Utopian Motherhood*. Doubleday, Garden City, New York.
Grobstein, Clifford. 1981. *From Chance to Purpose: An Appraisal of External Human Fertilization*. Addison-Wesley, Reading, Mass.
Hanmer, Jalna. 1984. A womb of one's own. In Arditti. Rita. Klein, Renate Duelli and Minden, Shelley , (eds), *Test Tube Women*. Pandora Press, Boston and London.
Keane, Noel P. with Breo, Dennis L. 1981. *The Surrogate Mother*. Everest House, New York.
Kieffer, George H. 1979. *Bioethics: A Textbook of Issues*. Addison-Wesley, Reading, Mass.
Mason, Jim and Singer, Peter. 1980. *Animal Factories*, Crown Publishers, New York.
Muller, Herman J., 1961. Human evolution by voluntary choice of germ plasm. *Science, NY* **134** (3480).
Murray, Finnie A. 1978. Embryo transfer in large domestic mammals. In Daniel, Joseph C., Jr, (ed), *Methods in Mammalian Reproduction*. Academic Press, New York, San Francisco, London.
OGN. 1983. Maintenance of brain-dead gravida held viable course. *Ob. Gyn News* **18** (11): 2.
Packard, Vance. 1979. *The People Shapers*. Bantam, New York.
Rostand, Jean. 1959. *Can Man Be Modified?* Basic Books, New York.
Scott, Russell, 1981. *The Body as Property*. The Viking Press, New York.
Seed, Randolph W. and Seed, Richard C., October 13, 1978. Statement before the Ethics Advisory Board of the Department of Health, Education and Welfare.
Seidel, George E., Jr. April/May, 1975. Embryo transfer. *Charolais Bull-O-Gram*.
Seidel, George E., Jr. 1981. Superovulation and embryo transfer in cattle. *Science, NY* **211** (4479): 351–358.
Shettles, Landrum P. 1955. A morula stage of human ovum developed *in-vitro*. *Fertility and Sterility* **6** (4): 287–289.
Schulman, Joanne. 1980. The marital rape exemption in the criminal law. *Clearinghouse Rev.* **14** (6): 538–540.
Shultz, Gladys Denny. May 1959. Journal mothers report on cruelty in maternity wards. *Ladies Home Journal*.
Singer, Peter. 1975. *Animal Liberation*. Avon Books, New York.
Star-Ledger (Newark, N.J.). March 31, 1983. Brain dead woman gives birth.
Westoff, Charles F. 1978. Some speculations on the future of marriage and fertility. *Family Planning Perspectives* **10** (2): 79–83.
Willadsen, S. M., Lenhn-Jensen, H., Fehilly, C. B. and Newcomb, R. 1981. The production of monozygotic twins of preselected parentage by micromanipulation of non-surgically collected cow embryos. *Theriogenology* **15** (1): 23–27.

11

Fathers' Rights, Women's Losses

Scarlet Pollock
and Jo Sutton

ILLEGITIMATE CHILDREN, OR THE LEGITIMACY OF FATHERHOOD

An illegitimate child is one who has no father. This is obviously not a biological definition. In a biological sense, every child has a father. It would be absurd to argue that every child should have a biological father. Illegitimacy is a social and political concept. The existence or non-existence of a mother is defined as irrelevant to the status of illegitimacy. What counts as important is solely that a child should have a father. Social and legal discrimination against illegitimate children exerts great pressure upon mothers to secure a man, a father, who can legitimate children. The status of illegitimacy imposed upon children whose father is not married to their mother, perpetuates the legitimacy of fatherhood.

The issue of illegitimacy is centered upon the social construction of what is a father and what is a family. Ideologically, a family should contain two parents: a female who is a mother and a male who is a father to the child/ren. Attempts to describe other arrangements are couched in language which expresses deviation and social deviance from this model, for example, one-parent families, fatherless families, broken homes. To be a legitimate family the two parents must be, or at least at one time have been, married. Marriage involves a set of legal rights and obligations which affirms the relations between men, women and children; within this framework men are legitimated as fathers.

In general, fatherhood is portrayed as simply a natural relation, meaning biological. The legal rights and obligations of men in marriage are perceived as little more than a biological imperative. There are, of course, 'absent' fathers or 'bad' fathers, but fatherhood, the norm and the ideal, is seen as

132

good and right and beyond question. It is socially justified in terms of the biological relation between a man and his sperm.

The international claims of fathers of illegitimate children can be seen through recent legislation in New Zealand, all Australian states except Victoria, Switzerland, Austria, France, the Netherlands and West Germany. In the U.S.A. a number of states have adopted the Uniform Parentage Act, and many have given unmarried biological fathers equal rights by judicial decisions based upon Constitutional rights. This 'equal rights' trend of the late 1960s and 1970s is not based upon equality between fathers and mothers, men and women, but between married men and unmarried men.

The direction of these changes has been to strengthen men's legal claims to children, and the chances of men gaining custody over children. It is to lessen the legal importance of marriage—a formal social contract between hetero-sexual partners. It will increase the claims of men over women and children irrespective of their social relationships.

In 1975 an agreement set out by the Council of Europe, and signed by the United Kingdom, designed the legal abolition of illegitimacy. This did not do away with the necessity of a father to legitimate a child's existence, as might seem simplest. Rather, it was proposed to extend the legitimacy of biological fathers' claims to the children of women to whom they were not married. The children would continue to be illegitimate, in the sense that the parents were not married, but the rights and obligations of a father would be established 'by voluntary recognition or by judicial decision' (1975, Article 3).

Since this time two British Law Commission Reports (1979, 1982) have appeared, which explore the legal alternatives for securing men's rights and obligations as fathers. Although these proposals are being discussed within the rubric of changing the status of illegitimacy, the Law Commission acknowledges that what is predominantly being addressed is the rights of men (1979, para 2.11). Outside of marriage, men are at present not able to establish paternity to a child nor claim rights of guardianship, custody or access, *without the consent of the child's mother*. This is a problem for men. Within marriage a woman's consent is not legally necessary; her husband is presumed to be the biological father, and is given the accompanying social and legal rights of a father (unless a competing claim is proved). What the proposed legislation would do is override the necessity for a woman's consent outside of marriage. The consent of the mother is made unnecessary, and men are enabled to take up the position of father.

It can be difficult to disentangle the position of fathers in relation to mothers, and to children, because the current debate conflates fatherhood in such a way as to concentrate only upon the relationship of a man to a child. This ignores the rights and privileges of men over women, supported by the position of father (see Sutton and Friedman, 1982). Thus, Samuels (1983) is able to argue that regardless of a man's behavior towards the mother, he

deserves the rights and privileges of being a father. This has serious consequences for women as well as for children.

Samuel points out that a biological father can be, and is 'all too often
unmeritorious' (1983: 88). The man may have 'deceived' the woman, 'jilted'
her, been 'interested only in sexual gratification'; he may 'even be guilty of
rape.' His relationship with the child may be no better than his relationship
with the mother. He may have 'failed to support the child' and his interest in
the child may be 'merely a means of blackmailing, harassing, pressurizing,
embarrassing or threatening the security of the mother' (ibid.). These are
seen as insufficient grounds to deprive an unmarried man of his right to be a
social father, as well as being the biological father, to a child. Furthermore,
this right is viewed as taking priority over the mother's judgement and
wishes.

The principle which is being affirmed is the legitimacy of fatherhood. The
rights and privileges of the position of father is bestowed upon men
regardless of their behavior towards women and children and irrespective of
the mothers' wishes. Men's rights are justified as stemming from biology, but
the action which is recommended is social and political. What we are
witnessing is the attempt to extend the existing power of fathers within
marriage, to beyond marriage.

In the face of high divorce rates, an increasing illegitimacy rate and a
growing number of one-parent families, there has been an upsurge in efforts
to reaffirm the family as the basic unit of our society. Fears are expressed
about the possible breakdown of family life, and about social instability.
Deviant families, particularly fatherless families, are portrayed to be disad-
vantageous for children, economically and socially. The image of family life
as secure, morally sound and vital for children is propounded at the same
time as 'breakdown' rates are made visible. The family is seen to be in need of
support.

We would argue that what is seen to be in need of support is the position of
men in the family, fathers. The Law Commission report on illegitimacy
(1982), for example, points both to the increasing numbers of illegitimate
births in England and Wales—77,400 in 1980 compared with 53,800 in
1976—and the increasing ratio of illegitimate births as a percentage of total
number of births in that year, reaching 11.8 per cent in 1980 (Haskey, 1982).
While these children may be legitimated through marriage or adoption in
subsequent years, the concern is repeatedly stated that it 'is likely to be that a
greater number of mothers than in the past now accept their illegitimate
children and bring them up themselves' (para. 2.2). This possibility is
presented as alarming, and the Law Commission's proposed Family Law
Reform Bill sets out to make it almost impossible for women to raise children
without men.

Interestingly, these figures point much less clearly to either a sharp increase in the proportion of illegitimate births or a marked trend towards fatherless families, than is suggested in the proposed legislation. For one thing, data collection methods changed during this period resulting in a greater likelihood of reported illegitimate births (Werner, 1982). Second, the number of unmarried women of childbearing age (15–44) in the population between 1977 and 1980 increased by 13 per cent. The increase in numbers of illegitimate births does not necessarily reflect an increasing trend (*ibid.*). Third, Werner suggests that the increasing numbers of separated mothers aged 30 or over in the 1970s, who were registered as having illegitimate children, were living with their future husband while awaiting divorce proceedings involving their first husband to be completed. Fourth, it is estimated that over a third of illegitimate children are born into relatively stable unions; 41 per cent live with their biological parents (mother and father) by the age of 11, and 65 per cent live in some kind of two-parent family (Leete, 1978; Lambert and Streather, 1980, quoted in Law Commission, 1982). These illegitimate children are not living in fatherless families, being brought up by women only.

Close to one in three marriages are now estimated to end in divorce (Haskey, 1982). This figure alone raises much alarm about the growth of fatherless families, since 90 per cent of one-parent families are headed by women (Letts, 1983). Once again, however, the picture is more complicated than this suggests. Despite the evidence that 7 out of 10 divorces are initiated by women (*Social Trends*, 1984), it does not appear to be the case that large numbers of women are electing to bring their children up without a father, or father figure. Only 4 per cent of households in 1982 consisted of lone female parents with dependent children (*Social Trends*, 1984), suggesting high rates of remarriage and cohabitation. Pre-marital cohabitation is overall increasing, and widowed, divorced or separated women are far more likely to be cohabiting than single (never married) women (*ibid.*). Remarriages have increased substantially since the Divorce Reform Act came into effect in 1971. Over half of the women who separated between 1970 and 1974, before the age of 35, had remarried within six years (*ibid.*). Haskey (1982) estimates that of women under 50 in 1979 who remarried during the second half of the 1970s, over one quarter remarried within 3 months, over half within the year and nearly three-quarters within 2 years of their divorce. Further, while one in five children are likely to experience divorcing parents and a large proportion of these children are likely to live with a lone parent for some period of their lives, a large proportion of lone parents will subsequently remarry and the child become part of a new (heterosexual) two-parent family unit (Haskey, 1983).

The trend towards women bringing up children without men is much less marked than references to high divorce rates or increasing illegitimacy rates suggest. Divorced women are highly likely to cohabit or remarry; mothers of illegitimate children, too. One-parent families are a transient state for the most part, for both women and children. Patterns of marriage and divorce are clearly changing, but this does not reveal a dramatic trend towards fatherless families.

Yet a high level of concern is expressed about the possibility of women bringing up children without men. The Law Commission (1982) assumes the availability of contraception and abortion, and emphasizes that illegitimate children are likely to be 'wanted' by their mothers. That is, the Law Commission suggests that women, by choice, are having illegitimate children and bringing them up without men. The report as a whole is addressed to this 'social problem' of women's choice and is designed to put a stop to it.

Legislation in this area is very likely, given the British government's commitment to the Council of Europe Convention of 1975. The Law Commission's proposal for legislation is very interesting, for it is based less upon an analysis of what is happening than on a concern of what might or could be happening. The figures which are used to argue for the Law Commission proposals to abolish illegitimacy are unrealistic. They do not, in fact, point towards marked increases in fatherless families. Yet this is an existing possibility which the Government intends to minimize. It is proposed that the rights of men over children are to be extended outside of marriage, while the possibility of women's independence be curtailed.

FATHERHOOD

Being a father is a social position of high patriarchal status and respect. It is a senior position of power. Fatherhood expresses the relationship between fathers and others, between senior males and less powerful others. Within the nuclear family this involves dominance over a woman and children. Fatherhood is the ideology and practice of the dominance of the senior male.

The path of social development for a male, in its narrow nuclear family sense, reaches its zenith at the birth of 'his' first child: he becomes a father and is enabled to practice fatherhood. This is an institutionalized relationship, through which a man gains social respect both within and outside the family unit. He is socially supported in practising the authority of a senior male.

Elsewhere (Sutton and Friedman, 1982) we have explored the authority of fatherhood as the means of instilling in family members a recognition and acceptance of, and acquiescence to, male authority in general. It is a means through which male supremacy is self-perpetuated. Fatherhood ensures that male children grow up 'normal'—that is, heterosexual, practising brotherhood, and eventually growing into fathers. Through fatherhood, girls are taught femininity—the proper place of women subordinate to men, the art of loyalty and service to men, and a thorough disrespect for women. While the rhetoric of mutual parenthood may seem to convey equality and exchange, the social position of each parent is hierarchically organized. The powerlessness of women is made clear and is continually affirmed by the father's authority over mothers and motherhood.

Arguments in support of the heterosexual family are couched in terms of the 'best interests' of the child. This is a circular argument for what is seen to be in the best interests of the child is to have a social father, and thus to live in a heterosexual family. The possibility for women to break away from this patriarchal family structure is extremely limited. It is currently being made more difficult as both right- and left-wing positions support the ideal family as if it were based upon equality, and in the best interests of children.

The family is not an equal place for men and women because men as fathers are granted social power over women and children. State concern with 'the problem of fatherless families' is less a consideration of poverty and stigmatization than an attempt to impose male authority. Posing fatherlessness as the problem, then presenting men as the solution, serves only to perpetuate political inequality for women and children.

If a particular father fails to practice fatherhood there are a variety of state supported agencies which may step in to ensure that authority relations are maintained (see, for example, Cavanagh on the practice of personal social services, forthcoming). Similarly, a man may not wish to exercise the power of his position over an individual woman and child/ren within a heterosexual relationship. Nevertheless, he retains his prerogative to do so and to draw upon structures of inequality. While he may make an exception of an individual woman, he does not give up his overall power as a male. Sex discrimination in employment, housing, state benefits, and so on, allow men greater access to resources. Men continue to be preferentially treated within social institutions and are the beneficiaries of discriminatory state policies and practices.

Challenging inequality is not only an individual issue. While men may participate in housework and childcare to a greater or lesser extent, they do not in consequence lose their male-dominant social privileges. The rights and authority of fatherhood protect men from the potential for sexual equality. To deny this assigned privilege would mean that men would have to renounce any claim to children.

A married man may at present claim rights of exclusive custody or care and control of children upon divorce. If the proposed legal changes on illegitimacy take place, as is likely, these may also be staked by unmarried men. Unmarried men will be able to claim child custody, care and control at any time. This possibility leaves it open for men, irrespective of marriage, to threaten to use the power of the state against women. It will put women as mothers in an even weaker position in relation to men than if they were a wife.

FATHERS AND CHILDBIRTH

We turn now to a recent trend which promotes fatherhood and hence, the authority of men in the family. The presence of men at childbirth affirms a relationship to women and children which is based on the social position of father. Their presence is not a simple expression of support for women who are giving birth, but an assertion of men's rights.

Fatherhood has increasingly become the subject of sociologists and psychologists, as well as social policy and film-makers. Recent literature on fathers' involvement in childcare has four predominant themes. First is the assessment of the quantity of men's involvement with children—how often they share in the tasks of childcare, how much time they spend looking after children and which tasks they are most likely to perform. Second, men's experiences of childcare are described, focusing upon how men feel and what they can say about being with children. Third, there is a theme which refers to the transition to fatherhood, exploring what it means to men to become fathers and how it affects their lives. Finally, research pursues the difficulties which men face in their attempts to practice fatherhood, and the improvements in social policies which are needed to help them. (See, for example, Lynn, 1974; Macy and Falkner, 1979; Lamb, 1981; Parke, 1981; Beail and McGuire, 1982; McKee and O'Brien, 1982).

In all of these approaches to the study of fatherhood, the perspective of men is paramount. We learn of men's needs, desires, experiences and problems. Assuming men's right to be fathers, these studies explore what is needed to support and encourage men to practice fatherhood.

The institution of fatherhood, and its relation of authority over mothers and children, is never questioned. Sex-stereotypical attitudes are regarded as a mere hangover of nineteenth-century traditions, unrelated to the social position of father. Without checking for evidence, fatherhood is assumed to provide women with support and children with a 'meaningful' relationship. Now and then, a doubt is expressed regarding the consequences for women of men's claim to children, given an increasing incidence of separation and divorce (McKee and O'Brien, 1982; Lewis, 1982a). However, this is no more than a passing reference in an otherwise uncritical stance towards men's rights of fatherhood.

Despite the concern of some of these researchers with sexual equality, there has been little analysis of the politics of fatherhood, and the consequences for women and children. More often the concern is expressed that the experience of man and the status of fathers has been overshadowed by the recent upsurge in feminist studies of motherhood. While the recent wave of feminist research on women and motherhood has helped to redirect our attentions in studies of the family, it is significant that studies of men and fathers have followed in its wake. The attempt to 'balance' feminist studies of motherhood by research into the needs, desires, experiences and problems of men, and the importance of fatherhood, reflects an all-too-familiar anti-feminist focus.

There is one fundamental difference between feminist research on motherhood and the recent focus upon fatherhood. This centers on the recognition and analysis of political inequality between men and women. Motherhood studies revealed women's experiences of being a mother in a relatively powerless relation to men in the family, and outside of it. Fatherhood studies do not address the question of power. Different roles or spheres for men and women are perceived, and an interest is shown in extending men's roles or spheres, yet this is approached without addressing the privileges of men or the consequences for women. As a result women's oppression becomes invisible once again while the privileges of men are affirmed and extended.

Specifically, the literature on fathers and childbirth begins during pregnancy. Men too, we are told, become pregnant. Observational studies support this hypothesis with data to suggest that men whose wives/girlfriends become pregnant commit sexual offenses (Hartman and Nicolay, 1966), are anxious (Fein, 1974), experience nausea, backache, stomach ache, headaches and toothaches during their 'pregnancy' (Trethowan and Conlon, 1965; Liebenberg, 1969). Within the rubric of scientific investigation, the underlying argument is that fantasies of pregnancy make men fathers.

While the research reports emphasize that fathers 'actively participate during labour,' delivery is a bit more problematic. Men, as yet, do not actually give birth. To overcome this problem, it is often suggested, men should be helpful and encouraged to take a more active part in the birth process. Beail, for example, tells us:

> 'One radical innovation being tried out in some American hospitals is to encourage fathers to deliver their babies themselves under the supervision of medical staff. This has not yet been tried out in Britain, but some British hospitals encourage fathers to be involved in a more ritualistic way by cutting the umbilical cord' (1982: 19).

This ritualistic cutting of the tie between mother and baby reveals the significance given to men at childbirth.

The general assumption about men in the delivery room is that they provide their wives with support. Women giving birth in hospital settings are vulnerable in the face of medical authority and hospital routines. Clearly, they need support. As Lewis (1982a) points out, this need for support has already been prescribed by the male-dominated medical profession to mean their husbands, rather than allowing women a choice of birth-companion. Studies which indicate women's preference for their husbands to be present 'may simply reflect their preference for having someone (rather than nobody) to give them moral support' (p. 68). Further, the support which men offer to women is likely to be both limited and inconsistent, given their concern with their own position as father. Observing fathers at birth, Woollett *et al.* (1982) found that the men largely ignored signs of discomfort from mothers once the child was born, and focused their attention on the newborn. They suggest that women who have been through childbirth, who share their experiences as women and as mothers, may be better able to provide the nurturance and support which is needed.

The importance of the presence of fathers at childbirth is held to be the promotion of their 'involvement' with the child and the beginning of a 'meaningful' relationship. Involvement is a very loosely applied term to suggest the quantity of childcare that fathers perform. A meaningful relationship implies a close rather than distant relationship. This distinction is implied to be a direct consequence of the quantity of childcare performed. Beyond this, we do not know. The quality of the relationship is not often explored except for what men feel about it.

Because fatherhood is unquestionably taken to be a good thing, even the evidence which might suggest otherwise is skewed to this perspective. The heterosexual family is protected as the ideal. The consequences for women and children are not open to question and are ignored.

The ways in which fathers relate to children stem from their social position in the family. Their privileged status, authority, rewards and access to resources as men, relative to women, allows for a particular form of involvement. They play rather than carry out the more mundane tasks (Clarke-Stewart, 1978; Lamb, 1981; White et al., 1982). They select what they do and the commitment they feel they are willing and able to make; mothers are left with the rest (Holly, forthcoming). They do not come into childrearing as workers, they come in as managers whose decision-making power is derived from the structures of sexual inequality.

The consequences of this type of childcare involvement is, indeed, meaningful for children, for it serves as an example of men's privilege to act in this way. The relation between fathers and mothers provides children with a view of the political inequality between family members. Acting from their position as senior male, fathers illustrate and effect sexual discrimination. Additionally, in the course of fathers' play with children. McGuire observes:

> 'Play with girls reflected mainly a combination of teasing, allowing aggression in a controlled situation, and demonstrating the father's power and strength. Play with boys was much more 'matey,' a 'put them up' situation where two equals could let off some steam together.' (1982: 118).

And further:

> 'while mothers will play with whatever is around in [their] joint play, fathers may be more selective, only choosing those items which they personally enjoy in the same way another child might play.' (ibid.).

Fathers' involvement in childcare has serious consequences for girls in particular, and also for boys who come to expect preferential treatment for being male. The attempt to promote fathers' rights and encourage men's involvement as fathers, is harmful for both women and children.

This discrimination may begin at birth. Woollett *et al.* (1982), observing fathers' interactions, note that fathers react positively to the birth of sons and express disappointment about daughters. Their comments to the newborn proudly affirm male status (father and sons) while they are negative about females (daughters, mothers and others). Patterns of holding, talking and touching are equally discriminatory. White *et al.* (1982) point out that sex discrimination in holding behavior by fathers illustrates the influence that fathers can have in the first months, even though they remain relatively unembroiled in repetitive caretaking tasks.

The support for fathers' presence at birth and encouragement of their involvement in childcare is based upon an apolitical perspective of family structure. The social position from which each family member speaks and acts is left unrecognized. The rhetoric of mutual parenthood glosses over these political relations, and obscures the effects upon women and children.

CONCLUSION

Attempts to give fathers 'equal rights' take in a society which actively discriminates against women and in favor of men. Men are constantly ascribed power and rights merely for being born male—the most pervasive inheritance of all. 'Equal rights' in this context means improving the rights and privileges of the powerful (men) in relation to the less powerful and subordinate position of women. This is a step backward on the road to sexual equality. The loss for women and children will be devastating.

Social policies which enhance men's status as fathers, and support their rights to claim children from women, are central to this process. From the encouragement of men's presence at childbirth to the promotion of the ideology of fatherhood, to judicial decisions in the custody of children —men's rights and status are being extended at the expense of women and children.

The British Law Commission's proposal to extend the existing rights of married men to unmarried men has arisen in the context of international governments' commitment to fatherhood and the rights of men. Unmarried men are to be given rights over children regardless of their relationship with the mother. Fatherless families are to be outlawed. Women's choice over how and with whom to have and raise children is to be denied. The structure of our families is to be kept within the rule of men. This is a move which misleadingly employs the language of equality while it directly aids male control over women and children. The reassertion of fathers' rights attacks the autonomy of women and children.

REFERENCES

Beail, Nigel. 1982. The role of the father during pregnancy and delivery. In Beail, N. and McGuire, J., (eds).

Beail, Nigel and McGuire, Jacqueline, (eds). 1982. *Fathers: Psychological Perspectives*, Junction Books, London.

Cavanagh, Kath. Forthcoming. The child abuse case conference: A feminist analysis. In Pollock, S. and J. Sutton, (eds).

Clarke-Stewart, Alison. 1978. And daddy makes three: The father's impact on mother and young child. *Child Dev.* **49** (2): 466–478.

Council of Europe. 1975. *European Convention of the Legal Status of Children Born Out of Wedlock*. Strasbourg.

Fein, Robert A. 1974. Men's experience before and after the birth of a first child: Dependence, marital sharing and anxiety, Ph.D. Thesis, Harvard University.

Hartman, A. Arthur and Nicolay, Robert C. 1966. Sexually deviant behaviour in expectant fathers. *J. Abnormal Psychology* **71**: 232–234.

Haskey, John. 1982. The proportion of marriages ending in divorce. *Population Trends* **27** (Spring): 4–8.

Haskey, John. 1983. Children of divorcing couples. *Population Trends* **31** (Spring): 20–26.

Holly, Lesley. Forthcoming. Where are the new fathers? In Pollock. S. and Sutton, J. (eds).

Law Commission Working Paper No. 74. 1979. *Family Law: Illegitimacy*, HMSO, London.

Law Commission. 1982. *Family Law: Illegitimacy*. HMSO, London.

Lamb, Michael E., (ed). 1981. *The Role of the Father in Child Development*. Wiley, Chichester.

Leete, Richard. 1978. Adoption trends and illegitimate births 1951–77. *Population Trends* **14**: 9–16.

Letts. Penny. 1983. *Double Struggle: Sex Discrimination and One-Parent Families*. National Council for One Parent Families, London.

Lewis, Charlie. 1982a. 'A feeling you can't scratch?': The effect of pregnancy and birth on married men. In Beail, N. and McGuire, J. (eds).

Lewis, Charlie. 1982b. The observation of the father-infant relationships: An 'attachment' to outmoded concepts. In McKee, L. and O'Brien, M. (eds).

Liebenberg, B. 1969. Expectant fathers. *Child and Family.* **8**: 265–277.

Lynn, David B. 1974. *The Father: His Role in Child Development*. Brooks/Cole, Monterey, California.

Macy, Christopher and Falkner, Frank. 1979. *Pregnancy and Birth: Pleasures and Problems*. Harper & Row, London.

McGuire, Jacqueline. 1982. Gender-specific differences in early childhood: The impact of the father. In Beail, N. and McGuire, J. (eds).

McKee, Lorna and O'Brien, Margaret (eds). 1982. *The Father Figure*. Tavistock, London.

Parke, Ross D. 1981. *Fathering*. Fontana, London.

Pollock, Scarlet and Sutton, Jo. (eds). Forthcoming, *Women and the Politics of Fatherhood*. The Women's Press, London.

Samuels, Alec. 1983. Illegitimacy: The Law Commission's report. *Family Law* **13** (3): 87–90.

Social Trends 14. 1984. HMSO, London.

Sutton, Jo and Friedman, Scarlet. 1982. Fatherhood: Bringing it all back home. In Friedman, S. and Sarah, E. (eds). *On the Problem of Men*. The Women's Press, London.

Trethowan, W. H. and Conlon, M. F. 1965. The couvade syndrome. *Br. J. Psychiatry* **III**, 57–66.

Werner, Barry. 1982. Recent trends in illegitimate births and extra-marital conceptions. *Population Trends* **30** (Winter): 9–15.

White, David, Woollett, Anne and Lyon, Louise. 1982. Fathers' involvement with their infants: The relevance of holding. In Beail, N. and McGuire, J. (eds).

Woollett, Anne, White, David and Lyon, Louise. 1982. Observations of fathers at birth. In Beail, N. and McGuire, J. (eds).

12

Pornography: Not a Moral Issue[1]

Catherine A. MacKinnon

> *'Pornosec, the subsection of the Fiction Department which turned out cheap pornography for distribution among the proles . . . nicknamed Muck House by the people who worked in it . . . produced booklets in sealed packets with titles like* Spanking Stories *or* One Night in a Girls' School, *to be bought furtively by proletarian youths who were under the impression that they were buying something illegal.'*
>
> George Orwell, *1984*

A critique of pornography[2] is to feminism what its defense is to male

[1] This article states the law as it stood at December 1984.

The title of this article is a play on the title of the anti-pornography film by the Canadian Film Board, *Not a Love story* (1983).

This article was previously published in the November 1984 issue of the *Yale Law and Policy Review*. *Women's Studies International Forum* is grateful to Professor MacKinnon and the *Yale Law and Policy Review* for allowing publication in *WSIF*.

Prior versions of this commentary were given as speeches to the Morality Colloquium, University of Minnesota, 23 February 1984; Women and the Law, Panel on Pornography, April 1983; Conference on Media Violence and Pornography, Ontario Institute for Studies in Education, 3-5 February 1984.

[2] This text as a whole is intended to communicate what I mean by pornography. The key work on the subject is Dworkin (1981a). No definition can convey the meaning of a word as well as its use in context can. However what Andrea Dworkin and I mean by pornography is rather well captured in our legal definition of the term. 'Pornography is the graphic sexually explicit subordination of women, whether in pictures or in words, that also includes one or more of the following: (i) women are presented dehumanized as sexual objects, things or commodities; or (ii) women are presented as sexual objects who enjoy pain or humiliation; or (iii) women are presented as sexual objects who experience sexual pleasure in being raped; or (iv) women are presented as sexual objects tied up or cut up or mutilated or bruised or physically hurt; or (v) women are presented in postures of sexual submission, servility or display; or (vi) women's body parts—including but not limited to vaginas, breasts, and buttocks—are exhibited, such that women are reduced to those parts; or (vii) women are presented as whores by nature; or (viii) women are presented being penetrated by objects or animals; or (ix) women are presented in scenarios of degradation, injury, torture, shown as filthy or inferior, bleeding, bruised, or hurt in a context that makes these conditions sexual.' The ordinance also defines 'the use of men, children or transsexuals in the place of women' as pornography. Pornography, thus defined, is discrimination on the basis of sex and, as such, a civil rights violation. This definition is a slightly

supremacy. Central to the institutionalization of male dominance, pornography cannot be reformed or suppressed or banned. It can only be changed. The legal doctrine of obscenity, the state's closest approximation to addressing the pornography question, has made the First Amendment[3] into a barrier to this process. This is partly because the pornographers' lawyers have persuasively presented First Amendment absolutism,[4] their advocacy position, as a legal fact, which it never has been. But they have gotten away with this (to the extent they have) in part because the abstractness of obscenity as a concept, situated within an equally abstract approach to freedom of speech embodied in First Amendment doctrine, has made the indistinguishability of the pornographers' speech from everyone else's speech, their freedom from our freedom, appear credible, appealing, necessary, nearly inevitable, *principled*.[5] To expose the absence of a critique of gender[6] in this area of law is to expose both the enforced silence of women and the limits of liberalism.

   This brief preliminary commentary focuses on the obscenity standard in order to explore some of the larger implications of a feminist critique of pornography for First Amendment theory. This is the argument. Obscenity law is concerned with morality, specifically morals from the male point of view, meaning the standpoint of male dominance. The feminist critique of

modified version of the one passed by the Minneapolis City Council on 30 December 1983, Minneapolis, Minnesota, Ordinance amending title 7, chapters 139 and 141. Minneapolis *Code of Ordinances Relating to Civil Rights*. The ordinance was vetoed by the Mayor, reintroduced, passed again, and vetoed again in 1984.

Many of the ideas in this essay were developed and refined in close collaboration with Andrea Dworkin. It is consequently difficult at times to distinguish the contribution of each of us to a body of work that—through shared teaching, writing, speaking, organizing, and political action on every level—has been created together. I have tried to credit specific contributions that I am aware are distinctly hers. This text is mine; she does not necessarily agree with everything in it.

[3] Congress shall make no law . . . abridging the freedom of speech, or of the press . . . *U.S. Constitution*. amendment I.

[4] Justice Black, at times joined by Justice Douglas, took the position that the Bill of Rights, including the First Amendment, was 'absolute' (Justice Black, 1960: 867; Cahn, 1962). For a discussion, see Kalven (1967). For one exchange in the controversy surrounding the 'absolute' approach to the First Amendment, as opposed to the 'balancing' approach, see for example Mendelson (1962, 1964); Frantz (1962, 1963). In the pornography context, see for example *Roth v. United States* (1957) (Douglas, J., joined by Black, J., dissenting); *Miller v. California* (1973) Douglas, J., dissenting). It is not the purpose of the current article to present a critique of absolutism as such, but rather to identify and criticize some widely and deeply shared implicit beliefs that underlie both the absolutist view and the more mainstream flexible approaches.

[5] The history of obscenity law can be read as a failed attempt to make this separation, with the failure becoming ever more apparent from the *Redrup* decision forward: *Redrup v. New York* (1967). For a summary of cases exemplifying such a trend, see the dissent by Justice Brennan, *Paris Adult Theatre I v. Slaton* (1973:73).

[6] Much has been made of the distinction between sex and gender. Sex is thought the more biological, gender the more social. The relationship of sexuality to each varies. See, for example Stoller (1974: 9-10). Since I think that the importance of biology to the condition of women is the social meaning attributed to it, biology *is* its social meaning for purposes of analysing the inequality of the sexes, a political condition. I therefore tend to use sex and gender relatively interchangeably.

pornography is a politics, specifically politics from women's point of view, meaning the standpoint of the subordination of women to men.[7] Morality here means good and evil; politics means power and powerlessness. Obscenity is a moral idea; pornography is a political practice. Obscenity is abstract; pornography is concrete. The two concepts represent two entirely different things. Nudity, explicitness, excess of candor, arousal or excitement, prurience, unnaturalness—these qualities bother obscenity law when sex is depicted or portrayed. Abortion or birth control information or treatments for 'restoring sexual virility' (whose, do you suppose?) have also been included.[8] Sex forced on real women so that it can be sold at a profit to be forced on other real women; women's bodies trussed and maimed and raped and made into things to be hurt and obtained and accessed and this presented as the nature of women; the coercion that is visible and the coercion that has become invisible—this and more bothers feminists about pornography. Obscenity as such probably does little harm;[9] pornography causes

---

[7] The sense in which I mean women's perspective to differ from men's is like that of Virginia Woolf's reference to 'the difference of view, the difference of standard' in Woolf (1966). Neither of us uses the notion of a gender difference to refer to something biological or natural or transcendental or existential. Perspective parallels standards because the social experience of gender is distinctive. (See MacKinnon, 1979: 107–141, and 1982, 1983; Woolf, 1938; see also Dworkin, 1976: 96.) I do not refer to the gender difference here descriptively, leaving its roots and implications unspecified, so they could be biological, existential, transcendental, in any sense inherent, or social but necessary. I mean 'point of view' as a view, hence a standard, that is imposed on women by force of sex inequality, which is a political condition. 'Male' is an adjective here, a social and political concept, not a biological attribute; it is a status socially conferred upon a person because of a condition of birth. As I use it, it has nothing whatever to do with inherency, preexistence, nature, inevitability, or body as such. Because it is in the interest of men to be male in the system we live under (male being powerful as well as human), they seldom question its rewards or even see it as a status at all.

[8] Criminal Code, *Can. Rev. Stat*. ch. c-34. § 159(2)(c) and (d)(1970): *People v. Sanger* (1918).

[9] The Report of the Commission on Obscenity and Pornography, 1970, majority report. The accuracy of the Commission's findings is called into question by:

   (a)   widespread criticism of the Commission's methodology from a variety of perspectives, for example, Sutherland (1975); Donnerstein (1980); Garry (1978); Diamond (1980); Cline (1974); Bart and Jozsa (1982);
   (b)   the Commission's tendency to minimize the significance of its own findings, for example, those by Mosher on the differential effects of exposure by gender;
   (c)   the design of the Commission's research. The Commission did not focus questions about gender, did its best to eliminate 'violence' from its materials (so as not to overlap with the Violence Commission), and propounded unscientific theories such as Puritan guilt to explain women's negative responses to the materials.

It should further be noted that it is unclear that scientific causality is what legally validates even an obscenity regulation:
   'But, it is argued, there is no scientific data which conclusively demonstrate that exposure to obscene materials adversely affects men and women or their society. It is [urged] that, absent such a demonstration, any kind of state regulation is "impermissible". We reject this argument. It is not for us to resolve empirical uncertainties underlying state legislation, save in the exceptional case where that legislation plainly impinges upon rights protected by the Constitution itself. . . . Although there is no conclusive proof of a connection between

attitudes and behaviors of violence and discrimination which define the treatment and status of half of the population.[10] To make the legal and philosophical consequences of this distinction clear, I will (I) describe the feminist critique of pornography; then (II) criticize the law of obscenity in terms of it; then (III) discuss the criticism that pornography 'dehumanizes' women, to distinguish the male morality of liberalism and obscenity law from a feminist political critique of pornography.[11]

This inquiry is part of a larger project that attempts to account for gender inequality in the socially constructed relationship between power—the political—on the one hand, and knowledge of truth and reality—the epistemological—on the other.[12] For example, the candid description Justice Stewart once offered of his obscenity standard, 'I know it when I see it' (*Jacobellis v. Ohio* (1964)), becomes even more revealing than it is usually understood to be, if taken as a statement that connects epistemology with power. If I ask, from the point of view of women's experience, does he know what I know when I see what I see, I find that I doubt it, given what's on the news-stands. How does his point of view keep what is there, there? To liberal critics, his admission exposed the obscenity standards's relativity, its partiality, its insufficient abstractness. Not to be emptily universal, to leave your concreteness showing, is a sin among men. Their problem with Justice Stewart's formulation is that it implies that anything, capriciously, could be suppressed. They are only right by half. My problem is more the other half: the meaning of what his view permits, which, as it turns out, is anything but

antisocial behavior and obscene material, the legislature of Georgia could quite reasonably determine that such a connection does or might exist.' (*Paris Adult Theatre I v. Slaton* (1973: 69-61) (Burger, C. J. for the majority); see also *Roth v. U.S.* (1957:501).

[10]Some of the harm of pornography to women, as defined *supra* at note 1 and as discussed in this article, has been documented in empirical studies. The findings of recent studies are that exposure to pornography increases normal men's willingness to aggress against women under laboratory conditions; makes both women and men substantially less able to perceive accounts of rape as accounts of rape; makes normal men more closely resemble convicted rapists psychologically; increases attitudinal measures that are known to correlate with rape, such as hostility toward women, propensity to rape, condoning rape, and predicting that one would rape or force sex on a woman if one knew one would not get caught; and produces other attitude changes in man such as increasing the extent of their trivialization, dehumanization, and objectification of women (Russell, 1982: 216; Malamuth and Donnerstein, 1984; Zillman, 1984; Check *et al.*, 1983; Donnerstein, 1984; Malamuth and Check, 1981; Malamuth, 1981a; Malamuth and Spinner, 1980; Mosher, 1971; Zillman and Bryant, 1984).

[11]The following are illustrative, not exhaustive, of the body of work I term the 'feminist critique of pornography'. Dworkin, 1981a; Leidholdt, 1983; Steiner, 1973; Brownmiller, 1975: 394; Morgan, 1977; Barry, 1979; Linden *et al.*, 1982, especially articles by Ti-Grace Atkinson, Judy Butler, Andrea Dworkin, Alice Walker, John Stoltenberg, Audre Lorde, and Sunsan Leigh Star; Walker, 1982b; and other articles in Lederer, 1982 (with the exception of the legal ones); Vidal, 1969; Lovelace, 1980; Millett, 1969; Rush, 1980. *N.Y.U. Rev. Law Soc. Change* (1978-1979) contains both feminist and non-feminist arguments.

[12]For more extensive discussions of this subject, see my prior work especially MacKinnon (1982, 1983).

capricious. In fact, it is entirely systematic and determinate. To me, his statement is precisely descriptively accurate; its candor is why it has drawn so much criticism.[13] Justice Stewart got in so much trouble because he said out loud what is actually done all the time; in so doing, he both *did it* and gave it the stature of doctrine, even if only dictum. That is, the obscenity standard—in this it is not unique—*is* built on what the male standpoint sees. My point will be: *so is pornography*. In this way, the law of obscenity reproduces the pornographic point of view on women on the level of Constitutional jurisprudence.

I

Pornography, in the feminist view, is a form of forced sex, a practice of sexual politics, an institution of gender inequality. In this perspective, pornography is not harmless fantasy or a corrupt and confused misrepresentation of an otherwise natural and healthy sexuality. With the rape and prostitution in which it participates, pornography institutionalizes the sexuality of male supremacy, which fuses the erotization of dominance and submission with the social construction of male and female (MacKinnon, 1982). Gender is sexual. Pornography constitutes the meaning of that sexuality. Men treat women as who they see women as being. Pornography constructs who that is. Men's power over women means that the way men see women defines who women can be. Pornography is that way.

In pornography, women desire dispossession and cruelty. Men, permitted to put words (and other things) in women's mouths, create scenes in which women desperately want to be bound, battered, tortured, humiliated, and killed. Or, merely taken and used. This is erotic to the male point of view. Subjection itself, with self-determination ecstatically relinquished, is the content of women's sexual desire and desirability. Women are there to be violated and possessed, men to violate and possess them, either on screen or by camera or pen, on behalf of the viewer.

One can be for or against this pornography without getting beyond liberalism. The critical yet formally liberal view of Susan Griffin, for example, conceptualizes eroticism as natural and healthy but corrupted and confused by 'the pornographic mind' (1981: 2-4, 251-265). Pornography distorts Eros, which preexists and persists, despite male culture's pornographic 'revenge' upon it. Eros is, unaccountably, *still there*. Pornography mistakes it, mis-images it, mis-represents it. There is no critique of *reality* here, only objections to how it is seen; no critique of that reality that

---

[13]Justice Stewart has been said to have complained that this single line was more quoted and remembered than anything else he ever said.

pornography imposes on women's real lives, those lives that are so seamlessly *consistent* with the pornography that pornography can be credibly defended by saying it is only a mirror of reality.

Contrast this view with the feminist analysis of Andrea Dworkin, in which sexuality itself is a social construct, gendered to the ground. Male dominance here is not an artificial overlay upon an underlying inalterable substratum of uncorrupted essential sexual being. Sexuality free of male dominance will require *change*, not reconceptualization, transcendence or excavation. Pornography is not imagery in some relation to a reality elsewhere constructed. It is not a distortion, reflection, projection, expression, fantasy, representation or symbol either. It is sexual reality. Dworkin's *Pornography: Men Possessing Women* (1981a) presents a sexual theory of gender inequality of which pornography is a core constitutive practice. The way pornography produces its meaning constructs and defines men and women as such. Gender is what gender means.[14] It has no basis in anything other than the social reality its hegemony constructs. The process that gives sexuality its male supremacist meaning is therefore the process through which gender inequality becomes socially real.

In this analysis, the liberal defense of pornography as human sexual liberation, as de-repression—whether by feminists, lawyers, or neo-Freudians[15]—is a defense not only of force and sexual terrorism, but of the subordination of women. Sexual liberation in the liberal sense frees male sexual agression in the feminist sense. What in the liberal view looks like love and romance looks a lot like hatred and torture to the feminist. Pleasure and eroticism become violation. Desire appears as lust for dominance and submission. The vulnerability of women's projected sexual availability—that acting we are allowed: asking to be acted upon—is victimization. Play conforms to scripted roles, fantasy expresses ideology—is not exempt from it—and admiration of natural physical beauty becomes objectification.

The experience of the (overwhelmingly) male audiences who consume

---

[14]Dworkin (1976).

[15]The position that pornography is sex—that whatever you think of sex you think of pornography—underlies nearly every treatment of the subject. In particular, nearly every non-feminist treatment proceeds on the implicit or explicit assumption, argument, criticism, or suspicion that pornography is sexually liberating in some way, a position unifying an otherwise diverse literature. See for example Lawrence (1955); Hefner (1962: 73, 1963: 43); Miller (1947: 286); English (1980: 20); Elshtain (1982: 42). To choose an example at random:

'In opposition to the Victorian view that narrowly defines proper sexual function in a rigid way that is analogous to ideas of excremental regularity and moderation, pornography builds a model of plastic variety and joyful excess in sexuality. In opposition to the sorrowing Catholic dismissal of sexuality as an unfortunate and spiritually superficial concomitant of propogation, pornography affords the alternative idea of the independent status of sexuality as a profound and shattering ecstasy.' (Richards, 1974: 81 (footnotes omitted). See also Schauer, 1979: 616).

pornography[16] is therefore not fantasy or simulation or catharsis[17] but sexual reality: the level of reality on which sex itself largely operates. To understand this does not require noticing that pornography models are real women to whom something real is being done (Lovelace and McGrady, 1980; Dworkin, 1981b: 65), nor does it require inquiring into the systematic infliction of pornographic sexuality upon women,[18] although it helps. The aesthetic of pornography itself, the *way* it provides what those who consume it want, is itself the evidence. When uncensored explicit—that is, the most pornographic—pornography tells all, all means what a distanced detached observer would report about who did what to whom. This is the turn-on. Why does observing sex objectively presented cause the male viewer to experience his own sexuality? Because his eroticism is, socially, a watched thing.

If objectivity is the epistemological stance of which objectification is the social proces (MacKinnon, 1982),[19] the way a perceptual posture is embodied as a social form of power, the most sexually potent depictions and descriptions *would* be the most objective blow-by-blow re-presentations. Pornography participates in its audience's eroticism because it creates an accessible sexual object, the possession and consumption of which *is* male sexuality, to be consumed and possessed as which *is* female sexuality. In this sense, sex in life is no less mediated than it is in art. Men *have sex* with their *image* of woman. Escalating explicitness, 'exceeding the bounds of candor,'[20] is the aesthetic of pornography not because the materials depict

[16]Spending time around adult bookstores, attending pornographic movies and talking with pornographers (who, like all smart pimps, do some form of market research), as well as analysing the pornography itself in sex/gender terms, all confirm that pornography is for men. That women may attend or otherwise consume it does not make it any less for men, any more than the observation that mostly men consume pornography means that pornography does not harm women. (See Lagelan, 1981: 5; Cook, 1978: 60.) Personal observation reveals that women tend to avoid pornography as much as possible—which is not very much, as it turns out.

[17]The 'fantasy' and 'catharsis' hypotheses, together, assert that pornography cathects sexuality on the level of fantasy fulfillment. The work of Donnerstein, particularly, shows that the opposite is true. The more pornography is viewed, the *more* pornography—and the more brutal pornography—is both wanted and required for sexual arousal. What occurs is not catharsis, but desensitization, requiring progressively more potent stimulation. (See works cited *supra* at note 9; Straus, 1974.)

[18]However, for one such inquiry, see Russell, 1982: 228 (a random sample of 930 San Francisco households found that 10 per cent of women had at least once 'been upset by anyone trying to get you to do what they'd seen in pornographic pictures, movies or books'). Obviously, this figure could only include those who knew that the pornography was source of the sex, which makes its findings conservative. (See also Russell, 1983: 27–41 (discussing the data base).) The hearings Andrea Dworkin and I held for the Minneapolis City Council on the ordinance cited in note 1 produced many accounts of the use of pornography to force sex on women and children (Public Hearings on Ordinances to Add Pornography as Discrimination Against Women, 1983).

[19]See also Sontag (1977).

[20]'Explicitness' of accounts is a central issue in both obscenity adjudications and audience access standards adopted voluntarily by self-regulated industries or by boards of censor. (See for example *Grove Press v. Christenberry* (1959: 489) (discussion of 'candor' and 'realism'): *Grove Press v. Christenberry* (1960: 438) ('directness'): *Mitchum v. State* (1971: 302) ('show it all'):

objectified sex but because they create the experience of a sexuality which is itself objectified. It is not that life and art imitate each other; in sexuality, they *are* each other.

II

The law of obscenity,[21] the state's primary approach[22] to its version of the pornography question, has literally nothing in common with this feminist critique. Their obscenity is not our pornography. One commentator has said:

> 'Obscenity is not suppressed primarily for the protection of others. Much of it is suppressed for the purity of the "community." Obscenity, at bottom, is not a crime. Obscenity is a sin.' (Henkin, 1963: 395)

This is, on one level, literally accurate. Men are turned on by obscenity, including its suppression, the same way they are by sin. Animated by morality from the male standpoint, in which violation—of women and rules—is eroticized, obscenity law can be seen to proceed according to the interest of male power, robed in gender-neutral good and evil.

Morality in its specifically liberal form (although, as with most dimensions of male dominance, the distinction between left and right is more formal than substantive) revolves around a set of parallel distinctions which can be consistently traced through obscenity law. Even though the approach this law takes to the problem it envisions has shifted over time, its fundamental norms remain consistent: public is opposed to private, in parallel with ethics and morality, and factual is opposed to valued determinations. These distinctions are gender-based: female is private, moral, valued, subjective; male is public, ethical, factual, objective (MacKinnon, 1983).[23] If such gendered concepts

---

Kaplan v. California (1973: 118).) How *much* sex the depiction shows is implicitly thereby correlated with how *sexual* (that is, how sexually arousing to the male) the material is. (See for example Memoirs v. Massachusetts (1966: 460) (White J. dissenting); Heffner. 1980; *Report of the Committee on Obscenity and Film Censorship*, 1981.) Andrea Dworkin brilliantly gives the reader the experience of this aesthetic in her account of pornography (Dworkin. 1981a: 25–47).

[21]To the body of law ably encompassed and footnoted by Lockhart and McClure (1954, 1960), I add only the most important cases since then: Stanley v. Georgia (1969); U.S. v. Reidel (1970); Miller v. California (1973); Paris Adult Theatre I v. Slaton (1973); Hamling v. U.S. (1973); Jenkins v. Georgina (1973); U.S. v. 12 200-ft Reels of Super 8mm Film (1973); Erznoznick v. City of Jacksonville (1975); Splawn v. California (1976); Ward v. Illinois (1976); Lovisi v. Slayton (1976): New York v. Ferber (1982).

[22]For a discussion of the role of the law of privacy in supporting the existence of pornography, see Colker (1983).

[23]These parallels are discussed more fully in MacKinnon (1983). It may seem odd to denominate 'moral' as *female* here, since this article discusses male morality. Under male supremacy, men define things: I am describing that. Men define women *as* 'moral.' This is the male view of women. My analysis, a feminist critique of the male standpoint, terms moral the concept that pornography is about good and evil. This is *my* analysis of them, as contrasted with their attributions of women.

are constructs of the male experience, imposed from the male standpoint on society as a whole, liberal morality expresses male supremacist politics. That is, discourse conducted in terms of good and evil which does not expose the gendered foundations of these concepts proceeds oblivious to—and serves to disguise the presence and interest of—the position of power that underlies, and is furthered by, that discourse.

For example, obscenity law proposes to control what and how sex can be publicly shown. In practice, its standard centers upon the same features feminism identifies as key to male sexuality; the erect penis and penetration.[24] Historically, obscenity law was vexed by restricting such portrayals while protecting great literature. (Nobody considered protecting women.) Having solved this by exempting works of perceived value from obscenity restrictions,[25] the subsequent relaxation—some might say collapse—of obscenity restrictions in the last decade reveals a significant shift. The old private rules have become the new public rules. The old law governing pornography was that it would be publicly repudiated while being privately consumed and actualized: do anything to women with impunity in private behind a veil of public denial and civility. Now pornography is publicly celebrated.[26] This victory for Freudian depression theory probably did not alter women's actual treatment all that much. Women were and still are sex. Greater efforts of brutality have become necessary to eroticize the taboo—each taboo being a hierarchy in disguise—since the frontier of the taboo keeps vanishing as one crosses it. Put another way, more and more violence has become necessary to keep the progressively desenitized consumer aroused to the illusion that sex is (and he is) daring and dangerous. Making sex with the powerless 'not allowed' is a way of keeping 'getting it' defined as an act of power, an assertion of hierarchy. In addition, pornography has become ubiquitous. Sexual terrorism has become democratized. Crucially, pornography has become truly available to women for the first time in history. Show me an atrocity to women, I'll show it to you eroticized in the pornography. This central mechanism of sexual subordination, this means of systematizing the definition of women as a sexual class, has now

[24]A reading of case law supports the reports in Woodward and Armstrong (1979), to the effect that this is a 'bottom line' criterion for at least some justices. The interesting question becomes why the tactics of male supremacy would change from keeping the penis hidden, covertly glorified, to having it everywhere on display, overtly glorified. This suggests at least that a major shift from private terrorism to public terrorism has occurred. What used to be perceived as a danger to male power, the exposure of the penis, has now become a strategy in maintaining it.
[25]One possible reading of Lockhart and McClure is that this was their agenda, and that their approach was substantially adopted in the third prong of the *Miller* doctrine. For the law's leading attempt to grapple with this issue, see *Memoirs v. Massachusetts* (1966), overruled in part, *Miller v. California* (1973). (See also *U.S. v. 'Ulyses'* (1933, 1934).)
[26]Andrea Dworkin and I developed this analysis in our class, 'Pornography', at the University of Minnesota Law School, Fall 1983. (See also Dworkin (1982: 141) (the issue of pornography is an issue of sexual acces to women, hence involves a fight among men).)

become available to it victims for scrutiny and analysis as an open public system, not just as a private secret abuse.[27] Hopefully, this was a mistake.

Re-examining the law of obscenity in light of the feminist critique of pornography that has become possible, it becomes clear that male morality sees that which maintains its power as good, that which undermines or qualifies it or questions its absoluteness as evil. Differences in the law over time— such as the liberalization of obscenity doctrine—reflect either changes in which group of men has power or shifts in perceptions of the best strategy for maintaining male supremacy—probably some of both. But it must be made to work. The outcome, descriptively analysed, is that obscenity law prohibits what it sees as immoral, which from a feminist standpoint tends to be relatively harmless, while protecting what it sees as moral, which from a feminist standpoint is often that which is damaging to women. So it, too, is a politics, only covertly so. What male morality finds evil, meaning threatening to its power, feminist politics tends to find comparatively harmless. What feminist politics identifies as central in our subordination—that is, the erotization of dominance and submission—male morality will tend to find comparatively harmless or defend as affirmatively valuable, hence protected speech.

In 1973 obscenity under law came to mean that which ' "the average person applying contemporary community standards" would find that . . . taken as a whole, appeals to the prurient interest . . . [which] depicts or describes, in a patently offensive way, sexual conduct specifically defined by the applicable state law; and [which], taken as a whole, lacks serious literary, artistic, political, or scientific value' (*Miller v. California* (1973)). Feminism doubts whether the average person, gender neutral, exists; has more questions about the content and process of definition of community standards than deviations from them; wonders why prurience counts but powerlessness doesn't; why sensibilities are better protected from offense than women are from exploitation; defines sexuality, hence its violation and expropriation, more broadly than does any state law, and wonders why a body of law which can't in practice tell rape from intercourse should be entrusted with telling pornography from anything less. In feminist perspective, one notices that although the law of obscenity says that fucking on streetcorners is not

---

[27]Those termed 'fathers' and 'sons' in Andrea Dworkin's article (1982), we came to term 'the old boys', whose strategy for male dominance involves keeping pornography and the abuse of women private, and 'the new boys', whose strategy for male dominance involves making pornography and the abuse of women public. In my view, Freud, and the popularization of his depression hypothesis, figures centrally in 'the new boys' approach and success. To conclude, as some have, that women have benefitted from the public availability of pornography, hence should be grateful for and have a stake in its continuing availability, is to say that the merits of open condoned oppression relative to covert condoned oppression warrant its continuation. This reasoning obscures the possibility of *ending* the oppression. The benefit of pornography's open availability, it seems to me, is that women can know who and what we are dealing with in order to end it. How, is the question.

supposed to be legitimized by the fact that the persons are 'simultaneously engaged in a valid political dialogue'[28] the requirement that the work be considered as a whole legitimizes something very like that on the level of publications like *Playboy*,[29] even though experimental evidence is beginning to support what its victims have long known: legitimate settings diminish the injury perceived as done to the women whose trivialization and objectification it contextualizes.[30] Beside, if a woman is subjected, why should it matter that the work has other value?[31] Perhaps what redeems a work's value among men *enhances* its injury to women. Existing standards of literature, art, science and politics are, in feminist light, remarkably consonant with pornography's mode, meaning and message. Finally and foremost, a feminist approach reveals that although the content and dynamic of pornography are about women—about the sexuality of women, about women as sexuality—in the same way that the vast majority of 'obscenities' refer specifically to women's bodies, our invisibility has been such that the law of obscenity has *never even considered pornography a women's issue.*[32]

To appeal to 'prurient interest' (*Miller v. California*, 1973: 24) means, I believe, to give a man an erection. Men are scared to make it possible for some men to tell other men what they can and cannot have sexual access to because men have power. If you don't let them have theirs, they might not let you have yours. This is why the *indefinability* of pornography, all the 'one

---

[28]*Paris Adult Theatre I v. Slaton* (1973). See *Miller v. California* (1973: 25, n.7): 'A quotation from Voltaire in the flyleaf of a book will not constitutionally redeem an otherwise obscene publication' (quoting *Kois v. Wisconsin* (1972): 231).

[29]*Penthouse International v. McAuliffe* (1980); *Coble v. City of Birmingham* (1980).

[30]Malamuth and Spinner: '. . . the portrayal of sexual aggression within such "legitimate" magazines as *Playboy* and *Penthouse* may have a greater impact than similar portrayals in hardcore pornography.' (Malamuth and Donnerstein, 1982: 130).

[31]Some courts, under the obscenity rubric, seem to have understood that the quality of artistry does not undo the damage. *People v. Mature Enterprises* (1973: 925, n. 14). 'This court will not adopt a rule of law which states that obscenity is suppressible but that well-written or technically well produced obscenity is not' (quoting, *People v. Fritch* (1963: 126). More to the point of my argument here is Justice O'Connor's observation that '[t]he compelling interests identified in today's opinion . . . suggest that the Constitution might in fact permit New York to ban knowing distribution of works depicting minors engaged in explicit sexual conduct, regardless of the social value of the depictions. For example, a 12-year-old child photographed while masturbating surely suffers the same psychological harm whether the community labels the photography "edifying" or "tasteless." The audience's appreciation of the depiction is simply irrelevant to New York's asserted interest in protecting children from psychological, emotional, and mental harm' (*New York v. Ferber*, 1982: 774–775) (concurring)). Put another way, how does it make a harmed child *not harmed* that what was produced by harming him is great art.

[32]Women typically get mentioned in obscenity law only in the phrase 'women and men' used as a synonym for 'people.' At the same time, exactly who the victim of pornography is, has long been a mystery. The few references to 'exploitation' in obscenity litigation do not evoke a female victim. For example, one reference to 'a system of commercial exploitation of people with sadomasochistic sexual aberrations' concerned the customers of women dominatrixes, all of whom were male (*State v. Von Cleef*, 1968: 505). The children at issue in *Ferber* were male. Justice Frankfurter invoked the 'sordid exploitation of man's nature and impulses' in discussing his conception of pornography in *Kingsley Pictures Corp. v. Regents* (1958: 692).

man's this is another man's that,'[33] is so central to pornography's *definition*. It is not because they are such great liberals, but because those other men might be able to do to them whatever they can do to those other men, and this is more why the liberal principle is what it is. What this obscures, because the fought-over are invisible in it, is that the fight over a definition of obscenity is a fight among men over the best means to guarantee male power as a system. The question is, whose sexual practices threaten this that can afford to be sacrificed to its maintenance for the rest? Public sexual access by men to anything other than women, objects, animals—is not the real system. The issue is *how public* that system will be, which the obscenity laws, their definition and patterns of enforcement, are major in regulating. The bind of the 'prurient interest' standard here is that, to find it as a fact, someone has to admit that they are sexually aroused by the materials[34] but male sexual arousal signals the importance of protecting them. They put themselves in this bind and then wonder why they cannot agree. Sometimes I think that what is ultimately found obscene is what does *not* turn on the Supreme Court, or what revolts them more, which is rare, since revulsion is eroticized; sometimes I think that what is obscene is what turns on those men that the men in power think they can afford to ignore; sometimes I think that part of it is that what looks obscene to them is what makes them see themselves as potential targets of male sexual aggression, even if only momentarily; sometimes I think that the real issue is how male sexuality is presented, so that anything can be done to a woman but obscenity is that sex that makes male sexuality look bad.[35]

Courts' difficulties framing workable standards to separate 'prurient' from other sexual interest, commercial exploitation from art or advertising,

---

[33]See for example *Miller v. California* (1973: 40–41) (Douglas, J. dissenting): 'What shocks me may be sustenance for my neighbors'; *U.S. v. 12 200-ft. Reels of Film* (1972: 137) (Douglas, J. dissenting): '[W]hat may be trash to me may be prized by others'; *Cohen v. California* (1970: 25) (Harlan. J.): 'One man's vulgarity is another's lyric'; *Winters v. New York* (1947: 510): 'What is one man's amusement, teaches another's doctrine'; Lawrence (1929: 195). 'What is pornography to one man may be the laughter of genius to another.' As put by Chuck Traynor, the pimp who forced Linda Lovelace into pornography, 'I don't tell you how to write your column. Don't tell me how to treat my broads,' quoted in Steinem (1983: 252).

[34]For the resolution of this issue for non-standard sexuality, see *Mishkin v. New York* (1966: 508).

[35]None of this is intended as a comment about the personal sexuality or principles of any judicial individual, but rather as a series of analytic observations that emerge from a feminist attempt to interpret the deep social structure of a vast body of case law on the basis of a critique of gender. Further research should systematically analyse the contents of the pornography involved in the cases. For instance, with respect to the last hypothesis in the text above, is it just chance that the first film to be found obscene by a state supreme court depicts male masturbation? (*Landau v. Fording*, 1966). Given the ubiquity of the infantilization of women and the sexualization of little girls, would *Ferber* have been decided the same way if it had shown 12-year-old girls masturbating? Is the depiction of male sexuality in a way that men think is dangerous for women and children to see, the reason that works like *Lady Chatterley's Lover* and *Tropic of Cancer* got in trouble?

sexual speech from sexual conduct, and obscenity from great literature make the feminist point. These lines have proven elusive in law because they do not exist in life. Commercial sex resembles art because both exploit women's sexuality. The liberal's slippery slope is the feminist totality. Whatever obscenity may do, pornography converges with more conventionally acceptable depictions and descriptions like rape does with intercourse because both express the same power relation. Just as it is difficult to distinguish literature or art against a background, a standard, of objectification, it is difficult to discern sexual freedom against a background, a standard, of sexual coercion. This does not mean it cannot be done. It means that legal standards will be practically unenforceable, will reproduce this problem rather than solve it, until they address its fundamental issue—gender inequality—directly.

To define the pornographic as the 'patently offensive' further misconstrues its harm. Pornography is not bad manners or poor choice of audience; obscenity is. Pornography is also not an idea; obscenity is. The legal fiction whereby the obscene is 'not speech' (*Roth v. U.S.* (1957))[36] has deceived few; it *has* effectively avoided the need to adjudicate pornography's social etiology. But obscenity law got one thing right: pornography is more act-like than thought-like. The fact that pornography, in a feminist view, furthers the idea of the sexual inferiority of women, a political idea, does not make the pornography itself a political idea. That one can express the idea a practice embodies does not make that practice into an idea. Pornography is not an idea any more than segregation is an idea, although both institutionalize the idea of the inferiority of one group to another. The law considers obscenity deviant, anti-social. If it causes harm, it causes anti-social acts, acts against the social order.[37] In a feminist perspective, pornography is the essence of a sexist social order, its quintessential social act.

If pornography is an act of male supremacy, its harm is the harm of male supremacy made difficult to see because of its pervasiveness, potency, and success in making the world a pornographic place. Specifically, the harm cannot be discerned from the objective standpoint because it *is* so much of 'what is.' Women live in the world pornography creates. We live its lie as reality. As Naomi Scheman has said,

> '. . . lies that we have lived, not just what we have told, and no story about correspondence to what is real will enable us to distinguish the truth from the lie' (1982).

So the issue is not whether pornography is harmful, but how the harm of pornography is to become visible. As compared with what? To the extent

---

[36]But cf. *Stanley v. Georgia* (1969) in which the right to private possession of obscene materials is protected as a First Amendment *speech* right. One justice noticed this incongruity in the oral argument in *Stanley*. (See 67 *Landmark Briefs*, 1975: 850.)

[37]*Report of the Commission* (1970: 1), charging the commission to study '[t]he effect of obscenity and pornography upon the public and particularly minors and its relation to crime and other antisocial behavior.'

pornography succeeds in constructing social reality, it becomes invisible as harm. Any perception of the success, therefore the harm, of pornography, I will next argue, is precluded by liberalism and so has been defined out of the customary approach taken to, and dominant values underlying, the First Amendment.

The theory of the First Amendment under which most pornography is protected from governmental restriction proceeds from liberal assumptions[38] which do not apply to the situation of women. First Amendment theory, like virtually all liberal legal theory, presumes the validity of the distinction between public and private: the 'role of the law [is] to make and guard the line between the sphere of social power, organized in the form of the state, and the area of private right' (Emerson, 1966). On this basis, courts distinguish between obscenity in public (which can be regulated, even if attempts founder, some seemingly in part *because* the presentations are public[39]) and the private possession of obscenity in the home (*Stanley v. Georgia* (1969)). The problem is that not only the public but also the private *is* a 'sphere of social power' of sexism. On paper and in life pornography is thrust upon unwilling women in their homes.[40] The distinction between public and private does not cut the same for women as for men (MacKinnon, 1984: 23–35). It is men's right to inflict pornography upon women in private that is protected.

The liberal theory underlying First Amendment law further believes that free speech, including pornography, helps discover truth. Censorship restricts society to partial truths. So why are we now—with more pornography available than ever before—buried in all these lies? *Laissez faire* might be an adequate theory of the social preconditions for knowledge in a nonhierarchical society. But in a society of gender inequality the speech of the powerful impresses its view upon the world, concealing the truth of powerlessness under that despairing acquiescence which provides the appearance of consent and makes protest inaudible as well as rare. Pornography can invent women because it has the power to make its vision into reality, which then passes, objectively, for truth. So while the First Amendment supports pornography believing that consensus and progress is facilitated by allowing all views, however divergent and unorthodox, it fails to notice that pornography (like the racism, in which I include anti-Semitism, of the Nazis and the Klan) is not

[38]This body of work is usually taken to be diverse (Emerson, 1966, 1970; Meiklejohn, 1948; *Whitney v. California* (1927: 375) (Brandeis, J., concurring, joined by Holmes, J.); Scanlon, 1972; Ely, 1975; Chafee, 1948). This literature is ably summarized by Ed Baker, who proposes an interpretative theory that goes far toward responding to my objections here, without really altering the basic assumptions I criticize (See Baker, 1978, 1982).
[39]*Erznoznik v. City of Jacksonville* (1975); *Breard v. Alexandria* (1951); *Kovacs v. Cooper* (1949).
[40]Walker, 1982a: 95; Russell, 1982; *Public Hearings*, 1983. Cf. *Paris Adult Theatre I v. Slaton* (1973: 71) (Douglas, J. dissenting): '[In] a life that has not been short, I have yet to be trapped into seeing or reading something that would offend me.' He probably hadn't.

at all divergent or unorthodox. It is the ruling ideology. Feminism, the dissenting view, is suppressed by pornography. Thus, while defenders of pornography argue that allowing all speech, including pornography, frees the mind to fulfil itself, pornography freely enslaves women's minds and bodies inseparably, normalizing the terror that enforces silence from women's point of view.

To liberals, speech must never be sacrificed for other social goals (Emerson, 1967: 16–25, 1970: 17). But liberalism has never understood that the free speech of men silences the free speech of women. It is the same social goal, just other *people*. This is what a real inequality, a real conflict, a real disparity in social power looks like. The law of the First Amendment comprehends that freedom of expression, in the abstract, is a system but fails to comprehend that sexism (and racism), *in the concrete*, are also systems. That pornography chills women's expression is difficult to demonstrate empirically because silence is not eloquent. Yet on no more of the same kind of evidence, the argument that suppressing pornography might chill legitimate speech has supported its protection.

First Amendment logic, like nearly all legal reasoning, has difficulty grasping harm that is not linearly caused in the 'John hit Mary' sense. The idea is that words or pictures can only be harmful if they produce harm in a form that is considered an action. Words work in the province of attitudes, actions in the realm of behavior. Words cannot constitute harm in themselves—never mind libel, invasion of privacy, blackmail, bribery, conspiracy or most sexual harassment. But which is saying 'kill' to a trained guard dog, a word or an act? Which is its training? How about a sign that reads 'Whites only?' Is that the idea or the practice of segregation? Is a woman raped by an attitude or a behavior? Which is sexual arousal? It is difficult to avoid noticing that the ascendancy of the specific idea of causality used in obscenity law dates from around the time it was first believed to be proved that it is impossible to prove that pornography causes harm.[41] Instead of the more

[41]The essentially scientific notion of causality did not *first* appear in this law at this time, however. See for example *U.S. v. Roth* (1957: 812–817, 826 n. 70) (Frank, J., concurring): 'According to Judge Bok, an obscenity statute may be validly enforced when there is proof of a causal relation between a particular book and undesirable conduct. Almost surely, such proof cannot ever be adduced.'

Werner Heisenberg, criticizing old ideas of atomic physics, in light of Einstein's theory of relativity, states the conditions that must exist for a causal relation to make sense: 'To coordinate a definite cause to a definite effect has sense only when both can be observed without introducing a foreign element disturbing their interrelation. The law of causality, because of its very nature, can be defined for isolated systems . . .' (Heisenberg, 1930: 63). Among the influences that disturb the isolation of systems are observers. Underlying the adoption of a causality standard in obscenity law is a rather hasty analogy between the regularities of physical and social systems, an analogy which has seldom been explicitly justified or even updated as the physical sciences have explicitly altered their epistemological foundations. This kind of causality may not be readily susceptible to measurement in social systems for the simple reason that social systems are not isolated systems; experimental research (which is where it *has* been shown that pornography

complex causality implicit in the above examples, the view became that pornography must cause harm like negligence causes car accidents or its effects are not cognizable as harm. The trouble with this individuated, atomistic, linear, isolated, tort-like—in a word, positivistic—conception of injury is that the way pornography targets and defines women for abuse and discrimination does not work like this. It does hurt individuals, just not *as* individuals in a one-at-a-time sense, but as members of the group 'women.' Harm is caused to one individual woman rather than another, essentially like one number rather than another is caused in roulette. But on a group basis, as women, the selection process is absolutely selective and systematic. Its causality is essentially collective and totalistic and contextual. To reassert atomistic linearcasuality as a *sine qua non* of injury—you cannot be harmed unless you are harmed through this etiology—is to refuse to respond to the true nature of this specific kind of harm. Such refusals call for explanation. Morton Horowitz says that the issue of causality in tort law is 'one of the pivotal ideas in a system of legal thought that sought to separate private law from politics and to insulate the legal system from the threat of redistribution' (1982: 201).[42] Perhaps causality in the pornography issue is an attempt to privatize the injury pornography does to women in order to insulate the same system from the threat of gender equality, also a form of redistribution.

Women are known to be brutally coerced into pornographic performances (Lovelace, 1980). But so far it is only with children, usually male children, that courts consider that the speech of pornographers was once someone else's *life*.[43] Courts and commissions and legislatures and researchers have searched largely in vain for the injury of pornography in the mind of the

causes harm) can only minimize what will always be 'foreign elements.' Pornography and harm may not be two definite events anyway; perhaps pornography *is* a harm. Moreover, if the effects of pornography are systematic, they may not be isolable from the system in which they exist. This would not mean that no harm exists; rather that because the harm is so pervasive, it cannot be sufficiently isolated to be *perceived* as existing according to this causal model. In other words, if pornography is only seen as harmful if it causes harm by this model, and if it exists socially only in ways that cannot be isolated from society itself, that means that its harm will not be perceived to exist. I think this describes the conceptual situation in which we find ourselves.

[42]The pervasiveness of the objectification of women has been considered as a reason why pandering should not be constitutionally restricted: 'The advertisements of our best magazines are chock-full of thighs, ankles, calves, bosoms, eyes, and hair, to draw the potential buyer's attention to lotions, tires, food, liquor, clothing, autos, and even insurance policies' (*Ginzburg v. U.S.*, 1966: 482 (Douglas, J. dissenting)). Justice Douglas thereby illustrated, apparently without noticing, that *somebody* knows that associating sex, that is women's bodies, with things causes people to *act* on that association.

[43]Two boys masturbating with no showing of explicit force demonstrates the harm of child pornography in *New York v. Ferber* (1982), while shoving money up a woman's vagina, among other acts, raises serious questions of 'regulation of "conduct" having a communicative element' in live sex adjudications (*California v. La Rue*, 1972: 113) (live sex can be regulated by a state in connection with serving alcoholic beverages). 'Snuff' films, in which a woman is actually murdered to produce a film for sexual entertainment, are known to exist. *People v. Douglas and Hernandez*, Felony Complaint (1983), alleges the murder of two young girls to make a pornographic film.

(male) consumer or in 'society,' or in empirical correlations between variations in levels of 'anti-social' acts and liberalization in obscenity laws.[44]
Speech can be regulated 'in the interests of unwilling viewers, captive
audiences, young children, and beleaguered neighborhoods' (Tribe, 1978:
662), but the normal level of sexual force—force that is not seen as force
because it is inflicted on women and called sex—has never been a policy issue.
Until the last few years experimental research never approached the question
of whether pornographic stimuli might support *sexual* aggression against
women[45] or whether violence might be sexually stimulating or have sexual
sequelae.[46] Only in the last few months are we beginning to learn the
consequences for women of so-called consensual sexual depictions that show
normal dominance and submission (Zillman, 1984). We still don't know the
impact of female-only nudity or of depictions of specific acts like penetration
or of even mutual sex in a social context of gender inequality.

The most basic assumption underlying First Amendment adjudication is
that, socially, speech is free. The First Amendment says, 'Congress shall not
abridge *the freedom of speech*.' Free speech exists. The problem for government is to avoid constraining that which, if unconstrained by government, *is*
free. This tends to presuppose that whole segments of the population are not
systematically silenced *socially*, prior to government action. The place of
pornography in the inequality of the sexes makes such a presupposition
untenable and makes any approach to *our* freedom of expression so based

[44]Both Susan Griffin (1981) and the oldest Anglo-Saxon obscenity cases locate the harm of
pornography in the mind of the consumer. See for example *Regina v. Hicklin* (1868: 371):
'tendency . . . to deprave and corrupt those whose minds are open to such immoral influences
and into whose hands a publication of this sort may fall.' The data of Court and of Kutchinsky,
both correlational, reach contrary conclusions on the issue of the relation of pornography's
availability to crime statistics (Kutchinsky, 1971, 1973; cf. Court, 1977). More recent investigations into correlations focused on rape in the United States have reached still other
conclusions. L. Baron and M. Straus have found a strong correlation between state-to-state
variations in the rate of reported rape and the aggregate circulation rate of popular men's sex
magazines, including *Playboy* and *Hustler*. 'Sexual Stratification, Pornography and Rape'
(1983). The authors conclude, at p. 16, that 'the findings suggest that the combination of a
society which is characterized by a struggle to secure equal rights for women, by a high
readership of sex magazines which depict women in ways which may legitimize violence, and by a
context in which there is a high level of non-sexual violence, constitutes a mix of societal
characteristics which precipitate rape.' See also *The Williams Report* (1981), and the opinions of
Justice Harlan on the injury to 'society' as a permissible basis for legislative judgments in this
area (*Roth v. U.S.*, 1956: 501–502 (concurring in companion case, *Alberts v. California*)).

[45]I am conceiving rape as *sexual* aggression. The work of Neil Malamuth is the leading research in
this area (Malamuth, 1981a, b; Malamuth, Haber and Feshback, 1980; Heim and Feshback,
1980). See also work by Malamuth and Donnerstein (1984); Check *et al.* (1983); Malamuth and
Check (1981); Malamuth and Spinner (1980). Of course, there are difficulties in measuring rape
as a direct consequence of laboratory experiments, difficulties which have led researchers to
substitute other measures for willingness to aggress.

[46]Apparently, it may be impossible to *make* a film for experimental purposes that portrays
violence or aggression by a man against a woman that a substantial number of male experimental
subjects do not perceive as sexual. (See *Public Hearings*, 1983: 31 (testimony of E. Donnerstein).)

worse than useless. For women, the urgent issue of freedom of speech is not primarily the avoidance of state intervention as such, but finding an affirmative means to get access to speech for those to whom it has been denied.

III

Beyond offensiveness or prurience, to say that pornography is 'dehumanizing' is an attempt to articulate its harm. But 'human beings' is a social concept with many possible meanings. Here I will criticize some liberal moral meanings of personhood through a feminist political analysis of what pornography does to women, showing how the inadequacy of the liberal dehumanization critique reflects the inadequacy of its concept of person. In a feminist perspective, pornography is seen to dehumanize women in a culturally specific and empirically descriptive—not liberal moral—sense, dispossessing women of the power of which, in the same act, it possesses men: the power of sexual, hence gender, definition. Perhaps a human being, for gender purposes, is someone who controls the social definition of sexuality.

A person, in one Kantian view, is a free and rational agent whose existence is an end in itself as opposed to instrumental.[47] In pornography, women exist to the *end* of male pleasure. Kant sees human as characterized by universal abstract rationality, with no component of individual or group differences, and as a 'bundle of rights.'[48] Pornography purports to define what a woman *is*. It does this on a group basis, including when it raises individual qualities to sexual stereotypes, as in the strategy of *Playboy's* 'Playmate of the Month.' I also think that pornography derives much of its sexual power, as well as part of its justification, from the implicit assumption that the Kantian notion of person actually describes the condition of women in this society, so that if we are there, we are freely and rationally there, when the fact is that women—in pornography and in part because of pornography —have no such rights.

Other views of the person include one of Wittgenstein's, who says that the best picture of the human soul is the human body (Wittgenstein, 1958: 178). I guess this depends upon what picture of the human body you have in mind. Marx's work offers various concepts of personhood deducible from his critique of various forms of productive organization. Whatever material conditions the society values, define person there, so that in a bourgeois society, a person might be a property-owner (Marx, 1970: ch. 1).[49] The problem here is that women *are* the property that constitutes the personhood, the masculinity, of men under capitalism. Thinking further in Marxian

---

[47]Kant (1969); Danto (1967); Radin (1982).
[48]Kant (1969); Danto (1967); Radin (1982). See also the 'original position' of Rawls (1971, 1980).
[49]Marx's concept of the 'fetishism of commodities' in which 'relations between men [assume], *in their eyes*, the fantastic form of a relation between things' (emphasis added) is presented in Marx (1970: 72), where his critique of capitalist society is epitomized.

theoretical terms, I have wondered whether women in pornography are more properly conceived as fetishes or objects. Does pornography more attribute life-likeness to that which is dead—as in fetishism—or make death-like that which is alive—as in objectification? I guess it depends upon whether, socially speaking, women are more dead than alive.

In Hume's concept of a person as a bundle or collection of sense perceptions, such that the feeling of self-identity over time is a persistent illusion,[50] we finally have a view of the human that coincides with the view of women in pornography. That is, the empiricist view of person is the pornographic view of women. No critique of dominance or subjection, certainly not of objectification, can be grounded in a vision of reality in which all sense perceptions are just sense perceptions. This is one way an objectivist epistemology supports the unequal holding and wielding of power in a society in which the persistent illusion of selfhood of one half of the population is materially supported and maintained at the expense of the other half. What I'm saying is that those who are socially allowed a self are also allowed the luxury of postulating its illusoriness and having that called a philosophical position. Whatever self they ineluctably have, they don't lose by saying it is an illusion. Even if it is not particularly explanatory, such male ideology, if taken as such, is often highly descriptive. Thus Hume defines the human in the same terms feminism uses to define women's dehumanization: for women in pornography, the self is, precisely, a persistent illusion.

Contemporary ordinary language philosopher Bernard Williams says 'person' ordinarily means things like valuing self-respect and feeling pain (1973a: 64).[51] How self is defined, what respect attaches to, stimuli of pleasure and to an extent stimuli and thresholds of pain, are cultural variables. Women in pornography are turned on by being put down and feel pain as pleasure. We want it; we beg for it; we get it. To argue that this is dehumanizing need not mean to take respect as an ahistorical absolute or to treat the social meaning of pain as invariant or uniformly negative. Rather, it is to argue that it is the acceptance of the social definition of these values—the acceptance of self-respect and the avoidance of pain as values—that permits the erotization of their negative—debasement and torture—in pornography. It is only to the extent that each of these values—is *accepted as human* that their negation becomes a quality of, and is eroticized in and as, woman. Only when self-respect is accepted as human does debasement become sexy and female. In this way, women's sexuality as expressed in pornography precisely negatives her status as human. But there is more: exactly what is defined as degrading to a human being, *however* that is socially defined, is exactly what

---

[50]Hume (1888: bk. 1, pt IV, sec. VI).
[51]Bernard Williams was principal author of the *Williams Report* (1981). Britain's equivalent to the U.S. Commission on Obscenity and Pornography, in which none of his values of 'persons' were noticed lacking in, or women deprived of them by, pornography.

is sexually arousing to the male point of view in the pornography, just as the one to whom it is done is the girl regardless of sex. In this way, it is specifically women whom pornography identifies with and by sexuality, as the erotic is equated with the dehumanizing.

To define the pornographic as that which is violent, not sexual, as liberal moral analyses tend to, is to trivialize and evade the essence of this critique, while seeming to express it. As with rape, where the issue is not the presence or absence of force but what sex *is* as distinct from coercion (MacKinnon, 1982, 1983), the question for pornography is what eroticism *is* as distinct from the subordination of women. This is not a rhetorical question. Under male dominance, whatever sexually arouses a man is sex. In pornography, the violence *is* the sex. The inequality is sex. Pornography does not work sexually, without hierarchy. If there is no inequality, no violation, no dominance, no force, there is no sexual arousal.[52] Obscenity law does the pornographers a real favor by clouding this, pornography's central dynamic, under the coy gender-neutral abstraction of 'prurient interest.' Obscenity law also adds the dominance interest of state prohibition to whatever the law of obscenity is seen to encompass.

Calling rape and pornography violent not sexual the banner of much anti-rape and anti-pornography organizing,[53] is an attempt to protest that women do not find rape pleasurable or pornography stimulating while avoiding claiming this rejection as *women's* point of view. The concession to the objective stance, the attempt to achieve credibility by covering up the specificity of one's viewpoint, not only abstracts from our experience, it lies about it. Women and men know men find rape sexual and pornography erotic. It therefore *is*. We also know that sexuality is commonly violent without being any the less sexual. To deny this sets up the situation so that when women are aroused by sexual violation, meaning we experience it *as* our sexuality, the feminist analysis is seen to be contradicted. But it is not contradicted, it is *proved*. The male supremacist definition of female sexuality as lust for self-annihilation has won. It would be surprising, feminist analysis would be wrong, and sexism would be trivial, if this were merely exceptional. (One might ask at this point, not why some women embrace explicit sado-masochism, but why any women do not.) To reject forced sex in the name of women's point of view requires an account of women's experience of being violated by the same acts both sexes have learned as natural and fulfilling and erotic when no critique, no alternatives and few transgressions have been permitted.

[52]This statement is a conclusion from my analysis of all the empirical data available to date, the pornography itself, and personal observations.
[53]Susan Brownmiller's book *Against Our Will: Men, Women and Rape* (1975) is widely considered to present the view that rape is an act of violence, not sex. Women Against Pornography, a New York based anti-pornography group, has argued that pornography is violence against women, not sex. This has been almost universally taken as *the* feminist position on the issue. For an indication of possible change, see 4 *NCASA News* 19–21 May 1984.

The depersonalization critique, with the 'violence not sex' critique, exposes pornography's double standard, but does not attack the masculinity of the standards for personhood and for sex that pornography sets. The critiques are thus useful, to some extent deconstructive, but beg the deeper questions of the place of pornography in sexuality and of sexuality in the construction of women's definition and status, because they act as if women can be 'persons' by interpretation, as if the concept is not, in every socially real way, defined by and in terms of and reserved for men and as if sexuality is not itself a construct of male power. To do this is to act as if pornography did not exist or were impotent. Deeper than the personhood question or the violence question is the question of the mechanism of social causation by which pornography *constructs* women and sex, defines what 'woman' means and what sexuality is, in terms of each other.

The law of obscenity at times says that sexual expression is only talk, therefore cannot be intrinsically harmful. Yet somehow pornographic talk is vital to protect. If pornography is a practice of the ideology[54] of gender inequality, and gender *is an ideology*, if pornography is sex and gender is sexual, the question of the relation between pornography and life is nothing less than the question of the dynamic of the subordination of women to men. If 'objectification . . . is never trivial' (Dworkin, 1981a: 115), girls *are* ruined by books.[55] To comprehend this process will require an entirely new theory of social causality—of ideology in life, of the dynamic of mind and body in social power—that connects point of view with politics. The development of such an analysis has been equally stymied by fear of repressive state use of any critique of any form of expression, by the power of pornography to create woman in its image of use, and by the power of pornographers to create a climate hostile to inquiry into their power and profits.

I said all that in order to say this: the law of obscenity has the same surface theme and the same underlying theme as pornography itself. Superficially both involve morality: rules made and transgressed for purposes of sexual arousal. Actually, both are about power, about the equation between erotic and the control of women by men: *women* made and transgressed for purposes of sexual arousal. It seems essential to the kick of pornography that it be to some degree against the rules; but it is never truly unavailable or truly illegitimate. Thus obscenity law like the law of rape, preserves the values, without restricting the ability to get, that which it purports to both devalue and to prohibit. Obscenity law, helps keep pornography sexy by putting state power—force, hierarchy—behind its purported prohibition on what men can

[54]This, again, does not mean that it is an *idea*. A new theory of ideology, prefigured in Andrea Dworkin's *Pornography* (1980) will be needed to conceptualize the role of pornography in constructing the condition of women.
[55]'Echoing Macaulay, "Jimmy" Walker remarked that he had never heard of a woman seduced by a book.' (*U.S. v. Roth*, 1957: 812 (appendix to concurrence of Frank, J.)). What is classically called seduction, I expect feminists would interpret as rape or forced sex.

have sexual access to. The law of obscenity is to pornography as pornography is to sex: a map that purports to be a mirror, a legitimization and authorization and set of directions and guiding controls that project themselves onto social reality, while purporting merely to reflect the image of what is already there. Pornography presents itself as fantasy or illusion or idea, which can be good or bad as it is accurate or inaccurate, while it actually, *hence accurately*, distributes power. Liberal morality cannot deal with illusions that *constitute* reality because its theory of reality, lacking a substantive critique of the distribution of social power, cannot get behind the empirical world, truth by correspondence. On the surface, both pornography and the law of obscenity are about sex. In fact, it is the status of women that is at stake.

REFERENCES

(a) Cases
Breard v. Alexandria, 341 U.S. 622 (1951).
California v. La Rue, 409 U.S. 109 (1972).
Coble v. City of Birmingham, 389 So. 2d 527 (Ala. Ct. App. 1980).
Cohen v. California, 403 U.S. 15 (1970).
Erznoznik v. City of Jacksonville, 422 U.S. 205 (1975).
Ginzburg v. U.S., 383 U.S. 463 (1966).
Grove Press v. Christenberry, 175 F. Supp. 488 (S.D.N.Y. 1959).
Grove Press v. Christenberry, 276 F. 2d 433 (2d Cir. 1960).
Hamling v. U.S., 418 U.S. 87 (1973).
Jacobellis v. Ohio, 378 U.S. 184 (1964).
Jenkins v. Georgia, 418 U.S. 153 (1973).
Kaplan v. California, 413 U.S. 115 (1973).
Kingsley Pictures Corporation v. Regents, 360 U.S. 684 (1958).
Kois v. Wisconsin, 408 U.S. 229 (1972).
Kovacs v. Cooper, 336 U.S. 77 (1949).
Landau v. Fording, 245 C.A. 2d 820, 54 Cal. Rpter 177 (1966).
Lovisi v. Slayton, 539 F. 2d 349 (4th Cir. 1976).
Memoirs v. Massachusetts, 383 U.S. 413 U.S. (1966).
Miller v. California, 413 U.S. 15 (1973).
Mishkin v. New York, 383 U.S. 502 (1966).
Mitchum v. State, 251 So. 2d 298 (Fla. Dist. Ct. App. 1971).
New York v. Ferber, 458 U.S. 747 (1982).
Paris Adult Theatre I v. Slaton, 413 U.S. 49 (1973).
Penthouse International v. McAuliffe, 610 F. 2d 1353 (5th Cir. 1980).
People v. Douglas and Hernandez, Felony Complaint # N.F. 8300382, Municipal Court,
    Judicial District, Orange County, California, 5 August 1983.
People v. Fritch, 13 N.Y. 2d 119, 243 N.Y.S. 2d 1. 192 N.E. 2d 713 (1963).
People v. Mature Enterprises, 343 N.Y.S. 2d 911 (1973).
People v. Sanger, 222 N.Y. 192, 118 N.E. 637 (1918).
Redrup v. N.Y., 386 U.S. 767 (1967).
Regina v. Hicklin, (1868) 3 Q.B. 360.
Roth v. U.S., 354 U.S. 476 (1957).
Smith v. California, 361 U.S. 147 (1959).
Splawn v. California, 431 U.S. 595 (1976).
Stanley v. Georgia, 394 U.S. 557 (1969).
State v. Von Cleef, 102 N.J. Super. 104, 245 A. 2d 495 (1968).
U.S. v. 'Ulysses,' 5F. Supp. 182 (S.D.N.Y. 1933), aff'd 72 F. 2d 705 (2d Cir. 1934).
U.S. v. Reidel, 402 U.S. 351 (1970).

U.S. v. *Roth*, 237 F. 2d 796 (1957).
U.S. v. *12 200-ft Reels of Super 8mm Film*, 413 U.S. 123 (1973).
Ward v. *Illinois*, 431 U.S. 767 (1976).
Whitney v. *California*, 274 U.S. 357 (1927).
Winters v. *New York*, 333 U.S. 507 (1947).

(b) Books and articles

Atkinson, Ti Grace. 1981. Why I'm against S/M liberation. In Linden, Robin Ruth, Pagano, Darlene R., Russell, Diana E. H. and Star, Susan Leigh, (eds), *Against Sadomasochism—a Radical Feminist Analysis*, p. 90. Frog in the Well, E. Palo Alto, California.

Baker, Ed. 1978. Scope of the First Amendment Freedom of Speech. *Univ. Calif. Los Angeles Law Rev.* **25**: 964.

Baker, Ed. 1982. The process of change and the liberty theory of the First Amendment. *5th. Calif. Law Rev.* **55**: 293.

Baron, L. and Straus, Murray. 1983. Sexual stratification, pornography, and rape. Unpublished manuscript. Family Research Laboratory and Department of Sociology, University of New Hampshire, Durham, New Hampshire.

Barry, Kathleen. 1979. *Female Sexual Slavery*. Prentice Hall, Englewood Cliffs, N.J.

Bart, Pauline and Jozsa, Margaret. 1982. Dirty books, dirty films, and dirty data. In Lederer, Laura, (ed), *Take Back the Night*, p. 204. William Morrow, New York.

Black, Justice. 1960. The Bill of Rights. *N.Y. Univ. Law Rev.* **35**: 865.

Brownmiller, Susan. 1975. *Against our Will: Men, Women and Rape*. Simon & Schuster, New York.

Butler, Judy. 1982. Lesbian S & M: The politics of disillusion. In Linden, Robin Ruth, Pagano, Darlene R., Russell, Diana E. H. and Star, Susan Leigh, (eds), *Against Sadomasochism*, p. 168. Frog in the Well, E. Palo Alto, California.

Cahn, Edmond. 1962. Justice Black and First Amendment 'Absolutes': A public interview. *N.Y. Univ. Law Rev.* **37**: 549.

Chafee, Zechariah. 1942. *Free Speech in the United States*. Harvard University Press, Cambridge, Mass.

Check, J.V.P., Malamuth, Neil and Stille, R. 1983. Hostility to women scale. Unpublished manuscript.

Cline, V. B. 1974. Another view: Pornography effects the state of the art. In Cline, Victor B., (ed), *Where Do You Draw the Line*? Brigham Young University Press, Provo, Utah.

Colker, Ruth. 1983. Pornography and privacy: Towards the development of a group based theory for sex based intrusions of privacy. *Law and Inequality: A Journal of Theory and Practice* **1**: 191.

Cook, J. 1978. The ψ-rated economy. *Forbes* (Sept. 18): 60.

Court, John. 1977. Pornography and sex crimes: A re-evaluation in the light of recent trends around the world. *Int. J. Criminol. Penol.* **5**: 129.

Danto, 1967. Persons. In Edwards, P., (ed), *Encyclopedia of Philosophy*, Vol. 6, p. 10. Macmillan, New York.

Diamond, Irene. 1980. Pornography and repression. *Signs: A Journal of Women in Culture* **5**: 686.

Donnerstein, Edward. 1980. Pornography Commission revisited: Aggression—erotica and violence against women. *J. Personality and Social Psychology* **39**: 269.

Donnerstein, Edward. 1984. Pornography: Its effects on violence against women. In Malamuth, Neil and Donnerstein E., (eds), *Pornography and Sexual Aggression*.

Dworkin, Andrea. 1976. The root cause. In *Our Blood: Essays and Discourses on Sexual Politics*, 96. Reprinted 1981. Perigee Books, New York.

Dworkin, Andrea. 1981a. *Pornography: Men Possessing Women*. Perigee Books, New York.

Dworkin, Andrea. 1981b. Pornography's 'exquisite volunteers,' *Ms* (March): 65.

Dworkin, Andrea. 1982. Why so-called radical men love and need pornography. In Lederer, Laura, (ed), *Take Back the Night*, p. 141. William Morrow, New York.

Elshtain, Jean Bethke. 1982. The victim syndrome: A troubling turn in feminism. *The Progressive* (June): 42.

Ely, John H. 1975. Flag desecration: A case study in the roles of categorization and balancing in First Amendment analysis. *Harv. Law Rev.* **88**: 1482.

Emerson, Thomas I. 1966. *Toward a General Theory of the First Amendment*, Random House, New York.

Emerson, Thomas I. 1970. *The System of Freedom of Expression*. Random House, New York.

English, Dierdre. 1980. The politics of porn: Can feminists walk the line? *Mother Jones* (April): 20.

Frantz, Laurent B. 1963. Is the First Amendment law?—A reply to Professor Mendelson. *California Law Rev.* **51**: 729.

Garry, Ann. 1978. Pornography and respect for women. *Social Theory and Practice* (Summer): **4**, 395.

Griffin, Susan. 1981. *Pornography and Silence: Culture's Revenge Against Nature*. Harper & Row, New York.

Hefner, Hugh. 1962, 1963. The Playboy philosophy. *Playboy* (December): 73; (February): 43.

Heffner, Richard. 1980. What G. PG. R and X really means. In *Congressional Record*, 126 (8 December), p. 172.

Heim, Maggie and Feshbeck, Seymour. 1980. Sexual reponsiveness of college students to rape depictions: Inhibitory and disinhibitory effects. *J. Personality and Social Psychology* **38**: 399.

Heisenberg, Werner. 1930. *The Physical Principles of the Quantum Theory*. University of Chicago Press, Chicago, Ill.

Henkin, Louis. 1963. Morals and the constitution: The sin of obscenity. *Columbia Law Rev.* **63**: 391.

Horowitz, Morton. 1982. The doctrine of objective causation. In Kairys, D., (ed), *The Politics of Law*, p. 201. Pantheon Books, New York.

Hume, David. 1988. Of personal identity. In Hume. David, (ed), *A Treatise of Human Nature*. Clarendon Press, Oxford.

Kalven, Harry. 1967. Upon rereading Mr Justice Black on the First Amendment. *Univ. Calif. Los Angeles Law Rev.* **14**: 428.

Kant, Immanuel. 1969. *Fundamental Principles of the Metaphysics of Morals*. Abbott, T., trans. The Liberal Arts Press, New York.

Kutchinsky, Berl. 1971. Towards an explanation of the decrease in registered sex crimes in Copenhagen. In *Technical Report of the Commission on Obscenity and Pornography*, Vol. 7. p. 263. U.S. Government Printing Office, Washington, D.C.

Kutchinsky, Berl. 1973. The effect of easy availability of pornography on the incidence of sex crimes: The Danish experience. *J. Social Issues* **29**: 163.

Langelan, Martha. 1981. The political economy of pornography. *Aegis: Magazine on Ending Violence Against Women* (Autumn): 5.

Landmark Briefs and Arguments of the Supreme Court of the United States: Constitutional Law. 1975. Vol. 67. p. 850 Kurland, P. and Casper, G. (eds), University Publications, Arlington, VA.

Lawrence, David Herbert. 1955. Pornography and obscenity. In *Sex, Literature and Censorship*, p. 195. Heinemann, London.

Lawrence, David Herbert. 1959. *Lady Chatterley's Lover*. Modern Library, New York.

Lederer, Laura. (ed). 1982. *Take Back the Night: Women on Pornography*. William Morrow, New York.

Leidholdt, Dorchen. 1983. Where pornography meets fascism. *WIN* (15 March): 18.

Linden, Robin Ruth, Pagano, Darlene R., Russell, Diana E. H. and Star, Susan Leigh, (eds). 1982. *Against Sadomasochism: A Radical Feminist Analysis*. Frog in the Well, E. Palo Alto, California.

Lockhart, W. B. and R. C. McClure. 1954. Literature, the law of obscenity and the constitution. *Minnesota Law Rev.* **38**: 295.

Lockhart, W. B. and R. C. McClure. 1960. Censorship of obscenity. *Minnesota Law Rev.* **45**: 5.

Lorde, Audre and Star, Susan Leigh. 1982. Interview with Audre Lorde. In Linden, Robin Ruth, Pagano, Darlene R., Russell, Diana E. H. and Star, Susan Leigh, (eds), *Against Sadomasochism*, p. 66. Frog in the Well, E. Palo Alto, California.

Lovelace, Linda and Michael McGrady. 1980. *Ordeal*. Citadel Press, Secausus, New Jersey.

MacKinnon, Catharine A. 1979. *Sexual Harassment of Working Women*. Yale University Press, New Haven.

MacKinnon, Catharine A. 1982. Feminism, marxism, method and the state: An agenda for theory. *Signs: A Journal of Women in Culture and Society* **7**: 515.

MacKinnon, Catharine A. 1983. Feminism, marxism, method and the state: Toward feminist jurisprudence. *Signs: A Journal of Women in Culture and Society* **8**: 635.

MacKinnon, Catharine A. 1984. The male ideology of privacy: A feminist perspective on the right to abortion. *Radical America* (February): 23.

Malamuth, Neil. 1981a. Rape proclivity among men. *J. Social Issues* **37**: 138.

Malamuth, Neil. 1981b. Rape fantasies as a function of exposure to violent sexual stimuli. *Arch. Sexual Behaviour* **10**: 33.

Malamuth, Neil and Check, J. V. P. 1981. The effects of mass media exposure on acceptance of violence against women: A field experiment. *J. Research in Personality* **15**: 436.

Malamuth, Neil and Donnerstein, Edward. 1982. The effects of aggressive-pornographic mass media stimuli. *Adv. exp. Social Psychology* **15**: 103.

Malamuth, Neil and Donnerstein, Edward. 1984. *Pornography and Sexual Aggression*. Academic Press, New York.

Malamuth, Neil and Spinner, Barry. 1980. A longitudinal content analysis of sexual violence in the best-selling erotica magazines. *J. Sex Research* **16**: 226.

Malamuth, Neil, Haber, Scott and Feshback, Seymour. 1980. Testing hypotheses regarding rape: Exposure to sexual violence, sex differences, and the 'normality' of rapists. *J. Res. Personality* **14**: 121.

Marx, Karl. 1971. *Capital*. International Publishers. New York.

Meikeljohn, Alexander. 1948. *Free Speech and its Relation to Self-Government*, Harper, New York.

Mendelson, Wallace. 1962. On the meaning of the First Amendment: Absolutes in the balance. *Calif. Law Rev.* **50**: 821.

Mendelson, Wallace. 1964. The First Amendment and the judicial process: A reply to Mr. Frantz. *Vanderbilt Law Rev.* **17**: 479.

Miller, Henry. 1947. Obscenity and the law of reflection. In *Remember to Remember*, p. 274. New Directions. N.Y.

Millett, Kate. 1969. *Sexual Politics*. Doubleday. New York.

Morgan, Robin. 1977. Pornography and rape: Theory and practice. In *Going Too Far. The Personal Chronicle of a Radical Feminist*, p. 165. Vintage Books, New York.

Mosher, William. 1971. Sex callousness towards women. In *Technical Report of the Commission on Obscenity and Pornography*, Vol. 8, p. 313. U.S. Government Printing Office, Washington, D.C.

NCASA News. 1984. National Coalition Against Sexual Assault (May).

N.Y. Univ. Rev. Law Social Change 1978–1979. Violent Pornography: Degradation of Women versus Right of Free Speech **8**: 181.

Orwell, George. 1949. *1984*. Harcourt Brace Jovanovich, London.

Public Hearings on Ordinances to Add Pornography as Discrimination Against Women. Committee on Government Operations, City Council, Minneapolis, Minnesota (12–13 December 1983).

Radin, Pamela. 1982. Property and personhood. *Stanford Law Rev.* **34**: 957.

Rawls, John. 1971. *A Theory of Justice*. Belknap Press of Harvard University Press, Cambridge, Mass.

Rawls, John. 1980. Kantian constructivism in moral theory. *J. Philosophy* **9**: 515.

The Report of the Commission on Obscenity and Pornography. 1970. U.S. Government Printing Office, Washington, D.C.

Report of the Committee on Obscenity and Film Censorship ('The Williams Report'). 1979. H.M.S.O., London. 1981. Cambridge University Press, Cambridge.

Richards, David A. J. 1974. Free speech and obscenity law: Toward a moral theory of the First Amendment. *Univ. Pa Law Rev.* **123**: 45.

Rush, Florence. 1980. *The Best Kept Secret: Sexual Abuse of Children*. Prentice Hall, Englewood Cliffs, New Jersey.

Russell, Diana E. H. 1982. Pornography and violence: What does the new research say? In Lederer, Laura, (ed), *Take Back the Night*, p. 216. William Morrow, New York.

Russell, Diana E. H. 1983. *Rape in Marriage*. Collier Books/Macmillan, New York.

Scanlon, Trevor. 1972. A theory of free expression. *Philosophy and Public Affairs* **1**: 204.

Schauer, F. 1979. Response: pornography and the First Amendment. *Univ. Pittsburgh Law Rev.* **40**: 605.

Scheman, Naomi. 1982. Making it all up. Transcript of speech. January (available from author).

Sontag, Susan. 1977. The pornographic imagination. *The Partisan Review* **34**: 181.

Star, Susan Leigh. 1982. Swastikas: The street and the university. In Linden, Robin Ruth, Pagano, Darlene R., Russell, Diana E. H. and Star, Susan Leigh, (eds), *Against Sadomasochism*, p. 131. Frog in the Well, E. Palo Alto, California.

Steiner, George. 1973. Night words. In Holbrook, D. (ed), *The Case Against Pornography*, p. 227. Library Press, New York.

Steinem, Gloria. 1983. The real Linda Lovelace. In *Outrageous Acts and Everyday Rebellions*, p. 243. Jonathan Cape, London.

Stoller, Robert. 1974. *Sex and Gender*. J. Aronson, New York.

Stoltenberg, John. 1982. Sadomasochism: Eroticized violence. Eroticized powerlessness. In Linden, Robin Ruth, Pagano, Darlene R., Russell, Diana E. H. and Star, Susan Leigh, (eds), *Against Sadomasochism*, p. 124. Frog in the Well, E. Palo Alto, California.

Straus, Murray. 1974. Levelling, civility and violence in the family. *J. of Marriage & Family* **36**: 13.

Sutherland, Lane V. 1975. *Obscenity—The Court, The Congress and the Presidents Commission*. American Enteprise Institute for Public Policy research, Washington, D.C.

Tribe, Lawrence. 1978. *American Constitutional Law*.

Vidal, Gore. Women's liberation meets the Miller-Mailer-Manson man. In *Homage to Daniel Shays: Collected Essays 1952–1972*, p. 389. Random House, New York.

Walker, Alice. 1982a. Coming apart. In Lederer, Laura, (ed), *Take Back the Night*, p. 95. William Morrow, New York.

Walker, Alice. 1982b. A letter of the times, or should this sado-masochism be saved? In Linden, Robin Ruth, Pagano, Darlene R., Russell, Diana E. H. and Star, Susan Leigh, (eds), *Against Sadomasochism*, p. 205. Frog in the Well, E. Palo Alto, California.

Williams, Bernard. 1973a. Bodily continuity and personal identity and individualization. In *Problems of the Self*, p. 1. Cambridge University Press, Cambridge.

Williams, Bernard. 1973b. Are persons bodies? Personal identity and individualization. In *Problems of the Self*, p. 1. Cambridge University Press, Cambridge.

Williams, Bernard. 1973c. *Problems of Self: Philosophical Papers 1956–1972*. Cambridge University Press, Cambridge.

Wittgenstein, Ludwig. 1958. *Philosophical Investigations*. (Anscombe, G. trans., 3d edn.). Basil Blackwell Oxford.

Woodward, Bob and Armstrong, Scott. 1979. *The Brethren*. Simon & Schuster, New York.

Woolf, Virginia. 1938. *Three Guineas*, Hogarth Press, London.

Woolf, Virginia. 1966. George Elliot. In *Collected Essays*. Vol. 1, p. 204.

Zillman, Dolf and Jennings, Bryant. 1984. Effects of massive exposure to pornography. In Malamuth, Neil and Edward Donnerstein, (eds), *Pornography and Sexual Aggression*, Academic Press, New York.

Zillman, Dolf. 1984. *The Connection Between Sex and Aggression*. L. Erlbaum, Hillsdale, N.J.

COMMENT: CATHARINE MACKINNON

The feminist critique of obscenity law explored in this article became part of the groundwork for the Antipornography Civil Rights Ordinances. These ordinances—conceived and drafted by the author with Andrea Dworkin, a feminist writer—have been introduced in several United States jurisdictions and have drawn increasing attention in the international community. Rather than strengthening the state with moral injunctions backed by the criminal apparatus of censorship, as this article shows obscenity laws do, the ordinances empower women to address pornography's harms as injuries of sex inequality.

III

*Feminist ethics and vision:
the meaning of feminism*

13

A Feminist World View[1]

Sheila Ruth

Feminists are struggling from one life into another. We do that in many ways and on several levels: we are struggling away from economic discrimination and dependence, from political disenfranchisement and only marginal participation in culture. We are exchanging 'male-identification' (alien definition of our being) for 'woman-identification,' positive, self-determined views of female excellence. We are testing new life-styles, even new kinds of community.

The struggle, both personal and political, is often very trying and painful; there is much to discourage us. Yet feminists, as I have experienced them, those I have read about and those I have met, tend to be rather high-spirited people, generally optimistic, at times even ecstatic, rather resilient and forward looking.

It has been my observation that feminists are sustained because we have a vision—I would be willing to say a spiritual vision. Although it is rarely articulated and often unconscious, it lies beneath, permeates and motivates what we write, say, and do. Feminists do not demand a better opportunity for jobs, careers, and incomes only for the increased wealth and comfort (although that is, of course, part of the issue), or else the gilded cage comfort of some marriage or of being kept or used or purchased would be acceptable, and it is not. Feminists do not demand more jobs, greater responsibility and power in political decision-making merely for the sake of power as an end in itself. Feminists' objections to 'separate spheres,' to being taken care of, to dependence, ignorance, or misogyny all have to do with the quality of human life, with autonomy, with the sense of self, with pride, dignity, freedom, joy, and meaningfulness. These are matters of the human spirit, spiritual matters. Feminists challenge the aggressiveness, stiffness, and uncaring character of

---

[1] Part of the following discussion is taken from Sheila Ruth, *Issues in Feminism: A First Course in Women's Studies*, published by Houghton-Mifflin, 1978–80.

masculist culture because it is inhumane, that is, it lacks the quality of excellence humans may or ought to aspire to. How could we do that unless we had some vision, however inchoate, however unformed, against which we measured present circumstances?

If we are to build new life-possibilities, whether for ourselves or for society, we cannot do so in a vacuum. We cannot develop a viable program if we know only what we do not want. We must have real alternatives derived from a positive set of values and goals, from a world-view created by feminists for ourselves, out of our own experience. Certainly the existing major sources of value and meaning available in our contemporary culture, traditional religion and popular culture, are inadequate if not totally destructive, because they are misogynist and masculist.

RELIGION

Religion as it is practiced through or by the social institutions of a people is as much a reflection and expression of that culture's ideals, attitudes, and needs as it is their creator. The Judao-Christian tradition of the West is, of course, no exception. As Western culture is patriarchal, so is its religion, so its god.

Although Christians (and sometimes Jews) argue that God is without sex, neither female nor male, that contention is contradicted by a host of beliefs indicating the maleness of their god. Currently some fathers of the various churches have opposed the ordination of women on the grounds that it would be clearly sacreligious, since the maleness of Christ proves that it is men who were meant for that office. (It could be argued that one must separate God and Jesus, but that does not hold *functionally*, in the minds of the faithful.) In medieval times the Church explained that women rather than men were likely to be witches because, among other things, since Christ was male, men had been saved from that awful danger. Today, the use of feminine pronouns to refer to the deity, *she* or *her*, brings a very hostile response. (Singer Helen Reddy shocked and dismayed her audience when, after receiving a recording award, she told them that she always trusted God, knowing that *She* would provide). Certainly the Catholic imagery of the Church standing analogously to Christ as a wife stands to a husband supports once more the identification of God as male.

So in our culture God is traditionally conceived to be male. What can be made of that? A great deal can and is made of that. The relationship between the concrete, material conditions of a culture, including its social organization, and its myths, mores and ideals are intricately close. The maleness of the western god, his character and behavior, is as much a source of the content of our culture's masculist perspectives as it is an indicator.

If men are to be god, their god must be male. Likewise, if God in his heaven is male, then on Earth men can be the only true gods. The entire conceptual system of Martial thought is elevated and deified by its incarnation in the person of the 'One true God,' the ultimate male, just as the socio-political structures of patriarchy are reinforced by their justification through theology.

The relationship between masculine theology and patriarchal society is the reason for its being both possible and necessary to insist upon the masculinity of the priesthood or the authority of the hierarchy, and it is the source of the masculine cast to the biblical imagery and to male privilege in church doctrine.

God, Mars, and Culture

To speak of a patriarchal religion, which incarnates the godness of maleness, and its effect on culture is to consider the cultural impact of the deification of masculist perspective, for as it was pointed out earlier, the forms of institutional religious worship are a reflection of cultural ideals expressed in a different language. What makes the religious expression of those ideals so important is its claim to absolute cosmic validity and its subsequent persuasive force over society.

What we find when we turn analysis sensitive to masculist conceptualizations upon the patriarchal Western tradition is precisely what we would expect to find: a Martial god, an authoritarian ethic, and a warrior-personality consciousness.

In patriarchy, God rules. He creates out of nothing. Superior and external to the rest, he orders, fixes, requires, commands, and does unto. He gets angry at disobedience, 'loves' on condition, rewards and punishes according to the meeting of his standards, and trains his followers through a series of trials and challenges. Jesus was supposed to have been the 'completion' of the person of God—gentle, merciful, and forgiving, but outside of his ultimate sacrifice and readiness to accept us—provided that . . .—one does not feel his 'sweetness' in excess of his power, not practically. Put all together, the Trinity as the One generally functions in the church more as the Power than as the Lamb.

That claims of the gentleness or lovingness of God are unconvincing among the laity is underscored smartly by the popular centrality of Mary as the image of mercy and kindness. Even in Catholicism, it is the female who captures the heart and serves the needs of the people, the Queen of Heaven, to whom most of the finest churches are dedicated; she is the Mother, free from the angry, frightening qualities of Mars/God, forgiving where he is stern, understanding where he is legalistic, accessible where he is distant. It is no accident that Mary is absent from Protestantism, which has been both more ascetic than Catholicism and unrelenting in its emphasis on sin and punishment.

God is good, we are told, although there are no standards outside of His own will against which we may judge Him. He is good (right) because he is God, that is, He is The Chief. Everybody else is expected to be good too, that is, obedient to the will of the Chief, not merely through coercion but through choice—ultimate obedience. If one is not good, God punishes. If one suffers sufficiently, one might be redeemed (forgiven), but that too is solely up to God. The pattern of the God/Person relationship is clearly disciplinarian and authoritarian.

Other relationships in which God resides are equally authoritarian, although in a different context. The relationships are generally expressed as dualistic oppositions in which God has ascendency: God contra nature, Spirit against body, life against death, God *vis-à-vis* humanity. The relations are ones of strain, either of striving or of contention.

And of course the ethos of strain and contention permeates the lives of the people who are both its subject and its instigators. One strives constantly to 'be good,' to conform, to measure up to an image which is not in harmony with what it is to be human because it is derived from only one aspect and one segment of humanity: maleness. One strives and strains and tries but, of course, usually fails and follows with guilt and penitence and atonement and forgiveness and striving and failing and so on.

The tone is anti-humanistic. You sinned, it bellows. You are bad. Your body is bad; sex is bad; pleasure is bad. You should be ashamed. Try harder, ever harder. Salvation is possible only through vicarious identification with the Sacrificial Lamb. Even the treatment of love is formally rather heavy, generally ascetic, weighted with obligation and prohibitions, not particularly self-affirming. Certainly the qualities of mirth and gaity have not been extant nor even a consideration until very recently, and then only under pressure of the new ethic. Levity, in fact, has usually been treated with suspicion and disdain if not outright suppression.

The character of this perspective, which is a masculist projection, permeates our culture conceptually and spiritually, expressing itself in our thoughts, institutions, attitudes, and expectations. It is difficult to be self-affirming, constructively self-confident, healthily self-loving in the face of an image of humanity that is 'sinful and debased.' It is difficult to put into positive ethical perspective the needs and directions of one's natural self in a context which is condemnatory and almost hysterically anti-nature. It is nearly impossible for self-affirming people to comprehend the healthy possibilities of worship, to know what or how or whether to worship when official worship is composed of self-abnegation.

For culture, the worship of Mars, the religion of masculism, means obeisance to all the warrior values, and that is very harmful for a people because it lends a distorted value base upon which to build society.

SOCIAL SCIENCE

The unsatisfying and self-contradictory aspects of traditional masculist religion are noted not only by scholars, but have become uncomfortably apparent to ordinary lay people as well. Feeling its failure to deliver as promised, its inauthenticity relative to itself as well as to contemporary culture, popular culture has turned for direction to something they deem much more worthy of respect and confidence, Science.

Science, both in its effects and as a concept, is an extremely important factor in the lives of twentieth-century people. Side by side with its data, procedures, and theories, stands the scientific world-view, a whole way of looking at truth and reality and of relating to life.

Some social analysts have suggested that in contemporary times science functions much as a god or as a substitute for God, providing a basis for truth and knowledge, an agent to be trusted and depended upon for salvation, even a ground of value. Placing very high conceptual priorities on the judgements and evaluations of science and scientists is part of our cultural ethos. A large segment of the intelligentsia and the moderately educated public maintain the belief that Science *is* Truth, the only dependable, sane truth for up-to-date, rational, right-minded people.

Of course, the corollary to the *Science is Truth* theme is the notion that we should all live our lives in accordance with the truths and findings of Science. Although the idea is rarely articulated in quite this way, a close appraisal of the new intellectual scene reveals the 'modern' imperative: 'Live your life in such a way that Science would be proud of you.' As medievals yearned to please God and stand in a state of grace, 'moderns' of the 1970s yearn to please the psychological community and to stand in a state of 'health.'

Because today's people want to be judged 'healthy,' social science has become very much like a faith. On at last two levels, as a technical-academic enterprise and as a 'philosophy' of life for popular culture, social science, especially psychology, serves as a kind of religion: it forms eternal verities about human nature and goals, decrees standards of perfection (health) towards which one is advised to strive, separates the 'good' people (healthy, normal, 'okay') from the bad (unhealthy, abnormal, not 'okay'), determines social priorities both for individuals and the state, and carries sufficient esteem in the community to socialize the population according to a certain vision of behavior.

Clearly the impact of the theories of social science on the conduct of our lives is tremendous. For women that is something of a disaster, for both the technical enterprise of the social sciences and the contemporary pop ethic that has evolved out of it are rabidly sexist.

The Formal Enterprise

For a variety of reasons—the relative newness of the study, the complexity of its subject matter, the absence of clearly articulated concepts and procedures—social science, at least for now and possibly forever, requires a far greater degree of interpretive latitude than its natural science counterparts. That is a polite way of saying that social science is still quite subjective and therefore resistant to the traditional forms of verification. Because of this, theories of the social sciences generally bear the mark of their creators, the people who develop them, and they tend to be 'culture bound,' reflective of their time and place.

The time, place, and greatest part of the personnel of the social sciences has always been predominantly male. For the most part it was men who developed the methods of research and the procedures for verification, it was they who originated the earliest axioms and perspectives from which current developments have evolved, and it was they who ultimately fixed the application of those perspectives, carrying theory out of the laboratory into the streets. With few exceptions, the few women who gained some recognition for their work were almost always adherents and popularizers of the already existent male-identified systems rather than creators of their own models. In fact, their female support of those anti-female systems lent them greater weight, not only in academe but, even more important, in the minds of the people who received them.

Theories struck from the pens of men immersed in the Victorian world-view brought all the familiar distorted misogynistic stereotypes into greater respectability, enshrined now as Science/Truth. At last it was not only experience that taught that women were petty, self-centered, and unprincipled, it was also 'explained' by science. Dr. Freud, for example, had shown how such traits followed from penis envy and castration needs.

Although some of the very most blatant expressions of misogyny have changed (the expression, not the beliefs), the situation is little better today. An anthropology chairman I asked to suggest a faculty person who might teach a course on *Women in Cross-Cultural Perspectives* answered that such a course was possible but unnecessary, because men do all the important work of society. In my salad days, before my raised consciousness, a psychologist to whom I confided that I had difficulty liking 'domineering' men told me that my *problem* was that I had a strong mother, and the solution was to spend more time with 'strong' men and 'traditional' women. (Fortunately, that therapy did not work.) A criminologist colleague recently enlightened me that his 5 years of research into prostitution revealed that women become prostitutes because they hate men. The examples abound *ad nauseum*.

Sexism in the social sciences is absolutely crucial to the formation and character of women's consciousness in contemporary society. The precepts of science have become the theoretical underpinnings of the public serving institutions of our culture—education, social services, or medicine—and through them misogynistic doctrines masquerading as scientific truth are being infused formally into our entire conceptual environment. Every teacher, social worker, nurse, doctor and veterinarian has received the rudiments of 'element,' strong male models, and clear sexual identity distinctions. It is a rare child who escapes Erikson or Piaget, a rare ob-gyn patient who eludes Freud. Women are getting extra doses of distortion, officially sanctioned and therefore extremely powerful and convincing.

The Psych-Hype Ethic

If the formal segment of social science is sexist and destructive, even more so is its popularized offspring, the contemporary culture's philosophy of life, what I call the Psych-Hype ethic, which is actually an anti-ethic.

Since science itself has ascended so high in the contemporary consciousness, it is not surprising that the popular scene, both the material environment and its conceptual framework, should be permeated by scientific or neo-scientific perspectives.

The scientific 'naturalistic' image of humankind, around which is build a whole genre of life philosophies, depicts a creature, temporarily existent on a minor planet, 'just' an animal like any other, subject only to its biological needs and impulses, bumping with difficulty against all other such creatures. All of this, of course, is in one sense very true. What transforms this picture from a basic description of the human condition into a fertile setting for the hype 'now'-ethic is a gross insensitivity to the complexities of such an image, a lack of sophistication in the business of trying to develop value systems out of 'factual data,' and a kind of immature manipulativeness on the part of its proponents.

The premise of the Psych-Hype begins: Hey, man, we're all here only for a short time; tomorrow we may all go up in smoke. So let's not get hung up on the small stuff, and let's get it on. That morality junk we grew up with is a bunch of crap to keep us in line; dump it, because it messes you over. What matters is feeling good and being 'happy.'

The Psych-Hype deepens: You gotta love yourself, man, take care of your needs. Trust your gut feelings, and put yourself first. Do what you want so long as you live and let live, and don't get on anybody else's case. Stay free. Don't let anybody tie you into something rigid, because you gotta stay loose (cool, laid back, mellow) and when something isn't good for you, (i.e., gets difficult—like a job, or a theory, or a relationship) you gotta split. Love everyone. Risk your innermost self and trust people. Don't be demanding. Be tolerant. (Different strokes for different folks.)

Such a vision is extremely seductive at first glance, especially to the young, who are seeking alternatives to the destructive and non-viable elements in our culture. Ostensibly it throws off the shackling inconsistencies and counter-humane tendencies of former theologies and moralities, it calls for freedom, love and trust, it integrates behavioral values with current knowledge and environment, and it liberates what it terms the 'feminine' in culture, the affective, feeling, emotional and spiritual side of experience.

On the surface it looks good. Actually, as it functions among people, the ethic is a hype; subliminaly it carries another message from the one it purports and practices another style, for it is a perfect rationale for exploitative behavior. Psych-Hype groupies tend to be extremely destructive. Demystify the theme to the bare bones of what is really being said and you have: do what you want without too much serious thought; do what feels easy. Love everyone, but keep your distance. 'Risk' your innermost feelings (i.e., reveal your fears), but exchange nothing deeply important with anyone. Don't get obligated; don't 'make demands' or get committed to anything, any place, or any person. Stay loose, that is relaxed, that is *not* feeling, reserved. On the other hand, 'feel,' free your 'feminine,' and let everyone else 'feel,' so long as it remains convenient, unscary, undemanding. Get 'spiritual;' trot off to Arike, TM, or the Andes for a short course in Nirvana, but persevere at nothing sustained. Put your own needs and interests first even when that is not appropriate, for 'obligation' or responsibility is only conformist sham.

Commentators on the life-style have variously called the ethic narcissistic (which it is), childish (which it is), inconsistent and counter-productive (which it is). I call it masculist, Mars all over. Leave aside the fact that its father is the body of theory and value created by (masculist) social science; its direction is decidedly male. Who needs to liberate the 'feminine,' the affective, the spiritual? Women have so much of that we are accused of being 'emotional' and irrational. Who has difficulty resolving the need to trust and risk with the fear of incurring emotional pain? Whose trip is it typically to keep one's distance, stay uncommitted and 'safe,' and yet be intensely loved? The inconsistencies and conflicts are basically male conflicts, and while we might have all sympathy with men's desire to work them out, we should consider the impact this world-view has on today's women.

Although the ethic/life-style poses as an alternative to out-dated, anti-human attitudes, in fact, so far as the concrete effects on women are concerned, it has turned out to be just a continuation of the same old thing.

So far as the 'new,' laid back 'okay' counter-culture young man is concerned, women are still subject to the classic servant/saint—witch/bitch dichotomy. Listen critically to Bob Dylan extolling the praises of his erstwhile lady, running gentle on his mind because she lets him, among other things, leave his sleeping bag rolled up behind her couch while he is off exploring railroad tracks. Bless him, he *will* return. One wonders whether he would so lovingly care for *her* things while she went off a-wandering or whether she *could* go off, his baby on her back. The old tender services of woman to man—waiting, serving, persevering, letting him have his way—are recreated intact in this and countless other pop songs, reminding women of their place just as surely as did the preachers of old.

Enter Jack Nicholson in *Five Easy Pieces*, poor alienated Psych-Hype hero par excellence, searching for himself, unsuccessfully, while he screws, abuses and generally exploits the women he encounters, nothing to stop him. The images of women in the film are classic: cheap waitresses, dykish lesbians, and up-tight spinsters, dumb or neurotic worthless broads with nothing to contribute, nothing to receive. Hip women in the audience are expected to contemplate the 'intense, universal, ramifications' of this 'important film,' to empathize with said hero, and applaud his rebellion. We are not supposed to question the treatment or fate of his female victims. As for the argument that the villain is the man, not the ethic, I suggest we test the tree by the fruit it produces.

From *Easy Rider* to savagely misogynistic rock groups, from T.A. or encounter weekends to a burst of angry young art, we are subjected to the same old stereotypes, insidiously hidden within the folds of a 'new' consciousness, powerfully compelling for appearing so young, rebellious, and 'radical.'

Questioning or challenging this ethic, furthermore, leads as certainly to the judgement of 'bad' woman as did challenging the old ethic, only in the new consciousness, the term *bad* is expressed in different language: hung-up, up-tight, heavy, or 'not okay.' The old lady is a good old broad, so long as she does her bit (serves), does not get heavy (assertive), and stays cool. The woman who does not choose to sleep with a particular man at a particular time can be comfortably put down as hung up, while her more serviceable sisters earn the praise of being game chicks or together, healthy girls. The woman who is not content to make coffee instead of policy is a drag. She who hesitates to play the game whole-heartedly and at once is obviously afraid to 'risk,' not ready for 'community,' needs to 'let go.'

An ethic which is an absence of ethic allows for any useful interpretation, for it is devoid of substance and principle. The new anti-'game' ethic is full of games, but clearly, they are not played equally by all; the pressures are not applied to each in equal strength. The loser, by the way, is said to suffer 'mind-fuck,' an apt phrase, one that women should be particularly sensitive to.

Given women's all-to-readiness to risk, to love, to give, to trust, to be kind and compassionate, to absorb another's pain, it isn't surprising that we are often the losers, that we miss the misogyny and the game, that we allow ourselves to be convinced that it is our responsibility to 'lay back,' both personally and politically. If women are beginning to realize and resist the sexism in traditional social scientific perspectives, very few are prepared for the onslaught of the subliminal woman-hating in what is supposed to be a philosophy for the new generation.

FEMINISM: AN ALTERNATIVE WORLD-VIEW

For a variety of reasons, then, neither traditional religion nor contemporary neo-scientific world-views will work for feminist women, for we are and wish to be both self-affirming and principled people. Furthermore, whether we are conscious of it or not, in our feminist heart of hearts, we have already rejected most of the non-ethics bequeathed to us in favor of values far more meaningful and constructive.

Feminists honor love, community, compassion, beauty, strength, feeling, intelligence, loyalty, and many other things, and they object, in a fundamental and practical way, to barbarity, to pointless pain and cruelty, in essence to the unbalanced and unbalancing supremacy of Mars over Venus. The perhaps utopian communities we envision, the people within them, are fashioned after this configuration of values, and such commitments are clearly discernable in our theories and ideal behavior.

Feminism is humanistic in ways that traditional male-defined 'humanism' often is not; it is highly altruistic and therefore highly motivating and sustaining. Yet very often there is hesitation or even refusal to articulate these commitments, to acknowledge them or identify them with feminism. It is not surprising that after centuries of being saddled by patriarchy with the constricting place of 'keeper of morals,' after being imprisoned on a rather questionable pedestal in the service of all-too-questionable 'moral-values,' after being held in contempt for the very character we were forced to display, that we should cast a wary eye to the talk of 'women's values.'

Yet we are women in many ways unlike the women of the pedestal, and these are values in many ways unlike the ones crammed down our throats. We cannot be led to *or away from* any perspective or behavior that we deem desirable because of masculist expectation, and we cannot allow ourselves to be defined by a reaction to patriarchal schemas anymore than we would be by our submission to them.

Given the spiritual poverty of the patriarchal panorama in which we live, feminist women in particular and society in general need a world-view, a configuration of values, that can help us guide our individual lives. I believe we already have one. All that needs to be done is to develop, crystallize, articulate, and acknowledge it.

COMMENT: SHEILA RUTH

It is interesting that in the ten years since the writing of this paper nothing has changed, except for the worse. Western society is even more spiritually bankrupt than it was in 1978, and a feminist world-view is more crucially needed than ever. What has changed is the awareness of this fact by feminists. 'Metaphysical feminism' is a reality, and works articulating feminist ethics and epistemology are cracking open the ancient and honored fallacies of traditional (patriarchal) philosophies.

The ideas in this article will be elaborated in a work now in progress, Feminist Spirit, *which will be finished early in 1988.*

14

The Visionary Task: Two Sights-Seeing

Janice Raymond

The possibilities of female friendship are founded on vision. Today vision is all the more important to talk about when the fabric of friendship among women seems often rent by disagreements, disruptions and dissensions.

There are many ways to speak about vision. Every meaning of vision, however, is possessed of a certain tension. This tension is linguistically present in its dual dictionary definition, but it is also experienced in any attempt to live out a vision. At one and the same time, vision is 'the exercise of the ordinary faculty of sight' and 'something which is apparently seen otherwise than by ordinary sight.' Another way of phrasing this is to ask how indeed it is possible to see with the ordinary faculty of sight, that is, to maintain a necessary realism about the conditions of existence, *and* to see beyond these conditions, that is, to overleap reality. Or, how do women live in the world as men have defined it while creating the world as women imagine it could be?

An undivided vision is based on two sights-seeing—near- and far-sightedness. In my opinion, this dual vision is the *essential tension* of feminism. Feminists must learn to live in and with that tension. This means not being crushed by the *contrast* between what the world is and the way it ought to be.

The state of female atrocity, or all of the ways in which women have been oppressed, abused, and rendered invisible under patriarchy, presents one view of women. The state of female friendship presents another. If women do not have a vision of female friendship, if women do not come to realize how profound the possibilities are of being for each other, as well as how buried these possibilities have been for us, I believe there is no true realism about the possibilities of feminism itself.

Dual vision poses a tension but not a contradiction. Realism about the conditions of man-made existence must be illuminated by a vision of feminist imagination. And the feminist visionary task must root itself in the real world else, like an electrical charge that has no ground, its energy becomes diffuse and dispersed in all directions (Hynes, 1981).

Hannah Arendt wrote:

'Humanity in the form of fraternity invariably appears historically among persecuted
peoples and enslaved groups . . . it is often accompanied by so radical a loss of the world,
so fearful an atrophy of all the organs with which we orient ourselves in a world common
to ourselves and others and going on to the sense of beauty or taste, with which we love the
world' (Arendt, 1968: 13).

Using the example of sisterhood instead of fraternity, we can apply these words
to the situation of women under patriarchy. Feminist literature, theory and
action have emphasized the ideal of sisterhood as a collective response to
women's oppression. Different schools of feminism have stressed the political
nature of feminism and the necessity to build a strong solidarity of sisterhood.

Indeed sisterhood is powerful, but perhaps not powerful enough when it
comes to the visionary task of which I speak. To resist the state of atrocity
that men have perpetrated against women may generate sisterly solidarity,
but it may not provide anything beyond the communion of resistance. It may
not provide, as Arendt says, '. . . a world common to ourselves and others
and going on to the sense of beauty or taste, with which we love the world,'
and I would add, 'are happy in it.'

At the same time that feminism is a political reality, it is also a way of life
full of struggle, risk *and promise*, the promise of *happiness in this world*.
Organized sisterhood against the conditions of female oppression and the
feminist struggle against all states of female atrocities serve as a powerful
bulwark against the forces and structures of patriarchy. But a purely political
feminism accentuating only conflict and resistance bears too similar a
resemblance to religious eschatologies which would have women believe that
true happiness is achievable only in the life to come.

Women must reject the sentimentality and false vision of patriarchal
romanticism precisely because men have dreamed false dreams for women.
This does not mean that women should reject vision. It does not mean that
women will shape our own vision so that we will not only enable our freedom
but create the conditions of female friendship.

In order to move beyond oppression and the struggle and conflict that
inescapably accompany resistance to oppression, there must be a vision of
'moreness.' Let it not be misunderstood that in advocating a movement
'beyond' struggle, I mean one that leaves the struggle behind. Rather one
revivifies the struggle hopefully by a moreness that enriches female life and
living. Friendship invigorates the reality of feminist resistance with this
moreness. It augments sisterhood with spirit, thereby infusing feminist
solidarity with an energy or vital force of affection.

Affection is a carefully chosen word in my discussion of vision and female
friendship. The more commonly understood meaning of affection is a
feeling, emotion, fondness, attachment and love for one another. There is
another meaning of affection, however, that conveys more than personal

movement of person to person. Affection in this sense means the state of influencing, acting upon, moving and impressing, and of being influenced, acted upon, moved and impressed. I maintain that women who affect other women stimulate response and action; bring about a change in living; stir and arouse emotion, ideas, and activities that defy dichotomies between the personal and political aspects of affection.

Elsewhere, I have suggested a new word, *Gyn/affection*, to describe this personal and political movement of women toward each other (Raymond, 1982). I define Gyn/affection as a synonym for female friendship, but it has a distinct meaning context of its own. The basic meaning of Gyn/affection is that women affect, stir, and arouse each other to full power through friendship. One task of feminism has been to show that 'the personal is political.' Female friendship gives integrity to that claim. The word Gyn/affection is meant to reunite the political and personal aspects of friendship.[1]

Sisterhood signals the kind of political community that is and has to be possible among women who are not necessarily friends. None of us is beyond sisterhood because feminist resistance to all forms of female oppression is ongoing. However, sisterhood and friendship have a richer meaning when they are brought together, that is when political sisterhood proceeds from a shared affection, vision and spirit, and when friendship has a more expansive political effect. We need to create a feminist politics based on friendship, and we need a philosophy of friendship that is realized in personal and socio-economic power for women. A genuine friendship goes beyond the Self's relations with other Selves to the society in which the female Self is allowed to grow. Thus the active and dynamic expression of female friendship involves more than feeling. It means the sharing of a common life and participation in a common world.

Worldliness and friendship must be intimately linked in the lives of women today who live with the basic tension that feminism presents—that of acting in a world that men have fabricated while yearning to go beyond it. Alice Walker has eloquently described the lucidity she experienced when her daughter told her that 'there's a *world* in your eye' (Walker, 1983: 393).[2] There must be a world in each of our eyes.

---

[1] The classical Greek philosophical tradition on friendship taught that friendship had a public nature. It was, in fact, the basis of the *polis*. Aristotle, for example, held that friendship fastened the moral and political fibres of the state together, and that friendship and justice coalesce. Of course, the citizens of this *polis* were all male. Women had no civic status, and therefore friendship *and* politics were affairs between men.

[2] In her essay, 'Beauty: When the other dancer is the Self,' Walker tells the story of her eye, wounded in early girlhood by a copper pellet from her brother's 'BB' gun. She trenchantly portrays years of feeling shame and ugliness, and the changes such feelings produced in a young life against the backdrop of her mother's and sister's refrain, 'You did not change.' Only when her almost three-year old daughter declares 'Mommy, there's a world in your eye' much later in Walker's life does the latter make peace with both her outer and inner vision. Rebecca's insight is no mere metaphor. It has significance for the visionary task of all women. It succinctly states the tension between the near- and far-sightedness with which my essay is concerned.

More than most philosophers, Hannah Arendt has discussed the concept of *worldliness*. Arendt's notion of worldliness, originally analyzed in the context of the history of the Jews and of Judaism, has much pertinence for feminist worldliness.[3] Because women have been the eternal victims of male cruelty and injustice; because survival has been the key focus of female existence and feminist political thought; because women have almost everywhere lacked involvement in and control over the political world in which we have lived; and because the world is man-made, many women have developed a *worldlessness* by *dissociation* from the world. Women in general have assumed this worldlessness almost by default, that is, by virtue of the passive positions most women have been forced into throughout history and in almost every culture. Other women, such as some feminist separatists, have made dissociation from the world a political ideal and reality. The difficulty in both cases is that when women make dissociation the basis for survival or for affinity, many come to conceive of their existence as independent from the rest of the world. Philosophically, this can make women narrow in vision; politically it can make them very vulnerable. Even radical and voluntary dissociation from the world, originally undertaken as a necessary and daring political stance, can culminate in women developing a worm's-eye view of the world and being more exposed to attack then ever before. The more women dissociate from the world, the further removed are women from a definite share of what should be a common world. This is the condition of any group within any diaspora, whether scattered voluntarily or forcibly. A Gyn/affective friendship cannot exist under these conditions of worldlessness.

On the other hand, the dissociation from the world that is not chosen for consciously defined feminist reasons—in other words, that experienced by women in general whose apprehension of the world is derivative from husbands or other men—is reinforced by these women's lack of knowledge that women are a common people. In contrast to other oppressed groups, women do not possess the past of a cohesive and self-conscious community with its own political traditions, philosophical vitality, and history. Or should I say that this past is one that most women know little about? The rootlessness of women in their own group identity contributes more than anything to the worldless, unrealistic, and unpolitical perception that many women have.

Female friendship—not just any kind of friendship—but the Gyn/affection of which I have spoken, is one way to rootedness, to the grasp of reality that women need, and to the experience of our own history. Female friendship, of this nature, orients women to the world, not as persons but *as women*. To paraphrase Arendt, when one is oppressed as a woman, one must respond as a woman. Female friendship cannot arise in a context where

[3] I am enormously indebted to Arendt's development of the typologies of dissociation and assimilation, and have drawn on many of her ideas in this section.

women have 'the great privilege of being unburdened by care for the world' (Arendt, 1978: 27), because Gyn/affection is a political virtue with a political effect.

Any strong and vital reality of female friendship cannot be created within a dissociated enclave of women who have little knowledge of or interest in the wider world. Female friendship is strongest and most affective when it takes shape *within an enclave of women who are located in the world* by virtue of their thinking and action and who do not dissociate from the world nor from each other. The feminist task of 'reconstituting the world,' to use Adrienne Rich's phrase (1978), can only come about in a worldly context and in struggle against the forces that threaten us. Reconstituting the world means reconstituting our lost bonds with our Selves. Strong friendships with strong women shape the world as women imagine it could be, while permitting women to move with worldly integrity in the world men have made.

The opposite of dissociation is *assimilation* to the world. This is another posture that many women have assumed as a location in the world. Assimilation is the stance of a woman who desires to succeed in the world of men and who forgets, or constantly tries to ignore, the fact of her femaleness. The assimilationist strives to lose her female identity, or to go beyond it, or to be regarded *as a person* in a world that grants the status of persons only to men. Realism, survival, worldliness are all acquired by assimilation to the male dominant world on its own terms.

Assimilation spells the end of any strong reality of female friendship even before it begins. For the assimilationist, men and/or male-defined structures are what counts. As women assimilate, they are reluctantly accepted into the ranks of male society mainly as exceptions and only insofar as they do not interfere with the homo-relational bonds[4] that men have established. In order to become part of the male dominant society, women have to believe (or pretend) that they are both persons and women, in the ways that men have defined both for women. What is demanded of assimilationist women by the male dominant world is that they behave in ways that distinguish them from ordinary women, e.g. they are encouraged to be bright, articulate, upwardly mobile professionals, but, at the same time, they must exhibit acceptable manners and modes of man-made femininity, e.g. charming behavior, wearing feminine clothing or make-up. The complicated psychology learned well by the assimilationist woman is how to *be* and *not be* a woman, or how to be the woman that men still recognize as their own creation while avoiding the woman who recognizes her Self and other women who are Self-defined.

---

[4] The fact, prevalence, and power of male homo-relations is disguised by such man-to-man rapport being institutionalized in every aspect of an apparently hetero-relational culture. It is women who bear the burden of living out the hetero-relational imperative. In truth, this is a male homo-relational society that is built on male-male relations, transactions and bonding at all levels. (See again, Raymond, 1982.)

Assimilation fosters private solutions. Everything is reduced to personal self-propulsion. It is a forward self-propulsion that does not depend on authentic Self-definition, Self-movement, and certainly not on Gyn/affection. Thus it locates women in an isolated sphere of action that is built upon a pseudo-individualism. For the assimilationist, the world becomes anywhere that is accessible to any 'rational' person without questioning the boundaries of the terrain or one's location within them. This world becomes an inauthentic one for women not by virtue of the *fact* that it is man-made but because that fact is not doubted and defied.

In a society that is not only hostile to women, but pervaded by what Andrea Dworkin has named woman-hating (1974), it is possible to assimilate only by assimilation to anti-feminism also. Explicitly or implicitly, assimilationists disidentify with other women, whether they are in the company of men or women, or both. The irony of this is that both men and women will always perceive them first and foremost as women. It is unfortunate that assimilationists do not recognize, or ignore, this basic fact, wishing it will go away, when it never will.

The road to assimilation is the road to conformism; a conformism very often creating new stereotypes that assume shape under the guise of liberation and 'new woman' rhetoric, but conformism nonetheless. Thus what we witness is a brand of assimilationism that often displays the verbiage and outward life-style of liberation. Assimilationists frequently view their freedom as an emancipation from the world of traditional women, as well as from the world of feminist women. Sometimes, they exaggerate declarations that they are not feminists, or they take pains to proclaim that they have moved beyond feminism. In the latter case, many women have taken the term *postfeminist* as a badge of maturity. The irony of such disidentifications with feminism is that often assimilationist women engage in quite extraordinary activities that *are* feminist in the sense that these endeavors require unconventional capabilities, courage, determination and persistence. One also thinks of women scientists, truck drivers, welders and presidents of colleges who are not only excellent at what they do, but very often more astute and humane than men in the same fields. However, many of these women, when asked, would deny any kind of woman-identification in a strong sense of the phrase. Assimilationist women want no social roots in any community of women. hetero-relations become their guiding ethic.[5] Their emancipation is their assimilation. Hence assimilation, like dissociation leads to a worldlessness that constricts rather than constructs female friendship.

---

[5] I use the word *hetero-relations* to express the wide range of affective, social, political and economic relations that are ordained between men and women by men. The literature, history, philosophy and science of patriarchy have reinforced the supposedly mythic and primordial relationship of *woman for man* (Raymond, 1982).

In addition to assimilation and dissociation, *victimism* is a third posture that women have assumed toward the world. I use the word to describe women whose primary female or feminist identity seems to be grounded in women's shared state of having been victimized by men. In relationships with each other, such women emphasize their heritage of shared pain, although the ways in which various women have been victimized differs by age, class, race and other factors.

I am not trying to minimize the pain of women's victimization by men in a patriarchal culture. It is extremely important that women understand and act on the full picture of female oppression. However, one-dimensional emphasis on the state of atrocity can have the unintended effect of stressing that what women have in common is only, or mostly, our shared pain. Such a perspective, as reflected in women's relationships, in women's sharing of experiences and in feminist literature and activism, can also create the impression that because women have been historically bound to and by men, that woman is *for man*, no matter how she might have to be forced to do his bidding.

Victimism drives women further away from strong female friendships by obscuring the historical reality that women have been and can be *for women* in other than sisterly suffering ways. Among many feminists, the emphasis on victimism bolsters the conviction that female friendship can only arise negatively, that is, because men are so bad, and/or in reaction to the atrocities promoted by a woman-hating culture. Here female friendship seems spawned by the results of the oppression of women. Thus in a better world, presumably one in which men were good, female friendship might not be necessary.

It is obvious that feminist analysis and action has to be well acquainted with the varieties of male terrorism perpetrated against women. It should be as obvious that a vision of Gyn/affection is a vital counterpart to the reality of women as abused, battered, and killed. Sustained and one-dimensional emphasis on victimism, however, reduces the history of women to an eternal state of atrocity over which women have never exerted any counter control. While it is necessary for women to recognize the prevalence and the longevity of anti-feminism across historical ages and cultural lines, the imperative for such recognition should not lead women to the conclusion that the force of anti-feminism is almost natural and without end—so overwhelming that any will to feminist action is lost.

Ultimately what victimism does is negate Self-definition and Self-responsibility in the world. When women do not define themselves beyond the role of sufferer, then women will settle for the world as men have made it. Victimism means annihilation by the world. It makes women world-sufferers rather than world-makers. It establishes women in the worlds negatively. Women's commonality is reduced to our shared oppression. There is the unstated, and hopefully unintended, premise that feminists might lose their feminist identity if anti-feminism disappeared from the world.

Women have indeed been broken by men. Yet men would make it the case that it is they who have been damaged by women. For example, they blame mothers who gave them too much or too little attention, or wives who dominate or are too dependent. Men have always claimed the wounded role. The overcoming of brokenness by women, as well as the rejection of men as broken creatures in need of women's restorative power, is necessary to the process of female friendship.

Women, as a people, cannot be held together nor move in the world linked primarily by a common enemy or by a negative identity of oppression. Only within the framework of female friendship can a woman live as a woman, working for a reconstituted world, without exhausting herself in the struggle against woman-hating, and without despairing at the enormity of the task.

The issue has been entitled 'Rethinking Sisterhood: Unity in Diversity.' Much emphasis in recent years of feminist writing and activity has been on the necessity to recognize and accept the diversity of women's lives and life experiences. Race, class, age, sexuality have all been in the forefront of this focus. Sometimes diversity has turned divisive. My work is meant to convey a sense of *hope* about the possibilities of friendship among women. It is not a naïve hope, but one that has been tempered by a diversity that has often turned divisive, as well as by a myriad of other obstacles to Gyn/affection that women have experienced in the 'maturity' of feminist movement. All of us, in our relationships with women, have met with a host of stumbling-blocks: unfulfilled expectations, betrayal, lack of real caring and the wall of entrenched differences between friends that becomes insurmountable. Dissociation, assimilation, and victimism have worked in their own ways to erase female friendship.

While it is not my intention to romanticize the subject of female friendship, I am calling for the regaining of hope about the present and future of friendship. This hope is grounded in several things: the reality of friendship that lives in my Self and in other women; the fact that women have been each other's best friends, relatives, faithful companions, emotional and economic supporters, and faithful lovers in all times and places; the continuity and consistency of these woman-to-woman affinities that veritably have formed historical and cultural traditions of female friendship in all epochs and cultures.

Hope is not necesary when things go smoothly, when there is a euphoria about the possibilities of women together as there was in the first stages of this particular wave of feminism. Many women have come through the feminism of the 60s and early 70s jaded, 'turned off,' or disillusioned by other women. Women who 'should have been different' turned out to be 'just as bad, if not worse than men.' Both hope and friendship are easy when things proceed well. Hope is hard to hold but is no less called for when things are not as good as we expected them to be, when sisterhood does not seem as powerful as it once was, or as once we felt it to be. Yet the failures of friendship can never destroy the presence of its past in our lives, and certainly not its possibilities.

A hopeful vision of female friendship is not based on some ontological essence of female energy and vitality that women naturally possess by virtue of a more refined capability for love, caring, and respect for others. Rather it is anchored in the historical and cultural facts of what women have created for our Selves in spite of the state of female atrocity. The obstacles to female friendship and the divisiveness that often attends diversity serve as correctives to a shallow sentimentalism about women's affinities with women. Such difficulties remind us that to ground Gyn/affection in an ontological capability of women to bond with each other is a false optimism that will betray itself.

Misplaced optimism and shallow sentimentalism are two sides of a similar coin. Another position to be avoided is pessimism about women's ability to originate and sustain Gyn/affection. Relationships disintegrate. Violence against women issues in horizontal violence against women issues in horizontal violence among women. Even something like the defeat of the ERA (for the moment) may dull the spirit of women working together to achieve simple and concrete goals for their Selves and other women. In the 'maturity' of feminist life and living, old directions are questioned.

A feminist vision realistically accepts these facts of worldly existence. Seeing with 'the ordinary faculty of sight,' or being in the world as men have created it, is to know that the possession of vision will not make such facts disappear. Yet the same vision when it sees 'something which is apparently seen otherwise than by ordinary sight' knows that such realism is not the whole perspective. Simultaneously two sight-seeing is needed. Vision, near- and far-sightedness, is neither false optimism nor disillusioned pessimism. But vision is imperative to build Gyn/affection. Female friendship alone cannot vanquish the oppression of women, nor can it guarantee that friendship lasts forever. But it can create and sustain hope in the midst of all the factors that militate against Gyn/affection.

REFERENCES

Arendt, Hannah. 1968. *Men in Dark Times*. Harcourt, Brace & World, New York.
Arendt, Hannah. 1978. *The Jew as Pariah: Jewish Identity and Politics in the Modern Age*. Feldman, Ron, ed. Grove Press, New York.
Dworkin, Andrea. 1974. *Woman Hating*. E. P. Dutton, New York.
Hynes, H., Patricia. 1981. *Conversation*. Montague, Massachusetts.
Raymond, Janice G. 1982. A genealogy of female friendship. *Trivia: A Journal of Ideas* I (1): 5–26.

Rich, Adrienne. 1978. Natural resources in *The Dream of A Common Language, Poems 1974-1977*. Norton, New York.
Walker, Alice. 1983. *In Search of Our Mothers' Gardens*. Harcourt Brace Jovanovich, New York.

15

The Feminist University

Berit Ås

I have a vision of a feminist university organized quite differently from universities we know from all over the world today.

Perhaps you will be amazed as I have been to learn that wherever you go, New York, Ann Arbor, Columbia, Missouri, Stockholm, Moscow, Mexico City, Tel-Aviv, Peking, Pyongyang . . . they are all alike . . . organized in faculties and departments with clear cut borderlines.

Like small countries, each of them defends their territories, while they try all the time to take a few resources from their neighbours. Kings and emperors arise, searching for disciples and successors to build the empire more solidly. And Young Men are coming up, firmly trained for years within one discipline.

It occurs in such a way, that when years of training are over, medical doctors can barely see anything else but illnesses, laboratories, big pharmaceutical firms and income opportunities. Lawyers, physicists, engineers and biologists, from one direction and often from one direction only, approach and attack the problem of this new world of ours; problems which are multifactorial, and dangerously complicated.

We might read about teamwork, but rarely do the teams work and survive, because the deep-rooted ideology of the outer world has long ago penetrated university life: compete, compete, compete. This undercurrent works directly against all intended programs.

I have had other experiences since my first years as a research leader. In doing research for transport authorities on accidents, I had to work together with architects, lawyers, road engineers and child educators.

It was necessary to solve a series of problems. In catastrophe research I worked with statisticians, sociologists, nuclear physicians (who were experts on the poisonous character of plutonium), and disaster committees of sociologists and medical people.

In my role in the governmental committee for changing smoking habits in the Norweigian population, I had to work with criminologists, marketing men, the World Health Organization in Geneva . . . and as a writer about consumer economy, traditional economy was never enough: psychology and sociology were potent theoretical instruments to understand consumer behavior.

You may be sure that for years and years I have crumbled when listening to experts talking above each other's heads, using similar words with different meanings, and from such different contexts that the only thing that could save them, was if the problem at hand was solved. That approach has been used in a few interdisciplinary congresses which I have attended, one on women where problems of the greatest importance to us were approached this way—pornography—from the point of view of the investors, from the media, from the legal authorities, social anthropologists and statisticians and Gallup experts. An interdisciplinary approach is necessary in a Feminist University.

Another main purpose is to cure the blind eye in patriarchal institutions. For example: whenever did economists care to provide models for the unpaid work which women do? There are several developed today in Women's Studies, which, for years I have had to struggle to include in general courses of social science.

A few sincere men, like Galbraith (1983) have written about this. A Swedish male statistician has calculated the number of hours spent in unpaid work compared to paid work in Sweden and found that the ratio was 7:6.[1]

But where have sincere sociologists of the past tried to understand how this tremendous workload was a barrier to the ideal of participation in competition?

The need for a feminist university comes from studies conducted all over the world, most often by women. This work shows:

That since universities were constructed by men, *for* men, women will not easily find their place within the structure however competent they are, nor will problems of the greatest importance to women be considered. This means that most of the world's scholars who are competing individuals, trained in well separated fields, will overlook the structure and inadequacies in 'the female world'[2] They will insist that they can understand the complicated issues of the world while staying blind in one eye.

This means that a woman's university like Mount Saint Vincent University

---

[1] Ingelstam, Lars. 1981. In the journal for the Swedish Statistical Bureau, *Velferd* (Welfare). The article is written in Swedish.

[2] Bernard, Jessie. 1981. *The Female World*, a brilliant exploration of a previously unchartered region—the special world of women. The Free Press, New York.

Ås, Berit. 1975. 'On female culture' an attempt to formulate a theory of women's solidarity and action. *Acta Sociologica* 18 (2–3). Special section on women's sociology: *Journal of Scandinavia Sociologist Association*, Munksgaard, Copenhagen.

will change differently from a man's university which is required to go co-educational. When I visited the Mount in the fall of 1979, I was not the least surprised to find that from a male student population of five per cent, came three candidates for the position of president in the student organization.

Returning this year, I am not the least surprised that the Mount has already acquired a strong male image through its student newspaper *The Picaro*, which carries a figurehead (a brand image I would say from the eight years I was in advertising), which gives association of male ideology which in strength will outdo every nice little pamphlet about the Mount being a woman's university. The editorial board is constructed in such a way that the 90 per cent Women Students are very strongly under-represented, and adult women, from continuing education, are practically invisible as journalists, or when it comes to the problems which might be of the greatest importance to them.

Students learn their proper role behavior from role models. I have looked at the composition of the faculty leadership and the head of faculty, and have found that this is, as in most other universities, a proper place for women students to learn that they might, under certain favorable conditions such as a women's university, not only achieve the post as chair in child education and home economics, but in biology and sociology too . . . and . . . as president.

First we have to tackle the problem of myths. Here and now I would not be the least surprised to be told that educational opportunities are similar for boys and girls in many countries. But they are not, and for the following reasons:

If we offer equal opportunities to two groups, one which is strong and has lots of resources, and another which is weak and meets barriers in many ill-defined areas, the strong group will use the opportunities to a greater extent and the gap between the sexes will increase.

Since conditions for women are not visualized and spelled out, and therefore not solved, the male society may blame the victim and comment on her low motivation or lack of fighting spirit.

Secondly: since girls and boys learn their roles and opportunities in contexts, in the institutions of society such as education, the economy, politics, etc., a feminist university must cope with this by taking away the hierarchical structures and hiring women scholars. Fortunately there are wonderful women scholars in mathematics, philosophy, physics; many of these women will tell how brilliantly girls perform if there are not boys in the class. The third and fourth solutions for a feminist university are therefore to do away with the hierarchal structures of scholars and hire, for example, the 23 women in my country who have more faith in their own competence than in the university committees which overlook them.

A fifth task for a feminist university would be to get away from discrimination practices which drain the energy out of women. We may use a concept developed by George Gerbner in an article by Gay Tuchmann[3] 'Women's depiction by the mass media.' Gerbner says that the media bespeaks women's 'symbolic annihilation.' According to Gerbner, just as representation in the media signifies social existence, so too, does under representation, trivialization and condemnation indicate 'symbolic annihilation.' Rather than keeping pace with women, by picturing, for instance, their increased participation in the labour force, the media discredits, isolates and undercuts. They discuss 'women's libbers,' present issues of liberation on shows which are distasteful to a general audience and muddy the distinction between women's liberation and sexual liberation and get away with it.

Let me take two examples from the Mount which have to do with the effect of such harassment.

Remember, we talked about myths and symbolic annihilation and the impact these two important areas have on the construction of a feminist university. There is a myth in the world that all people are getting a better education. This is wrong. United Nations publications from 1980[4] and 1981[5] report consistently that the gap between boys and girls in educational opportunities in primary schools as well as in secondary schools is widening in all countries. And no instruments which are forceful are built to counteract these developments. (Another good reason for having a feminist university.)

Another myth tells us that conditions for women are improving in all the nations of the world. The truth is that the conditions for most women in most countries, independent of the country's economic system is worsening. Yet women do between 66 and 75 per cent of all the work in the world.[6]

A myth says that competence determines the position of a person in a hierarchy. Research findings on all levels of exams show that a paper with girl's name on it will get a lower grade that the same paper or thesis, delivered with a boy's name on it.

A study by Philip Goldberg (1974) many years ago now, shows this, and has been replicated in several class levels by Dale Spender (1980) by Norwe-

---

[3] Tuchman, Gaye. 1982. Women's depictions by the mass media. *Signs* 4 (2): 528–543.

[4] Deble, Isabelle. 1980. *The School Education of Girls*. Published by the United Nations Educational, Scientific and Cultural Organization, 7 place de Fonterroy, 75700, Paris, France.

[5] Dupont, Beatrice. 1981. *Unequal Education: A Study of Sex Differences in Secondary-School Curricula*. United Nations Educational, Scientific and Cultural Organization, France.

[6] The former Foreign Minister of Sweden, Karin Soder, quoted the figure of 75 per cent at the Center Party's convention in 1976. The Finnish professor Elina Haavia-Manilla of the University of Helsinki reported at the Moscow Conference of Political Scientists in August 1979, that the U.N. had recently issued the figures of 66 per cent (the amount of women's work in the world), 10 per cent (the size of the total salary volume given to women for their work) and 1 per cent (women's part of all private property).

gian social scientists[7] and by Swedes, evaluating similar official documents from the authorities, signed by women and men.[8]

Adult men and women, teachers and journalists (Tuchman, 1982) are prejudiced in the same ways, which means that not only do we learn our sex-roles, but also their legitimacy (Payne, 1980). We learn it so well that confronted with the fact that boys in coed classes take about two-thirds of the teacher's attention, the teacher, as well as the students, perceive it as if girls and boys are treated similarly.

If girls get as much as 40 per cent of the attention, boys usually complain (Spender, 1982). Jon Elliot had the feeling that girls did not ask questions to the same extent as boys, neither did they give information or elaborate extensively on the topics, the way boys did. When he went over the discussions he found that when a girl tries to take the floor, the boys stop her immediately, try to silence her and ridicule what she said.

'It is,' Jon Elliot says, 'the boys who determine the rules by which all have to behave (quoted in Spender, 1982). Boys are willing to make degrading remarks about women's sexuality, girls and female teachers. This very important research material is seldom taught in universities, neither are the findings from other areas of women's experience. These findings should be taught to the women they concern, so that they can have some tools for recovering their dignity and self-respect. This would be part of the curricula of a women's university.

Boys are seldom punished for this behavior. Teachers say that boys will outgrow it—they are going through a phase in their development (Spender, 1982).

Girls learn early the hidden messages in all general education—that they have to wait (Spender, 1978) and that boys do not like them, and that this is legitimate.

Men need women as a negative reference group and are not willing to perceive women in roles different from the sex object and/or as wife and mother.

There is a strong tendency in all male institutions (I am not claiming that every man does this!) to show this degrading behavior against women. But it is adjusted subtly to the women involved.

Navy personnel may tell—as male members of fraternities sometimes do—that in foreign ports they gather all the ugliest women to participate in a 'beauty contest' on board, the crippled, blind, or sick, to elect the Pig of the Port. Indian or white men may rape young Indian women, as we have been

[7] Utne, Birgit Brock and Runa Haukaa. 1980. *Kunuskap uten makt* (Knowledge without power): *Kvinner som larere og elever* (Women as teachers and students). The University Press, Oslo (written in Norwegian).
[8] Einarsson. January 1981. *Språk och kön i skolan.* (Language and Sex in School) report. Lärarhögskolan i Mälmo, Sweden (written in Swedish).

reading, without facing severe penalties. This extreme violence toward women must be treated as a severe dysfunction of society.

At this university (the Mount) it may take the form which I saw a few weeks ago. A nice poster in one of the elevators at Seton Academic Centre, announced the coming of a woman singer. It had been decorated with a mustache. Symbolic disabling has not yet been seen on men represented on posters. If women are very competent they must be very masculine. Or they must be ugly. So, on a poster of Heather Bishop her teeth have been blackened. The Norwegian female leader of the Labour Party had this done to her picture during the last election. And then finally, the announcement of this lecture. Again in the elevator at Seton. The university emblem had two breasts drawn over it, over my name.

Sexual annihilation means draining women of competence, of self reliance and dignity and telling them; 'You are just a sex symbol.'

I do not accept it. Not for myself, for my women students, for my daughters or for all small girls in this world. So the feminist university will have some very particular features.

It will be for all women of all ages and with education backgrounds from primary schools to doctoral degrees. To increase the confidence of women who have their self respect totally destroyed, the university will provide education and research facilities and production opportunities for those women who need to work their earlier experiences out of their systems. Female Danish scholars have suggested that we build on Paolo Freire's educational traditions, developed among illiterate people in Latin America (Freire, 1971).

Men may attend the feminist university for certain periods if they accept as a working hypothesis that: possibly the whole world would change if women, one day, in this world and in the future of men's minds, become persons.

The feminist university is now searching for sites, preferably in areas where women have a strong historical heritage. It will build upon an ideology of giving supressed people their dignity once again. It will organize faculty and administration in a new way learned from experiments in the Quaker communities, on board ships, from women refugees and smaller schools, in a way characterized by multiple leadership and frequent rotation of jobs.

The teaching goals are to provide education and research facilities and production opportunities for women of all ages and of different educational backgrounds.

The curricula, issuing from the need to liberate women of different nations, classes and races, should build, in addition to conventional know-ledge, on results available from Women's Studies, cross-cultural and in an interdisciplinary context.[9]

[9] Summary of paper to be presented at a Canadian Conference: *The Need for an International Feminist University*. June 1984.

198   BERIT ÅS

REFERENCES

Elliot, Jon. 1974. Sex Role Constraints on Freedom of Discussion: A neglected reality of the classroom. *The New Era*, reprinted in *Spare Rib*, 27.
Freire, Paolo. 1971. *Pedagogy of the Oppressed*. Herder & Herder, New York.
Galbraith, John Kenneth. 1983. The economics of the American housewife. *Atlantic Monthly* **232** (2).
Goldberg, Phillip. 1974. Are women prejudiced against women? In Stacey, Judith *et al.,* (eds), pp. 37–42, *And Jill Came Tumbling After: Sexism in American Education*. Dell Publishing, New York.
Payne, Irene. 1980. Sexist ideology and education. In Spender, Dale and Elizabeth Sarah, (eds), pp. 32–38, *Learning to Lose: Sexism and Education*. The Women's Press, London.
Spender, Dale. 1978. Don't talk, listen! The *Times Educational Supplement*, November 3.
Spender Dale. 1980. *Man Made Language*. Routledge & Kegan Paul, London.
Spender, Dale. 1982. *Invisible Woman: The Schooling Scandal*. Writers & Readers, London.
Tuchman, Gaye. 1982. Women's depiction by the mass media. *Signs* **4** (2): 528–543.

16

Compulsory Heterosexuality and Psych/atrophy: Some Thoughts on Lesbian Feminist Theory

Betsy Ettorre[1]

INTRODUCTION

In popular feminist folklore, there is an expression, 'A woman without a man is like a fish without a bicycle.' As an introduction to this paper and as an addition to this folklore, one might also say: 'Lesbianism without psychiatry is like a cat without a skateboard' or 'Lesbianism without psychiatry is like ontology without motor accidents.'

Lesbians and psychiatrists are as different as chalk and cheese and yet both groups of individuals live in a society where the 'institutional and ideological domination of heterosexuality is a fundamental part of male supremacy' (Bunch, 1978: 180). For the majority, if not all psychiatrists, heterosexism, the institutional and ideological domination of heterosexuality as a fundamental part of male supremacy, is a necessary given, while for lesbian feminists, heterosexism with its functionaries, like psychiatrists who serve to eradicate the lesbian world, is indeed *problematic*. In other words, if lesbians are feminists, their view of the heterosexist world is most probably totally different from—and furthermore *opposed* to—the view psychiatrists have of

[1] Betsy Ettorre is a research sociologist at the Addiction Research Unit, Institute of Psychiatry, London. She has lectured throughout Britain on lesbianism and is best known for her work *Lesbians, Women and Society* (Routledge & Kegan Paul, 1980). While her theoretical interests are rooted primarily in lesbian feminism, she has also developed an interest in the issue of 'women and dependency.' She is currently working on a policy study of the overall provision for alcoholism treatment within the mental health services in Great Britain and is involved in organizing a London based survey on women consumers and their relation to drug and alcohol agencies.

them as lesbians, as well as the view psychiatrists have of the heterosexist world.

On the one hand, lesbian feminists would see themselves as women—identified, self-affirming and self-loving women. Lesbian feminists would assert that their primary identification with women gives them energy and that lesbians develop a positive sense of themselves by looking to other women for support rather than to men or (in relation to heterosexist structures) the family. On the other hand, psychiatrists would probably argue (whether consciously or unconsciously) that most 'normal' women (thus excluding lesbians) wouldn't be able to have that 'normal' level of self-love or self-affirmation. As Mary Daly suggests, to the extent that 'They [psychiatrists] are successful, their female patients are paralyzed by a lack of Self-Respect, for these doctors engender the debilitating disease of self-hatred' (Daly, 1979: 230). Furthermore, psychiatrists see lesbianism as a 'disease entity.' They view lesbians as 'over sexed,' 'wanting to be men,' 'penis envious,' 'unfeminine,' etc.[2]

The time has come for psychiatrists' misconceptions about women, particularly lesbians, and for anti-feminist psychiatric practice to end. Littlewood and Lipsedge (1982) point out that a recent survey on psychiatrists in Great Britain reveals that psychiatrists regard themselves as more radical than other doctors, especially in the areas of religion and politics. Why don't psychiatrists take this 'self-assumed radicalism' into the area of lesbianism? The answer is most probably not that psychiatrists are unable to change their attitudes towards lesbians but they don't want to change. Psychiatrists won't change their attitudes because assuming a feminist or radical definition of lesbianism would challenge the whole patriarchal, heterosexist, clinical world from which their power emerges. Psychiatrists have a vested interest in helping to maintain conflicting social images and social definitions between what is 'normal' and what is 'pathological.' The maintenance of the conflict around these issues is the heart of the psychiatric profession—it is how it beats! For instance it is in psychiatrists' interest to have the power to say not only *what* is 'normal woman' or who is a pathological' or 'deviant' woman but also what is normal sex for both men and women. Psychiatrists have the moral responsibility to control certain forms of social weakness, i.e., mental illness, and apparent causes for social vulnerability, i.e., depression, neurosis, etc. This responsibility more often than not extends to women help-seekers.[3] The Black Health Workers and Patients Group tells us that psychiatrists as 'the guardians of morals'

[2] In 1976, I did a review of literature of the work of psychiatrists and psychoanalysts from the years 1920–1976. At that time, I found a plethora of negative attitudes held by psychiatrists towards lesbians. See Ettorre, 1978, especially pp. 10–48.

[3] For an illuminating expose of women's relationship to seeking help within the system of mental health care, see Phyllis Chesler (1972). Her discussion on lesbians is most definitely set within a feminist framework (pp. 182–205).

established wide ranging theories about women, for example concerning 'their small brains and aptitude for hysteria' (The Black Health Workers and Patients Group, 1983: 53). Within this oppressive view, lesbians were seen to be 'moral degenerates' (Fassler, 1979: 239).

One of the strengths lesbians have in relation to psychiatry is that historically, the lesbian world existed long before the profession of psychiatry ever began. Over the last years, feminist writers have been gradually unearthing a rich lesbian heritage.[4] As more lesbians become aware of their unique heritage, they are able to discover, what Mary Daly calls, 'the Sister Self,' the original intuition of integrity. As Lesbians truly search for their 'Sister Selves,' they find that 'Remembering is the Remedy' (Daly, 1979: 338) and that psychiatrists have never been and are not necessary for lesbian liberation.

A LESBIAN FEMINIST VIEW OF PSYCHIATRY AND COMPULSORY HETEROSEXUALITY

The purpose of this paper is to present a lesbian feminist critique of psychiatry. It could be called a meta-patriarchal journeying into a field which 'confronts old molds/models of question—asking by being itself an other way of thinking/speaking' (Daly, 1979: xiii).

Before journeying on, let us ask ourselves the question: 'What *is* lesbian feminist theory?' In my view feminist theory is a contemporary political theory which extends the traditional feminist analysis of sexual politics to an analysis of sexuality itself, as it is structured into our society today. Furthermore, lesbian feminist theory as a critique of male supremacy and heterosexism is 'a perspective, analysis and commitment that can be embraced by anyone gay or straight, female or male, etc.' (Bunch, 1978: 180–181). Two areas in the development of lesbian theory are of particular importance:

(1) that the initial ideas of lesbian feminist theory can be found in early radical feminist writing.
(2) that the current basis of lesbian feminist theory is represented by what is termed the 'Compulsory Heterosexual Perspective.'

Firstly, early radical thinking is the belief that patriarchy is the primary system of power relations which not only reflects but also structures human life as we know it and experience it today. Adrienne Rich gives us a clear picture of the roots of the radical feminist critique of patriarchy when she says:

'For the first time in history a pervasive recognition is developing that the patriarchal system cannot answer for itself; that it is not inevitable, that it is transitory; and that the

---

[4] See especially Lillian Faderman (1981) which gives a detailed account of lesbian friendship over distinct historical periods.

cross-cultural, global determination of women by men can no longer be either denied or defended. When we acknowledge this, we tear open the relationship at the core of all power-relationships, a tangle of lust, violence, possession, fear, conscious longing, unconscious hostility, sentiment: the sexual understructure of social and political forms. For the first time we are in a position to look around at the kingdom of the Fathers and take its measure. What we see is the one system which recorded civilization has never actively challenged and which has been so universal as to be a law of nature'. (Rich, 1976: 39).

For Rich, as for many feminists, patriarchy is experienced as the sexual understructure of all social and political forms in society. Patriarchy saturates *all* of human life. Within this view, biology and socialization become the source of sexual oppression.

Secondly, the current strain of lesbian feminist theory, the 'Compulsory Heterosexuality Perspective,' has a critical focus on the institution and ideology of heterosexuality itself. This perspective grew from dissatisfaction with the somewhat limiting, one dimensional analysis of radical feminism and this perspective is outlined in the work of Charlotte Bunch (1978) and the article 'Compulsory heterosexuality and the lesbian existence' by Adrienne Rich (1979).

In an article entitled 'Lesbian feminist theory,' Katherine Arnup presents a clear synthesis of the ideas behind the compulsory heterosexuality perspective. She says:

'The heterosexism perspective challenges the entire notion of choice in the area of sexuality. No longer can we talk about lesbianism as if it were the innate sexual orientation of a small number of women. Neither can we talk about heterosexuality as if it were the normal mode of relating. Rather we must see heterosexuality itself as a political institution which has been maintained through a whole cluster of forces within which women have been convinced that marriage and a sexual orientation towards men are inevitable if unsatisfying or oppressive components of their lives.' (Arnup, 1983: 54).

Charlotte Bunch reflects a similar analysis when she states:

'All of society's institutions are based on the assumption that every woman either is or wants to be bonded to a man both economically and emotionally and that she depend on the idea that heterosexuality is both the only and natural and superior form of human sexuality' (Bunch, 1978: 180).

The concept of compulsory heterosexuality has broad implications for feminist theory because it enables all women to explore the pressures under which we all function in our day to day lives. It helps us to examine the forces which operate to determine our sexuality. Let us continue on our journey by, first, clarifying the feminist definitions of lesbianism and psychiatry and then by moving on to a discussion of the implications of these definitions in contemporary society.

LESBIANISM AND PSYCHIATRY: SAPPHIC MEANINGS VS PSYCH/ATROPHY

For feminists, the words lesbianism and psychiatry need to be redefined in non-traditional ways in the light of our experiences as women. The word 'lesbianism' rather than relating to a strictly sexual meaning, refers to an all-encompassing view of women as women-identified or as women creating their Female Selves. Lesbianism is, in reality, a 'social vehicle' for women; a feminist process whereby women gather a greater sense of self/sensual awareness through the process of self-healing or self-affirmation. The actual root meaning of the word, 'Lesbian,' comes from the Greek word 'Lesbios,' meaning 'one of the island of Lesbos' and the *English Oxford Dictionary* also includes the meaning 'from the home of Sappho.'[5] Sappho was a well-known Greek poetess who lived during the 3rd century B.C. on the island of Lesbos in the Aegean Sea. Historically, Sappho has been seen as a lesbian who herself advocated lesbianism as a way of life for women. Whether or not this is true, Sappho set up a sexually-segregated community of women on Lesbos and she, furthermore, helped to stir these women's imaginations to a heightened awareness of their sensuality. One feminist writer, Judith P. Hallett, argues that an understanding of Sappho and her work has to be seen within the historical context from which she emerged. Hallett says:

> 'That Sappho's verses were basically intended as public, rather than personal, statements, that they aimed at instilling sensual awareness and sexual self-esteem in young women, and that even those written in the firstperson may not express her own feelings seem more obvious if we consider other examples of poetry from a similar social and cultural milieu written in a generation prior to hers' (Hallett, 1976: 461).

It appears that Sappho's influence had more to do with stirring women's sensuality than with advocating traditional lesbian practice and it is a great pity that this influence has been obscured in history. Blanche Wiesen Cook whose work focuses on the cultural tradition of intense female bonding, provides us with a possible reason for the obscuring of Sappho's *real* influence. She says:

> 'Entirely obscured from view were the many networks, both contemporary and historical, of egalitarian and nurturing friendships among creative and publicly active women. Like the historical denial of women's history generally the historical denial of the vast range of women loving women has not been an accident. . . . In a hostile world in which women are not supposed to survive except in relation with and in service to men, entire communities of women were simply erased. History tends to bury what it seeks to reject.' (Wiesen Cook, 1979: 720).

In other words although history bestowed a certain level of notoriety upon Sappho, it falsely reports that she was an advocator of traditional lesbianism rather than a stirrer of women's feminist potential. Perhaps, the creation of a women's community in the 3rd century B.C. was an all too threatening recognition for the male world. Nevertheless, as lesbianism becomes defined as a 'choice women make in response to a sexist society' (Weitz, 1984), or as women creating their Female Selves, traditional definitions may disappear and perhaps, all women will see that what we need is not only an end to lesbian oppression but also the freedom of choice for all women.

[5] For these meanings, I found more extensive explanations in the *English Oxford Dictionary* than in the *Merriam Webster Dictionary*.

Within a feminist analysis, the term, 'psychiatry' is 'Amazingly Deceptive' in relation to women. Psychiatry comes from a coupling of the Greek words, psyche and iatros, which literally mean 'soul healer.' Since feminist theory asserts that only women can heal themselves, the idea of psychiatrists as being soul healers is meaningless. As Mary Daly states:

> 'The reign of healing is within the Self, within the Selves seen by the Self and seeing the Self. The remedy is not to turn back but to become the healing environment' (Daly, 1978: 339).

In a similar vein of thought, Nor Hall emphasizes how healing for women must always be sought in the wound itself. She suggests that the female void cannot be cured by conjunction with the male, but rather by internal conjunction, by an integration of its own parts, by a remembering or a putting back together of the mother–daughter body (Hall, 1980: 68).

Abandoning the term psychiatry, feminists may find it useful to use the word Psych/Atrophy as a more accurate term. In Psych/Atrophy we have a term which exposes how traditional psychiatry (and psychiatrists, traditionally, as what Daly would call, 'mind gynaecologists') attempt to invade the Psyche or souls of women. Our new term for psychiatry. Psych/Atrophy comes from the Greek words, psyche and atrophia, meaning 'soul-atrophy' or 'not giving food to the soul.' Within a feminist framework, this root or radical definition of Psych/Atrophy provides us with a clearer understanding of how the profession of 'mind gynecologists' or traditional psychiatrists operate in relation to women who search for their Female Selves and furthermore, how this profession obstructs, opposes and contradicts the feminist process of Self-Healing.

Thus far, this paper has been an excavation of the Unknown as well as exposition of the relevant areas of lesbian feminist theory. Let us journey on to some of the real conflicts between lesbians and psychiatrists. More specifically, to understand why and how lesbians are no longer psychiatric scapegoats but Revolting Hags (as Daly would suggest). Examining how lesbians are Revolting Hags *vis-a-vis* psychiatrists as 'soul starvers,' I propose to examine five inter-related areas of lesbian feminist practice. They include: Discarding the 'sexual' label (1); Resisting Reversal (2); Erasing the Victim Role (3); Social Change not Individual Solutions (4); Psychic Deliverance and Amazonian Asylum (5).

1. Discarding the 'sexual' label

Many pre-feminist lesbians in search of an understanding of themselves sought out various psychological and psychiatric theories whether in their original or popularized versions. Very quickly, they discovered that lesbians (they) were 'the medical psychiatric scapegoats and that every homosexual act was a symptom of mental disease' (Szasz, 1971: 272). Gradually lesbians discarded the 'disease' label imposed upon them by the psychiatric profession and they (lesbians) attempted to find a meaningful frame of reference for life in a hostile society. It is interesting to know that even today the International Classification of Diseases which is used as the primary means of justifying psychiatric diagnoses views lesbianism as a sexual deviation and disorder. Lesbianism is defined as a sexual deviation because 'it is an abnormal sexual inclination or behaviour . . . which does not serve approved social and biological purposes' (World Health Organization, 1977: 196). For psychiatrists today, lesbianism is defined and diagnosed as a sexual disorder or a mental disease. In recent years, this view has been challenged by lesbian feminist theorists and they argue that there are probably more similarities between heterosexual women and lesbians than meet the eyes of psychiatrists. Indeed in lesbian works, such as Tanner's, *The Lesbian Couple* (1978), Wolf's, *The Lesbian Community* (1979), Klaich's *Woman plus Woman*, Krieger's *The Mirror Dance* (1983), Martin and Lyon's *Lesbian/Women* (1972), Abbott and Love's, *Sappho was a Right-on Woman* (1972), Stewart-Park and Cassidy's *We're Here* (1977), as well as my own work *Lesbians, Women and Society* (1980), we see how within feminist theory, contemporary lesbians have shifted their definition of lesbianism from a sexually focused one to a women-focused one and placed it in a socio-political context.

As more lesbians challenge the traditional view of psychiatrists, they break down the false polarization which exists between heterosexual women and lesbians. As Mary Daly suggests that Revolting Hags become 'disposed and enspirited . . . they create themselves and new space: semantic, cognitive, symbolic, psychic and physical spaces' (Daly, 1979: 340). In effect, lesbians have discarded the 'sexual' label pinned upon them by psychiatrists. This process of discarding the 'sexual' is really a strategy to combat male mystification through the false polarization of women by dividing them (women) into heterosexual and lesbian 'sexual' categories.

2. Resisting reversal

Reversal, like false polarization, is another form of male mystification and psychiatrists as enactors (par excellence) of this male supremacy role tell lesbians that they (lesbians) really 'want to be men,' not (as proven by the experiences of lesbians) that they are women and closely bound to women. This process of covering up the real 'nature' of lesbianism and reversing the phenomenon is discussed in Faderman's expose of the effects of Kraft-Ebing's work on the writings of Radclyffe Hall.[6]

---

[6] Faderman (1981) refers specifically to Hall's *The Well of Loneliness* which was published in Great Britain in 1928. It is interesting to note that *The Well of Loneliness* became an infamous novel and was banned by the English courts for over 30 years. See Brittain (1968) for a discussion of the case of Radclyffe Hall.

Faderman tells us that Kraft-Ebing was a 19th-century sexologist and psychiatrist whose work, *Psychopathia Sexualis*, published in 1882, put forward the idea that if a woman loves a woman, she must really be a man. These ideas had a profound effect upon Radclyffe Hall who was 'responsible for bringing the congenitalist theories to popular fiction and thereby disseminating them widely after they were no longer the most accepted theories among medical men' (Faderman, 1981: 317). Although there are probably a minority of psychiatrists who would uphold the congenital invert theory today,[7] many psychiatrists believe that lesbians want to be men (which is a variation on the congenital inversion theme). By mobilizing their practice around these ideas, psychiatrists attempt to kill the Female Spirit or Female Selves in Lesbians. In addition, they play out their role of 'thought or mind police' (Heather, 1976: 100) in relation to women. Lesbian feminist theory combats this 'mind policing' work of psychiatrists by seeing psychiatrists' moralizing as a form of lesbian oppression and furthermore, by seeing 'lesbian oppression in many ways as emblematic of women's oppression' (Arnup, 1983: 55). As Bunch tells us:

> 'We need to discover what lesbian consciousness means for any woman just as we struggle to understand what class or race consciousness means for women of any race or class'. (Bunch, 1975: 52).

3. Erasing the victim role

In their discussion of ethnic minorities and psychiatry in Great Britain, Littlewood and Lipsedge (both psychiatrists) make some telling comments about the origins of the psychiatric profession. They say:

> 'The modern psychiatrist is a descendant of the 19th Century mental asylum keeper. . . . He was a paternalistic figure whose popular image has been described as both divine and satanic: divine because of his power over the sick and satanic because of his demonic knowledge' (Littlewood and Lipsedge, 1982: 22).

These authors go on to say that the physical coercion of the pre-psychiatric hospital (which Scull calls museums of madness)[8] was replaced by moral authority: the ideal psychiatrist was a 'father to his children.'

As we see, women right from the beginning of the psychiatric era have been at a disadvantage in relation to psychiatrists who were expected to be superior beings—either gods or devils. These ideas expose the real nature of psychiatry as Psych/Atrophy. Psych/Atrophy in practice is a male-instigated degradation of victims and, as Daly points out, 'within this type of degradation, there is a hidden paradigm, the Female as Other, as Victim' (Daly, 1979: 332).

---

[7] Yes, they exist. I had a personal experience of meeting with them at a conference on sexual behavior in Liverpool, England in April 1979.

[8] Scull's analysis of the psychiatric profession is not feminist based. But he does present some critical ideas on the organization of insanity within oppressive structures. His *Museums of Madness* (1974) exposes some of the inhumanity which existed in the 'pre-psychiatric' era.

In an article entitled 'The rapists—lesbians and psychiatrists,' an anonymous lesbian feminist, writing in the feminist classic, *Our Bodies, Ourselves* (Boston Women's Health Book Collective, 1971: 63–65), described how she was placed in a Victim Role by psychiatrists. She states:

> 'Doctors told me I was utterly dependent, had anxiety neurosis, was a borderline schizophrenic and had a poor prognosis.' (Anonymous, 1971: 64).

Recalling how she had been treated, she offers two main reasons for this negative treatment by psychiatrists: (a) she failed to conform to psychiatrist's idea of what a woman's life should be and (b) she believed more in herself than in their (psychiatrist's) theories about her.

In a similar way of thinking, Jill Johnston in *Lesbian Nation* discusses that the emphasis in psychiatry for lesbians is on 'conformity and adjustment rather than Liberation' (Johnston, 1973: 189). By victimizing lesbian women, psychiatry favors individual solutions rather than social change and by inhibiting this change, psychiatrists attempt to control and thwart lesbian consciousness among women.

4. Social change not individual solutions

Earlier in this paper I have implied that by placing lesbians in the victim role as 'non-conformist,' 'sick' and 'deviant women,' psychiatrists inhibit social change for women and, in turn, for society at large. Psychiatrists are not only agents of the compulsory heterosexist order but also agents of social control.[9] In this context it is interesting to note that in a recent editorial in the *British Journal of Addiction* it is stated that 'psychiatrists should be social change agents' (by another psychiatrist of professorial distinction) (Editorial, 1983:3). This type of thinking is totally 'out of sync' or out of 'Psyche' within lesbian feminist theory as well as within any critical social theory. Most psychiatrists have a vested interest in maintaining the status quo and the established social order which is patriarchal. Clearly, the purpose of any social control agent, such as a psychiatrist, is to stabilize the kind of society which now exists and thus prevent it from changing. Heather describes how psychiatry contributes to this effort in three particular ways:

> '(a). Psychiatry serves the industrial machine by repairing its broken parts and putting them back, literally, into working order. In wartime, psychiatry's task is to get the shell-shocked back to the front line; in peace time it has the analogous task of returning the producer/consumer to the work bench, the kitchen sink and the supermarket.
>
> (b). Psychiatry re-inforces the increasingly restricted range of human possibilities

[9] There have been a number of theories highlighting this aspect of psychiatry. One of the clearest explanations of this theory is presented by Peter Conrad (1981) where he outlines his ideas on how the medical profession attempts to define and control deviant behavior with medical means and in the name of health. See also Sedgewick (1982) for a similar point of view.

demanded by society by legislating what is normal, sane, allowable behaviour and what is not.

(c). Psychiatry serves the function of disguising the casualties of a harsh competitive and callous social system by portraying them as consequences of individual psychopathology.' (Heather, 1976: 101)

As we can see, to imply that psychiatrists are social change agents rather than agents of social control is not only misleading but also a distortion of their real social function. Within lesbian feminist theory, psychiatrists could never be viewed as social change agents and if so, only when compulsory heterosexuality and male supremacy is totally eliminated from society. At that time, there would be neither a need for the type of mind control which psychiatrists attempt to enact or the need for a rigid 'hanging on' to the established social order. Both of these needs characterize psychiatrists current role in society.

5. Psychic deliverance and Amazonian asylum

From the above discussion, we have seen that within a lesbian feminist framework psychiatrists fail in their role as 'soul healers' and that, in effect, they have been conniving to repress and depress Female Being and are indeed perpetuating Psych/Atrophy.

To the degree that lesbians have been possessed by the spirit of patriarchy, they have been slowly expiring psychically. It is not surprising that lesbians may become 'dispirited' that is 'depressed, downcast, lacking independent vigor and forcefulness' (Daly, 1979: 340) in the face of Psych/Atrophy.

Lesbians not only need to heal themselves but also to deliver themselves from the debilitating images which, although officially mostly outdated today live on in people's minds and have a profound psychic effect. One of these images is the image of 'Evil,' which as Faderman points out, was perpetuated by the non-aesthete writers of the 19th century such as Adolphe Belot, Alphonse Daudet, Emile Zola, Catulle Mendes and Guy de Maupassant (Faderman. 1981: 277-294).

That literary figures colluded with the early psychiatric profession to associate lesbianism with vice and unmitigated evil gave strength to that definition and to those images which have their vestiges in the contemporary world of pornography.

Lesbians as Victims of Psych/Atrophy could find real asylum neither in psychiatric asylums nor in patriarchal society hostile to their needs. The current response to psychiatry has been an active resistance to psychiatry's negative images of women. For all women, both lesbian and heterosexual, this response has been a self-healing and self-affirming process which is based on self-love and *not* the internalization of self-hate. Lesbian Feminist Theory enables many lesbians to experience what I would term, the Fury of the Rage, as a real Amazonian Asylum. This type of Asylum of resistance and rage has been built up over centuries of being locked up, mis-labeled, burned as witches and having one's Spirit possessed and dissected by the psychiatric profession or their precursors. Once the rage is experienced, lesbians are no longer powerless, they create their own Asylum and they actively challenge the heterosexist structure and practices of society.

CONCLUSION: FINDING A REASON?

My purpose in writing this paper has been to re-define or to re-search the concepts of lesbianism and psychiatry within lesbian feminist theory and to present these concepts within a lesbian feminist critique of Psych/Atrophy. I have examined the roots of lesbian feminist theory in an attempt to understand how compulsory heterosexuality (the view that heterosexuality is both the only natural and superior form of human behavior for men and women) establishes the foundation for a lesbian feminist critique. Also, I have preposed to view lesbian feminist practice in relation to psychiatry and in relation to five strategies which relate to how Psych/Atrophy mystifies the experience of all women as Victim or the Other.

In conclusion. I would like to share a quote I found in Virginia Woolf's *Moments of Being*. In this moving verse, Woolf describes her recollections of one of many intense experiences in her life when she sees, in a profound sense, a flower bed near to her front door.

> 'When I said about the flower, "That is the whole," I felt that I had made a discovery that I had put away in my mind something that I should go back to, to turn over and explore. It strikes me now that this was a profound difference. It was the difference in the first place between despair and satisfaction this difference I think arose from the fact that I was quite unable to deal with the pain of discovering that people hurt each other; that a man I had seen had killed himself. The sense of horror held me powerless. But in the case of the flower I found a reason; and was thus able to deal with the sensation. I was not powerless. I was conscious—if only at a distance that I should in time explain it.' (Woolf, 1976: 83).

Over time, many lesbians have come to realize that they/we are not powerless but conscious. Whether or not the lives of particular lesbians have merged with the creation of unreason, we have found a reason. I think it is time psychiatrists accept this reason.

REFERENCES

Abbott, Sidney and Love, Barbara. 1982. *Sappho was a Right-on Woman*. Stein & Day, New York.

Anonymous. 1971. The-rapists-lesbians and psychiatrists. In Boston Women Health Book Collective. eds. *Our Bodies, Ourselves*, pp. 63–65. Simon & Schuster, New York.

Arnup, Katherine. 1983. Lesbian feminist theory. In *Resources for Feminist Research* **XII** (1): 53–55.

Black Health Workers and Patients Group. 1983. Psychiatry and the Corporate State. In *Race and Class* **XXV** (2): 49–64.

Boston Women's Health Collective. 1971. *Our Bodies, Ourselves*. Simon & Schuster, New York.

Brittain, Vera. 1968. *Radclyffe Hall: A Case of Obscenity*. Femina Books, London.

Bunch, Charlotte. 1978. Lesbian-feminist theory. In Vida, Ginny, ed., *Our Right to Love*, pp.180–182. Prentice Hall, Englewood Cliffs.
Chesler, Phyllis. 1972. *Women and Madness*. Avon Books, New York.
Conrad, Peter. 1981. On the medicalization of deviance and social control. In Ingleby, David, (ed), *Critical Psychiatry: The Politics of Mental Health*, pp. 102–119. Penguin Books, Harmondsworth.
Daly, Mary. 1979. Gyn/Ecology: The Metaethics of Radical Feminism. The Women's Press, London.
Editorial. 1983. Alcoholism and the involvement of psychiatry. *Br. J. Addict. Alcohol.* **78**: 1–3.
Ettorre, E. M. 1978. The sociology of lesbianism: Female 'deviance' and female sexuality. Unpublished Ph.D. thesis, University of London.
Ettorre, E. M. 1980. *Lesbians, Women and Society*. Routledge & Kegan Paul, London.
Faderman, Lillian. 1981. *Surpassing the Love of Men: Romantic Friendship and Love Between Women from the Renaissance to the Present*. William Morrow, New York.
Fassler, Barbara. 1979. Theories of homosexuality as sources of Bloomsbury's androgyny. *Signs: Journal of Women in Culture and Society* **5** (2): 237–251.
Hall, Nor. 1980. *The Moon and the Virgin*. The Women's Press, London.
Hallett, Judith P. 1979. Sappho and her social context: Sense and sensuality. *Signs: Journal of Women in Culture and Society* **4** (3): 447–454.
Heather, Nick. 1976. *Radical Perspectives in Psychology*. Methuen, London.
Johnston, Jill. 1973. *Lesbian Nation: The Feminist Solution*. Touchstone Books, New York.
Klaich, Dolores. 1974. *Woman plus Woman*. New English Library, London.
Krieger, Susan. 1983. *The Mirror Dance: Identity in a Women's Community*. Temple University Press, Philadelpia.
Littlewood, Roland and Maurice Lipsedge. 1982. *Aliens and Alienists: Ethnic Minorities and Psychiatry*. Penguin Books, Harmondsworth.
Martin, Del and Lyon, Phyllis. 1972. *Lesbian Woman*. Bantam Books, New York.
Rich, Adrienne. 1976. *Of Woman Born*. Bantam Books, New York.
Rich, Adrienne. 1980. Compulsory heterosexuality and lesbian existence. *Signs: Journal of Women in Culture and Society* **5** (4): 631–660.
Scull, Andrew, T. 1979. *Museum of Madness*. Penguin Books, Harmondsworth.
Sedgwick, Peter. 1982. *Psycho Politics*. Pluto Press, London.
Stewart-Park, Angela and Jules Cassidy. 1977. *We're Here*. Quartet Books, London.
Szasz, Thomas, S. 1971. *The Manufacture of Madness*. Paladin, St. Albans.
Tanner, Donna, K. 1978. *The Lesbian Couple*. Lexington Books, Lexington, Massachusetts.
Weitz, Rose, 1984. From accommodation to rebellion: The politicization of lesbianism. In Darty, Trudy and Potter, Sandre, (eds), *Women—Identified Women*. pp. 233–248. Mayfield, Palo Alto.
Wiesen Cook, Blanche. 1979. Women alone stir my imagination: Lesbianism and the cultural tradition. *Signs: Journal of Women in Culture and Society* **4** (4): 718–739.
Wolf, Deborah Goleman. 1979. *The Lesbian Community*. University of California Press, Los Angeles.
Woolf, Virginia. 1976. *Moments of Being*. Triad/Granada, London.
World Health Organization. 1977. *Manual of the International Statistical Classification of Diseases, Injuries and Causes of Death*, Vol. I. HMSO, London.

COMMENT: BETSY ETTORE

As a lesbian feminist, I can honestly say that this paper emerged very much from seven and a half years of struggle at what I see as the bastion of male/ medical domination, the Institute of Psychiatry, London. Very soon after I took up my post there as a research sociologist in December 1978, I was aware that declaring myself openly as a lesbian feminist would have interesting results, if not painful repercussions. On the day that my book Lesbians, Women and Society *was published in 1980 and some of my 'more sympathe-*

tic' colleagues were organizing a small party in my honor, I felt the target of an attack when a senior male colleague commented on my 'book about perverts.'

While I tried not to allow myself to take 'things' personally, I knew that male doctors in general and male psychiatrists in particular had a vested interest in seeing feminists and indeed lesbian feminists as 'non-women' or just plain 'crazy.' I would never be a sycophant or pander to the needs of my male colleagues. For me, challenging the patriarchal structure became the order of the day and it was no easy task.

Since I am a woman as well as a lesbian, I often feel the need for self-healing, a need generated by my own experiences of struggle within male dominated settings. My paper which some individuals, both men and women, may find overwhelmingly critical of psychiatry and psychiatrists was written as an attempt at self-healing. This should be known. Also, this paper was written with other women in mind (i.e., those who have shared similar experiences to my own). I wanted them to be better able to build a feminist framework, sensitive to their needs as women and more hopeful than the 'disease framework' currently on offer from psychiatrists.

Although some of my feminist colleagues were and are critical of me for entering into the sort of struggle I have described above, I always feel that it is only within the wound that true healing comes about, not in collusion with male authority or men's interests.

Given that it is almost a year since I have left the Institute of Psychiatry, I can now look back at my experience with a sense of achievement. Luckily, I am now working where the needs of women as a social group and the issue of gender as key theoretical concern are taken seriously. My hope is that all who read this work will see very clearly that psychiatrists and psychiatry have very little, if anything at all, to offer lesbians. We must explore at a profound level how we will collectively liberate our own psyches.

17

We Are the Ones We Have Been Waiting for: Political Content in Alice Walker's Novels[1]

Barbara T. Christian

'Because women are expected to keep silent about their close escapes I will not keep silent'
(Walker, 1979: 23)

There is no question that Alice Walker's works are directed towards effecting social change, that she is a writer with political intent. Black women writers have little choice in this regard. Even if they could manage blindness, deafness to the state of black people, their status, as black, female, writer, a triple affliction, would, at some point, force them to at least consider the effect of societal forces on the lives of individuals. I make this bold-faced statement at the beginning of this essay on political content in Walker's novels, because it seems to me that our supposedly most radical avant garde critics seem to insist upon the unimportance of external reality, that the text ought to be dispersed, deconstructed—that writers do not mean what they write, do not even know what they write, that language is devoid of meaning, and is primarily a system of signs that refer to other signs rather than to anything that exists. Probably many of these critics would agree, if they thought they could say it aloud, that the best text would be silence, and that such a term as a political writer is a backward reactionary one.

I am particularly concerned with emphasizing my disagreement with this point of view, since I believe it would demolish much of the tradition (a bad word, I am told) of Afro-American writers, who have always had to refer to that reality out there which has its all too real foot on their necks. Further, for women, whatever their race, who have been silenced for so long, the very

[1] The first version of this essay was presented at the Women and Literature Conference. San Francisco State. April 14, 1985.

essence of this supposedly radical literary theory would reduce their words to sound and fury without meaning. It strikes me ironic that as groups who have traditionally been silenced begin to 'penetrate' the literary market, we learn that neither the world nor meaning exists. That a text is but a reference to other texts.

Like many other black women writers, Walker intends her works to effect something in the world. That is why she speaks and that is why she writes. But in her work, intention is not the only political factor. The process of political changing, the envisioning of social transforming is central to her work. Her forms, themes, imagery, critiques are marked by her belief in a coherent yet developing philosophy of life (an ideology in other words), which has some relationship to external reality. Her works are not merely *her* fictions, they are her fictions in relation to the world.

The core of her works is clearly her focus on black women, on the freedom allowed them as an indicator of the health of our entire society. This focus may seem a simple one. But if one considers the reality of black women's conditions in American society, her focus must involve a complexity of vision, if that condition is to be probed. In looking at what it means to be a black woman in the world, one must confront the vortex of sexism, racism, poverty so integrated that the parts of the whole can hardly be separated.

Many of Walker's literary ancestors had attempted to illuminate one part of this vortex, racism, primarily because of the tremendous oppression black women and men have suffered because of their race. But in so doing these writers have not *consciously* probed the salient fact, that racism is most invidiously expressed in sexist terms and that often the forms used most effectively by racist institutions are based on this interrelationship. Thus, the slave was to relate to the master, the black to the white, as woman was to relate to man, in a submissive, obedient manner essentially, as a role to the *real* person, who was master, white, male. I wrote about this construct in *Black Women Novelists* (1980: 3–34) by analysing the patriarchal plantation system, the major ideology that buttressed American slavery. And last year, I discussed this interrelationship as an underlying theme in all of black women's fiction, though often unconsciously perceived by the writers themselves (Christian, 1985: 171–186).

But Walker is certainly *conscious* about demonstrating the relationship between these two oppressions. One reason why her maternal ancestors had not approached this interrelationship was their fear that the other, the powerful other, whites, were listening, could read their published works, and that any critique of the behavior of black people would further be used by whites to further oppress the race. Walker, however, insists on placing black people at the center of her work both as subject and as audience. In portraying the sexism that exists in black communities and demonstrating its relationship, though not source in racism, she is speaking to her community about itself and its many participants. Walker's focus is itself an important political one, a breaking of silence which overthrows the oppressive stance fostered by racism, that white people are all that is important, that they are to blame for everything, that black people have no responsibility to themselves, their families, their institutions. Like Audre Lorde (1978: 32), another contemporary Afro-American woman poet, Walker proclaims that speaking the truth is necessary to survival, especially for those of us who were not meant to survive.

Walker's critiquing of her own community, her demonstration of the relationship between sexism and racism is already focal in her first novel, *The Third Life of Grange Copeland* which was published in 1970. At at time when the prominent black writers of the day emphasized confrontation between the beleaguered black community and the powerful white society, Walker's novel showed how that confrontation affects the relationships between black women, men, and children in other words the family. If the family is the core of the community, within which values are nurtured, the place where black people relate to each other on the most intimate level, then one needs to look at that interaction in order to discuss political reality, political possibility. As in her other two novels, *Meridian* and *The Color Purple*, Walker traces the development of three generations of a black family. In contrast to her second and third, however, the focus in *Grange Copeland* is on the Copeland men, their mistaken acceptance of the definition of maleness as power, an attribute they cannot possibly attain, and how that results in their brutalization of their wives and children.

This subject was certainly a taboo one in the early 1970s since black writers were intent on idealizing nationhood. What Walker did was to show how racism is capable of distorting the individual's relationship to his own kin, because he is encouraged to blame everything on the white folks and not accept responsibility for his own actions. No nationhood was possible if violence in the family persisted. Too, she does not hesitate to expose the destruction of black women by their own relations. But Walker also shows the coming to consciousness of Grange Copeland in this novel, his awareness that his resistance against whites must begin with his love of himself and his own family. This is a part of the novel that many who condemn it for its pessimism refuse to acknowledge, stunned as they are by a critique that they do not wish to confront. Yet this coming to consciousness is an essential part of every Walker novel—an integral part of her political statement.

Walker's first novel is an indicator of her political stance, but also of her insights into political process. As in her other two novels, *Grange Copeland* also analyses how economic struggle is linked to racism and sexism for the people she focuses on are southern sharecroppers. Her protagonists must contend with the restrictiveness of the economic order, of capitalism on their lives, even as they do not understand its nature. The effects of capitalism on the southern black family cannot be understood only in terms of the present. Thus all her novels span generations, in other words, are rooted in history.

The process by which Walker interweaves the overall history of the Copeland family with the story of each generation of that family is an important aspect of her political vision. She uses quilting, a Southern womanist form, as a model for her first novel. Just as her maternal ancestors took bits of waste material and transformed them into patterned works, at once useful and beautiful, so Walker stitches together motifs repeated in each generation into a coherent pattern. Thus we are able to see how essential the motifs of racist terror and sexual violence are to the pattern of this family's history. Only when Grange learns to love himself and his granddaughter Ruth is the destructive pattern changed and a regenerative pattern begun. Even so the force of the previous history is so strong that the old pattern of destruction threatens the new one, as Brownfield Copeland attempts to destroy his father, Grange. By concluding the novel with the appearance of Civil Rights workers, Walker suggests the necessity not only for the personal change that Grange Copeland undergoes, but also that the pattern of this quilt will not be changed for long unless social change begins to occur.

Paradoxically, although Walker uses a womanist form in her first novel, the adult Copeland women are destroyed precisely because they do not understand the social forces that are arrayed against them as black women. Convinced by their culture that they can be 'the perfect wife' regardless of their economic and social context, they are defeated by the men in their own families, as well as by white society. Walker courageously opposes the widespread belief that black women always 'endure,' as she shows how terrifying are the oppressions that assail them. Such a portrayal was practically heresy in 1970, when black women were being continually exalted for their superhuman ability to survive anything, the implication being that they did not need, as urgently as others, relief from their condition. Although Margaret and Mem Copeland are destroyed, Ruth, the girl-woman of the Copelands' third generation has the possibility of surviving for she is given by her grandfather the knowledge about her culture and about white society that she will need. As importantly, she has a greater possibility of 'surviving whole' because a social movement against racism may affect her life.

This historical dimension which is prevalent not only in *Grange Copeland* but in all of Walker's novels enables her to analyse the process by which the social order becomes oppressive, particularly of black women while giving her the space to show how they come to consciousness about the nature of their condition. Paradoxically, even as she focuses on the intimate relationships between black women and men, black parents and children, black women and black women, she is able to relate the quality of these relationships to the larger sweep of history. And her novels show, through this historical dimension, not only the repression that blacks have suffered but also their resistance to it. Thus a knowledge of their own history is one source for the coming to consciousness that her protagonists go through, a reminder that black people before them, black women before them have resisted powerful attempts of dehumanization. History, too, is an impetus for black women, a source of their understanding of their right to be themselves whatever the prevailing black ideology may be, as well as an indicator of the often painful process through which they must go to retain their integrity as human beings. Since much of the 'history' that is written omits black women, Walker and her sisters who write are reclaiming that history even as they create visions of new alternatives. And in so doing, they are primary political actors.

> 'They were women then
> My mamma's generation
> Husky of voice—stout of
> Step
> With fists as well as
> Hands'

(Walker, 1973: 5).

Meridian, Walker's second novel is an even more graphic illustration of the importance of herstory to black women's lives. One of the novel's major themes is both a rich critique of the ideology of black motherhood in this country and a celebration of the true meanings of motherhood. By tracing the history of black people, not through battles or legislation, but in terms of the lives of mothers, Walker demonstrates how motherhood is 'an angle of seeing life,' of valuing all life, of resisting all that might destroy it—in other words that motherhood is not merely a biological state but an attitude towards life.

Even as she probes the meaning of motherhood, Walker's use of herstory also allows her to highlight the insidious ways in which both black and white society restrict, punish individual mothers even as they canonize motherhood. The political meaning of this analysis is tantamount to the freeing of woman, who solely has the potential of being a mother, and who has, for much of the world's history, been reduced to that role. Walker then, extends the definition of womanhood beyond the restrictive definition of biological motherhood, even as she beautifully expands the meaning of that state.

But Walker also extends the true meaning of mother, of cherishing life, to that of the revolutionary. For the novel *Meridian* relates this attitude to the spiritual/political principles of the Civil Rights movement, a social movement opposed to violence, the destruction of life, even as it had violence inflicted upon its members by the ruling classes. *Meridian* poses a major political question: 'When is it right to kill? Why isn't revolutionary murder, murder?' How does the acceptance of the culture of violence effect those who struggle for positive social transformation. 'What would the music be like?' It is a question critical to our world when revolutions sometimes self-destruct, and when sometimes the only actual change after a political revolution is a changing of the guards. Walker of course does not fully resolve the question but she does probe its meaning reminding us that those who consider killing in order to effect change must prepare themselves to go through their own personal revolution—that social change is impossible without personal change. The flawed Meridian pursues the question of revolutionary violence in the novel, an issue she can perceive, because from her point of view she has violated life at its deepest level. Because she feels guilt about giving up her son to others and about aborting her second pregnancy, Meridian is propelled on a search for spiritual and political health. Having sinned against biological motherhood, she becomes a mother by 'expanding her mind with action' which is directed toward the preservation of all life.

Meridian's form is itself a graphic image of revolution. It is both circular and ascending, the meaning of the word *meridian*, as Walker intersects the personal histories of Meridian, Truman and Lynne, actors in the Civil Rights movement, with the collective history of black people. Within this form, Walker carefully connects bits and pieces of these histories, as she creates an even more intricate quilt in this second novel. The meridian-like movement of the novel indicates a process of coming to consciousness for Meridian, which Truman at the end of the novel, can use as a source of inspiration and process if he is to become whole. In *Meridian* then, Walker suggests a process for all those who seek social change. Meridian must go backward in time in order to move forward beyond the point that she is at, continually seeking the connections between her personal history and communal history. It is through this process that Walker the writer is able to show the interrelationship of sexism, racism and economic deprivation not only on individuals and their families but also *on the political movements they create*. And how, as well, these areas of oppression must be struggled through, rather than ignored or talked out of existence. Only then is ascension possible.

> '*The Nature of this Flower Is to Bloom*
> Rebellious. Living.
> Against the Elemental Crush.
> A Song of Color
> Blooming
> For Deserving Eyes.
> Blooming Gloriously
> For its Self.
> *Revolutionary Petunia*.'
>
> (Walker, 1973: 70)

The forms that Walker creates then have political content. Perhaps, even more than *Meridian*, the form of her most recent novel, *The Color Purple* is dramatically political, for she employs a technique that is both associated with every day life and with women. *The Color Purple* is written entirely in letters. Not only is this a *tour de force* for Walker, the novelist, letters along with diaries were the only forms allowed women to record their herstory. Letters both express Celie's view of herself and her view of the world even as they show her development from a victimized girl to a woman who becomes strong enough to change her condition and to love herself. Letters are both a source of subjective information, Celie's feelings about herself, and objective information, the world in which she moves. Letters proclaim the woman-centered focus of this novel, a political statement in itself.

Also Walker distinguishes her woman protagonist as a black woman by her language. Like Walker's other two novels, *The Color Purple* traces three generations of a family, most emphatically this time from a woman's point of view. Like *Grange Copeland* the novel is a story about a rural Southern family, though not sharecroppers but small land-owners. But *The Color Purple* is distinguished from these other two novels by its use of black folk language which too develops in complexity as Celie becomes stronger, more articulate, older. By using this language in contrast to standard English, Walker affirms the value of Afro-American culture. This is no small political assertion. Attempts are always made to discredit the language of a people in order to discredit them; for it is in their language that a people's values are expressed. If there is any significant idea (and there are many) that Walker has learned from her literary maternal ancestor Zora Neale Hurston, it is this one.

Perhaps the most obvious measure of *The Color Purple's* political direction is the novel's focus on sexism within the black community. This is not a new subject for Walker. All her work exposes how sexism, is, tragically, a part of black mores, a question of power in the black community as it is in all other human cultures we know. But in *The Color Purple*, Walker protests incest, a taboo subject in the black community. Just as she approached in 1970 the taboo subject of family violence in *Grange Copeland*, in 1976 the myth of black motherhood and the idea that revolutionary violence should at least be questioned in *Meridian*, in 1983 Walker again approached a taboo subject among black ideologues. Her exposing of incest in *The Color Purple* has precipitated more discussion within her community on sexism than ever before, as Walker insists that black people adhere to the value of life for black women. By critiquing her community she affirms our right to take responsibility for ourselves, by speaking to her community as her audience, she demonstrates how central black people are to her vision.

As if breaking the silence about incest in black families were not enough, the intrepid Walker gives *The Color Purple* a distinctly womanist thrust by having Celie triumph over brutality, wife-beating, incest—through her sisters—through Shug who becomes her lover and friend, through Nellie her blood sister who writes letters to her from Africa, and whose letters she finally can answer, and through Sophie, her sister-in-law who resists her husband as well as white peoples' attempts to beat her down. Again Walker explores another taboo subject, for physical as well as spiritual love between women is the core of the novel. By presenting this love as natural and freeing, Walker protests homophobia in the black community. Sisterhood among women is *The Color Purple's* theme and form as Walker proclaims bonding among black women as a necessary ingredient if we are to be free.

Walker, however, does not ignore racism among women. Through Sophie's experience with the Mayor's wife which results in this black woman being jailed and taken away from her children, Walker questions whether sisterhood across racial lines is possible until white women descend from the unnatural pedestal they stand on and eliminate racism in themselves. But Walker also insists that sexism, though affected by racism, is not derived from it. Nellie's sections in Africa has as one of their focuses the sexism African women are afflicted with as Walker exposes another taboo subject amongst black ideologues. Nellie's sections also emphasize the impact of colonialism and imperialism on African peoples as Walker protests in one bold stroke the doctrine of white supremacy and capitalist expansion.

But *The Color Purple* goes beyond the protest of sexism, racism, and homophobia. Perhaps the novel's most significant contribution to Walker's expanding political vision is the pivotal role the erotic plays in Celie's movement toward freedom. The title of the novel itself is a celebration of the beauty, the pleasure of living and how that celebration is at the core of spiritual and political growth. It is through Celie's awareness of her right to the passion, creativity, satisfaction possible in life that she empowers herself. Once she experiences the erotic, the sharing of joy, she fights for her right to participate in it. Celie's story beautifully exemplifies Audre Lorde's words in her essay 'The Uses of the Erotic, the Erotic as Power' 1984: 58):

> 'In touch with the erotic I become less
> willing to accept powerlessness or those
> other supplied states of being which are
> not native to one such as resignation,
> despair, self-effacement, depression, self-denial.'

Like Lorde, Celie comes to *demand* from all of her life—her relationships, her work, whatever she is engaged in—that deep satisfaction. In guiding her to that knowledge Shug, her friend and lover, helps Celie to initiate change in all these aspects of her life. And in changing herself, Celie helps to change her entire community. Political change in *The Color Purple* occurs because of life-affirmation. From my point of view then one of the most important political statements of *The Color Purple* is its emphasis on the right to happiness for even the most oppressed of us all, for poor black women, and that our happiness can be imagined, pursued, achieved through the growing strength of the community of black women:

> 'We are the Ones We have been Waiting for'
>
> (Jordan, 1980: 42).

From her first novel, *The Third Life of Grange Copeland* to her most recent, *The Color Purple*, Walker shows how lasting political change is impossible without personal transformation. But she also emphasizes in her work that personal change is inevitably linked to a community of changers. The individual cannot effect lasting change for the self without some corresponding societal change. And for Walker, personal change is most indelibly achieved through the process of working for change with others.

In *Grange Copeland*, change begins to occur for the Copeland family when Grange, like so many others, goes North, the traditional escape for Southern blacks since slavery. When he discovers, as did so many others, the ineffectiveness of this solution he begins to work for change in his granddaughter's life in the South. But though his personal transformation has meaning, he is killed by the system he opposes. In ending the novel with Civil Rights workers, a growing community of changers, Walker suggests that other Granges are beginning to come together in their need and desire to change their society. Walker's second novel *Meridian* explores that historical development for the novel is as much about the principles of the Civil Rights and Black Power movements as it is about her characters. Meridian, her major protagonist, both affirms and challenges the underlying concepts of these movements of the 60s. As a black woman, as a black mother, she struggles to be free within herself even as she encounters sexism, elitism, violence within the Movement. The themes of *The Color Purple* build on Meridian's pilgrimage to freedom, for Walker's most recent novel explores basic tenets of the women's movement of the 1970s. Thus she protests violence against women and racist violence among women, while celebrating the bonding that women must develop in their struggles to achieve selfhood. Too, she expands feminist thought by placing the erotic, the right to satisfaction in women's lives at the center of the novel. Black women loving each together and working together are the community of changers in *The Color Purple*, through which individual black women and men come to demand and experience more of life.

Walker therefore scrutinizes historical movements that have had significant effects on the lives of black women. In celebrating these movements she both celebrates and critiques them. Walker's peculiar sound as a political writer has much to do with her contrariness, her willingness at all turns to challenge the fashionable beliefs of the day, to examine them in the light of black women's herstory, of her own experiences, and of dearly won principles that she has previously challenged and absorbed. It is significant that 'the survival whole' of black people which Walker focused on in *Grange Copeland* is extended to the value of life she illuminated in *Meridian* and is further developed into the relationship between freedom and happiness in *The Color Purple*, particularly for her women characters. While Margaret Copeland and men are destroyed in *The Third Life of Grange Copeland*, Meridian 'expands her mind with action.' But in pursuit of spiritual health, Meridian goes through a period of 'madness,' paralysis of the body, then self-abnegation. Celie completes the cycle of Walker's women. Like Mem Copeland she is physically abused; like Meridian she goes through a painful period of healing. Celie, however, comes to full bloom in her entire self, physically and spiritually.

Survival whole—the value of all life—the right to happiness—these are increments in an ever-expanding philosophy of Walker's fiction. And for her, these goals can only be imagined as possible, pursued, and believed in, if we take responsibility for ourselves, and undergo the process of struggle historically, personally and collectively necessary to make ourselves physically, passionately, spiritually healthy. Only then can we achieve a sense of the oneness of creation, as symbolized by the color purple. Further, for Walker, black women must do this for themselves and each other, if the unnatural hierarchies of sexism, racism, and economic exploitation are to be eliminated: 'We are the ones we have been waiting for.'

REFERENCES

Christian, Barbara. 1980. *Black Women Novelists, The Development of a Tradition*. Greenwood Press, Westport, Conn.

Christian, Barbara. 1985. *Black Feminist Criticism, Perspectives on Black Women Writers*. Pergamon, New York, Oxford.

Jordan, June. 1980. Poem for South African women. In *Passion*. Beacon Press, Boston.

Lorde, Audre. 1978. A litany for survival. In *The Black Unicorn*. W & W Norton, New York.

Lorde, Audre. 1984. *Sister Outsider*. The Crossing Press, Tramansberg, New York.

Walker, Alice. 1973. Women. In *Revolutionary Petunias and Other Poems*. Harcourt Brace & Jovanovich, New York.

Walker, Alice. 1979. On stripping bark from myself. In *Good Night Willie Lee I'll See You in the Morning*. Dial Press, New York.

Walker, Alice. 1983. Introduction. In *In Search of Our Mothers Gardens*. Harcourt Brace & Jovanovich, New York.

18

Friends or Foes: Gerontological and Feminist Theory[1]

Shulamit Reinharz

Gerontology is an interdisciplinary field in which women have made important contributions for which they have received recognition, e.g., Carroll Estes, Jacquelyne Jackson, Eva Kahana, Marjorie Fiske Lowenthal, Bernice Neugarten, Matilda Riley, Ethel Shanas, and Lillian Troll, to mention a few. This has occurred without much specific feminist consciousness in the field. Whereas a handful of gerontologists have consistently integrated feminist- and age-consciousness in their work, e.g., Sharon Curtin, Zena Blau, Arlie Hochschild, only recently have older women become highlighted, or in some cases included, among the concerns of gerontologists. Only in 1973 did the 26th Annual Conference on Aging, sponsored by the Institute of Gerontology at the University of Michigan, devote itself to women (Institute of Gerontology, 1973); only in 1978 did the Baltimore Longitudinal Study add women to its study of normal aging; only in 1978 did the Gerontological Society of America give aging women significant emphasis at its annual meeting; and only in 1981 did the White House Conference on Aging have a special committee to deal with older women's concerns (Markson, 1983).

Feminist theory has been proliferating since about 1970. Nearly from the start, feminist theorists working within the three major perspectives—radical, liberal and socialist (see Jaggar, 1983; McFadden, 1984)—have been developing analyses of aging (see, e.g., Bart, 1979; Bell, 1970; de Beauvoir,

[1] I would like to thank the following people for helpful discussions or correspondence concerning this paper: Thelma Nason, Mary Gilfus, Kathy Kautzer, Mickey Friedman, Denise Connors, Kathy MacPherson, Robbie Pfeiuffer, Karl Pilemer, Becky Thompson, Morrie Schwartz, Paula Rayman, Karen Fields, Mary Ann Wilner, Janet Giele, Connie Cutter, Loraine Obler, Paula Doress, Oliva Espin, Buffy Dunker, Brinton Lykes, Hortensia Amaro, Ruth Jacobs and Annette Rickel.

1970; Demetrakopoulos, 1983; Jacobs, 1979; Olson, 1982; Nett, 1982; Rubin, 1979; Sontag, 1972). For some of these women, doing feminist work sparked an interest in gerontological issues. In one instance, the opposite process occurred, i.e., doing gerontological research became the impetus for the development of feminist consciousness. Specifically, Bart (1975: 4) reported that Helena Lopata's research on widowhood (1973) led her to feminism because 'she was so infuriated at the lack of preparation women have for living lives without their husbands. . . .' To Lopata, the helplessness of (some) widows revealed the damaging effect of their socialization as women. Examples of this helplessness continue to appear regularly in advice columns:

> 'I would like to hear from anyone who has lost her husband. My wonderful husband suddenly passed away on Dec. 20. I cannot express how I feel. We had 36 years in which we shared everything. He was always there. I felt safe and protected; now I feel so alone, scared, not knowing where to turn. How can you live when your life is so empty? There's an empty house just full of furniture—no life. I have married children who are great, but let's face it—they have lives of their own. It's my life that's incomplete. I really don't know how I can make it without him.' (Confidential Chat, *The Boston Globe*, 2/5/85.[2]

Conceptual linkages between feminism and gerontology fall into five main categories: (1) the struggle over the extent to which 'their group' is defined by biology or by social conditions; (2) the strategic use of statistics to demonstrate the existence of inequality and to press for policy changes; (3) the struggle over whether to consider the group as a whole, or to be concerned primarily with those subgroups which suffer the greatest inequities; (4) the struggle over the choice of a strategy which demonstrates the group's strengths or unfair treatment, and (5) the struggle to prevent or challenge a backlash which would arise among powerful groups or other relatively powerless groups.

What feminism and gerontology have in common is an attempt to create social consciousness, social theory and social policy which will improve the life chances of a specific group. One question that arises for both is the extent to which each recognizes subgroups within the major social group, and how they are handled conceptually. Feminist theorists have long recognized that women represent a highly diversified group with cross-cutting allegiances to work, family, race, class, religion, ethnic group, age group and more. Yet, feminist theory asserts that superceding these differences is the commonality of femaleness which among other things, means relative powerlessness. Feminism seeks to understand why—what are the crucial variables that determine the status of women?

Like feminism, gerontology considers the elderly both as a single group within a society (and cross-culturally) and as a set of subgroups. It has long

---

[2] Fortunately, this letter continues with the widow saying she will try a widows support group. The emergence of these groups is the product of the work of another feminist, Phyllis Silverman (1986).

recognized that variables such as socio-economic class, marital status, work status, ethnicity and more create profoundly different subgroups among the elderly. Gerontologists are concerned with relations, i.e., interdependence, hostility, love and affection, between old and young, in a way analogous with feminist concern with the relations between women and men. There are many other parallels. Writers exploring old age such as Tillie Olsen (*Tell me a Riddle*) suggest a need for an older person to have a psychological space of her own just as Virginia Woolf explained the need for younger women to have rooms of their own to be themselves and to do their work. The relations we must understand are those between women as well as those between men and women. For example, consider the nursing home. Nursing homes are a women's issue—both because women comprise the vast majority of the patients, and also because they comprise the vast majority of the workers whose low pay fuels nursing home profits. This very pairing creates its own problems:

> '. . . for predominantly female nurses caring for predominantly female patients, there is a dilemma arising from the patient as an image of the nurse's future self, engendering conflicting responses of total rejection and profession of care to the best of the nurse's ability.' (Evers, 1981: 114).

Both gerontological and feminist theory attempt to identify the significant common dimensions of 'their' groups: some perspectives stress the common dimension of humaneness, other stress bodily experiences, while still others focus on how members of the group are treated by others, specifically examining oppression, hatred, trivialization and exploitation. Both types of theorists have examined media images at length, and have sought to show how these images act as forces of discrimination and social control. In both fields, the way 'the group' is treated is perhaps the most significant of these commonalities. People's meaning to others more often than not becomes the meaning they have for themselves. This meaning shapes people's identity, attitudes, and behaviors. When the group is not perceived as powerful, then the group member loses the power to define the culture, shape the institutions, or control her/his intimate relations. Powerlessness and denigration breed intimidation which has to be unlearned in new types of relationships and new institutions. Gerontologists have shown that the meaning that the elderly have in our society, particularly the meaning of being physically unattractive and relatively powerless, is frequently internalized by the elderly themselves. In response, some new institutions—such as senior citizen centers, elder hostels, retirement communities—and some new language—senior citizen, gray panther—have been developed to reduce the stigma.

It is my contention that just as the women's movement inherited the experiences and successes of the civil rights movement (Evans, 1979), the fledgling anti-ageism movement is now inheriting the experiences and successes of the women's movement. Gerontology is the theory that furnishes the ideology of the anti-ageism movement. A full-fledged social movement to combat ageism has not yet arisen, but in its nascent form it is heavily influenced by feminist models for social change and well populated by feminist activists. In addition, the anticipated elderly-advocacy social movement can be predicted to be grounded in the conceptual and practical links between anti-sexism and anti-ageism that have already formed.

A CONFLICT MODEL FOR UNDERSTANDING WOMEN AND THE ELDERLY

Regardless of the particular type of feminist theory, their shared perspective on aging is that it occurs within a context of inequalities—sexism, racism, antisemitism, heterosexism, capitalism, elitism, beautyism, etc. These forces allow a small social group to retain power and rewards while other groups are blamed for their induced deficiencies. This conflict perspective characteristic of feminist theory has also been adopted by old age activists who analyse discrimination against the aged in the context of the entire social system. Advocates of the elderly rebel against the structural–functional sociological model of disengagement as the 'normal' aging process, just as feminists dispute the structural–functional model of the sexual division of labor as the 'normal' distribution of tasks in a society. Both groups argue to physicians and psychoanalysts that 'anatomy is not destiny.' Both argue that being defined as inherently passive is inaccurate for the defined group, but perpetuated nevertheless because it is self-serving for the defining group.

Prominent among elderly-advocates who have articulated this conflict position is Maggie Kuhn, national convenor of the Gray Panthers. She argues that the most significant independent variables in explaining the conditions of elderly people are not the biological effects of their chronological age, but the way in which facets of the social–economic structure interweave to deprive the elderly of status, power and control over their own lives. For this reason the Gray Panthers took up opposition to the Vietnam War as its initial focus for action. Today they are concerned not only with nursing home reform and the development of national health insurance, but also with decent housing for all, environmental protection and nuclear disarmament (Kuhn, 1984: 7). Kuhn questions the value of social services for the elderly, which she calls 'novocaine,' and prefers the formation of age-integrated political action groups.

BODILY KNOWLEDGE AND LIES

Epidemiologists and demographers have shown that women live in ways that extend their longevity. As is well known, rates of alcoholic addiction, crime, auto accidents, heart disease, cancer and suicide are far higher for men than for women (Waldron: 1976). Lois Verbrugge, one of the acknowledged experts on this subject, claims that mortality rates have been higher for men and morbidity rates and health services use have been higher for women as long as vital statistics, health surveys and medical/hospitals records have been available in the U.S. (Verbrugge, 1985: 156–157). The fact that women outlive men and therefore increasingly outnumber men in old age makes it mandatory that theories of old age recognize the extent to which 'the elderly' about whom we are talking are likely to be women. Because women predominate among the elderly and among the caretakers of the elderly, old age can largely be defined as a 'woman's issue' (see Minkler and Estes, 1984).

To argue against the repressive slogan that 'biology is destiny' is not to say that biology is insignificant or an enemy. On the contrary, some feminist theoreticians and writers see woman's body as a source of knowledge, insight and wisdom. For example, when a girl reaches puberty the appearance of the monthly cycle ushers in a new age of responsibilities and possibilities. It signals membership in the community of potentially reproductive women. As the monthly cycle reappears, it becomes a reminder of the passage of time and its circularity. Menstruation provides a continuous message about generational connections, and the choices of making or not making new lives. Later, menopause is a reminder that a new life stage is beginning and that death awaits us all. Tillie Olsen (1965: 201) reprints a poem by Jane Cooper which reflects this 'bodily wisdom' of the older woman whose body is both foe and friend as it generates conflicts and questions:

'My body knows it will never bear children.
What can I say to my body now,
this used violin?
Every night it cries out desolately
from its secret cave.
Old body, old friend,
why are you so unforgiving? . . .'

Our bodies need to be protected in order that we may continue to derive wisdom from them. In this arena of health, feminist activists and theorists address issues of older women with strategies previously successful with younger women (Golub and Freedman, 1985). For example, *Ourselves Growing Older* will be published by the Boston Health Book Collective as an extension of *Our Bodies, Ourselves*. The self-help groups and women's health centers designed to serve young women are being followed by menopause collectives and rap groups (Beeson, 1975) and the *HotFlash Newsletter*. The idea that we can control birth is being extended to the idea that we can control menopause. Feminists argue that women should attempt to be less dependent on physicians and should attempt to learn more about our bodies, ourselves. The efforts of younger feminists to help women accept our bodies as they are (sometimes fat, always with body hair) is being extended to a message to older women to accept our bodies as they are

(usually with gray hair, skin spots, wrinkles and sags, etc.) The consciousness-raising technique in which younger women share their personal experiences honestly and openly is being extended to older women stating their age,
honestly and openly. For many older women, this is impossible.

> 'Diana Menuhin, tall, and thin as a dancer in her prime, will not disclose her age. "I can't
> tell you how old I am," she says slowly, her eyes reflecting an inner mischief. "Don't
> ask." Pause. "Tell them I'm ageless." Pause. "Don't you know women *lie* about their
> age." ' (Christy, 1985: 67).

Feminist attention to sexist language has led to efforts to redefine and replace
damaging words. In this way, gray becomes silver, wrinkles become age lines,
menopause becomes womenpause. Everything becomes positive. The feminist stance that young women do not need make-up stretches across the
generations to include older women not needing face-lifts. Feminist work to
uncover the tragedy of DES is stretched to include suspicion of estrogen
replacement therapy (MacPherson, 1985). Finally, feminist analysis of
advertising extends our initial understanding that women are portrayed in
violence-encouraging, sex-role restricting, and soft-porn ways. It includes
the recognition that old women vanish from ads when they lose their sex
appeal for men, appearing only to sell food they can cook, medications they
can take, or being foolish in a modern female, version of 'Uncle Tom.'

When seeing older women's bodies naked or scantily clothed, Gloria
Steinem realized the extent to which all of us are manipulated by images of
'what we should look like' (1983: 163). She believes that if were able to really
look at each other's bodies, we would get new images of what we are rather
than be burdened by what we should be.

> 'A cheerful, seventyish woman with short white curls held back by an orange ribbon,
> wearing a satiny green leotard that hugs her gently protruding stomach like a second skin.
> From her, I learn the beauteous curve of a nonflat stomach.' (Steinem, 1983: 163).

THE REDEFINITION OF MENOPAUSE AND THE
SELF

Menopause can be defined physiologically in terms of the gradual cess-
ation of menstruation or sociologically as the gradual termination of the
possibility of bearing children. When menstruation ceases, the ovary still
contains eggs, but there is a decline in ovarian estrogen production which in
turn increases the pituitary's output of hormones (FSH and LH) which can be
measured in the blood. Menopause may be accompanied by hot flashes,
vaginal dryness and depression. Just as menstruation and possible pre-
menstrual symptoms can render women of a younger age patients, the
possible symptoms of menopause make women of an older age candidates
for new market products, medicalization, and treatment as mental patients
(see Daly, 1978: 249). There are other continuities and sources of potential

identification between menstruating and menopausal women. According to Evelyn Shaw and Joan Darling, both may share a 'cultural menopause.'

> '[T]he Westernized woman has created a cultural menopause. Despite the fact that she continues monthly menstruation as a member of the species, she has made herself as infertile as women whose reproduction has been ended by natural biological menopause. . . . Even if she created a menopause earlier, the Westernized woman often reacts to biological menopause with distress, depression, and a sense of loss—not of her fertility, but rather of her control over the choice to have offspring or not.' (1985: 72–73).

Menopause is heavily laden with meaning. For some gerontologists it is the cut-off point between young and old women. For women themselves, menopause may become an object of competition. Women can compete as to who is 'really young,' i.e., a woman who is still menstruating is younger than one who is not, regardless of chronological age. Other women compete for a 'freedom status' on the basis of who is already free of menstruation. Older women can use contact with their adult children, number of grandchildren, or accomplishments of adult children as other forms of competition among themselves. All of these behaviors signify ways in which older women derive their identity through others, or through their bodily functions, rather than through themselves as autonomous individuals, an objective which may be very difficult to reach.

SHARING OF TERMINOLOGY AND ORGANIZATIONAL FORMS

Several theorists of aging have begun to apply the terminology and analytic framework of feminism to issues of aging (Feldman, 1975; Levin and Levin, 1980). Ageism (the parallel of sexism) is now discussed in gerontology textbooks. So too the fight against ageism inherits the conceptual and political work of feminists. Laws to combat age discrimination are being fashioned in the model of sex discrimination. Problems that women were discovered to face, e.g., physical abuse, drug abuse, are identified as problems to look out for among the elderly. Women who had been coordinators of the Task Force on Older Women of the National Organization of Women became founders of grass roots organizations designed for the special needs of older women—the Alliance for Displaced Homemakers (founded in 1972; Shields, 1981) and the Older Women's League (OWL, founded in 1980). These organizations challenge the ability of age anti-discrimination laws to protect older women seeking work, and the ability of Social Security to protect the divorced, separated or widowed woman who cannot find paid employment.

The terminology and strategy of some feminist scholarship also parallels some concerns within gerontology. To explain women's status, Hacker reconceptualized women as a minority group (1951). The elderly, too have been conceptualized as a minority group (see Streib, 1976). To repair the 'gynopia' (see Reinharz, 1985) of historians, women's 'herstory' has been discovered, invisible women made visible, and history has been rewritten. So too, the forgotten elderly have been rediscovered, and elderly heroes and heroines identified. The myth of the vaginal orgasm finds its parallel in the myth of sexual disinterest among the elderly. The discovery of the normalcy of clitoral orgasm may find its parallel in the discovery of the normalcy of sexuality among nursing home residents or the normalcy of forms of sexuality for the elderly other than heterosexual intercourse. The means by which elderly solitary women might derive sexual pleasure has not yet been discussed.

ADDING AGEISM CONSCIOUSNESS TO FEMINIST CONSCIOUSNESS

Now that the women's movement is maturing, so too are its early activists, several of whom have become interested in the meaning of aging in our society. Betty Friedan, for example, is extending her ideas about 'women's liberation' to an interest in 'elderly liberation.' When feminist-consciousness ages, it adds ageist-consciousness. Gloria Steinem received a great deal of attention on her 50th birthday when she claimed her age rather than hiding it. When told that she didn't look her age, she answered that this is what her age looks like. Although still 'young,' Jane Fonda and other feminist celebrities publicly celebrate their aging rather than mourning or denying it. These women are asking to be seen as pioneers of positive woman-defined aging. They work to combat the very stereotypes that keep other women alienated from themselves. Of course it is necessary not to let the media manipulate women into thinking that they can 'claim their age' only if they look like Gloria Steinem or Jane Fonda, which the media define as 'looking good.'

Just as aging feminists add age-consciousness to their feminism, so too aging women are likely to add feminism to their consciousness, or to deepen their feminism where it already exists. Gloria Steinem carried the placard 'Women Get More Radical with Age' at the 25th reunion of her graduation from Smith College. Her sign was taken from her 1979 article, 'Why Young Women are More Conservative' (reprinted in Steinem, 1983) which argued that, although there are exceptions, and in contrast with men, women in general don't begin to challenge the politics of their lives until later. Women are more conservative when young because during their youth women are most valued for their full potential as workers, wives, sex partners and child bearers. Steinem suggests that only when women enter the paid-labor force, discover how women are treated there, marry, have children and experience aging (which she calls a greater penalty for women than for men), do they become radicalized. Once this connection between women's youth and the attractiveness of the status quo is recognized, it is easier to understand why the 19th-century wave of feminism was started by older women. Steinem sees hope in aging women: 'One day, an army of gray-haired women may quietly take over the earth' (1983: 218).

HAVE FEMINISTS NEVERTHELESS BEEN UNFAIR TO OLDER WOMEN?

Regardless of the above, some advocates of the elderly continue to say that feminists are blatantly insensitive to older women (Datan, 1981). Some of this attack on feminists may be part of a general disrespect for feminists who continue to be objects of ridicule. Some critics are more specific. Feminists have been accused of disregarding age altogether and treating 'all women as though age were not a significant category or as though women were ageless' (Fuller and Martin, 1980: xi). This accusation is sound to a certain extent. After all, feminists, just as everyone else, have been socialized in our aging-phobic or geronto-phobic culture.

It must also be recognized that the very development of feminist consciousness among some women stems from a rejection of the world of their mothers, a 'limited world' which may consist of voluntarism, housework, living for one's husband and children, and sacrificing one's education and career. It may be difficult for older women to understand their daughters' disinterest in marriage or in having children, when the mothers were socialized to expect to have children and grandchildren. To some young feminists, the world of their mothers seems unattractive, 'politically incorrect,' a product of 'false consciousness.' These women have yet to learn about the sisterhood of women across the life cycle. One college student recently told me that her friends accuse her of immaturity when she tells them how fond she is of her own mother. Whereas young feminists see their rejection of their mothers as a sign of their radical politics, the severing of bonds may actually reflect a male definition of radical activity, flowing from the boy's breaking the tie with the father as the means of liberation. By contrast, what is radical for women is the ability to bond with women, to forge sisterhood with other women rather than separateness (see Steinem, 1983). Consider the words of this older woman who sees herself as more radical than her daugher, but sharing the same issues:

> 'My daughter is a senior in college. She already talks about her 'youth' with a sad nostalgia. She is worried because she is not married. . . . Everybody confirms in her a sense of time passing, that she will be left behind, unsold on the shelf. She already peers in the mirror for wrinkles and buys creams and jellies to rub into her skin. Her fear angers me but leaves me helpless. . . . I want to beg her not to begin worrying, not to let in the dreadful daily gnawing already. . . . How can a woman respect herself when every day she stands before her mirror and accuses her face of betraying her, because every day she is, indeed a day older.' (Moss, 1978: 67).

Psychologists have played a role in encouraging intergenerational alienation when they argue that parents who see their children as friends and confidants are acting in an age-inappropriate manner. In a similar vein, Troll (1983: 63–64) accuses psychologists of assuming that in order to avoid disturbed relationships among themselves and an unhealthy relationship with their children, young married couples must 'separate themselves effectively from their parents.' She acknowledges that this equation of generational 'separation' with 'mental health' is still upheld by many professionals. The ability to separate from, i.e., reject, the 'world of our fathers and mothers' is defined in gerontology books as necessary in industrialized societies in which labor must be mobile, and the drags on one's ability to compete eliminated. In our society, the parallel in divorce between spouses is the attenuation of the strength of intergenerational ties, leaving perhaps little more than visiting rights (rites?).

In feminist writing, the flip side of the daughter's rage against her mother is sometimes visible, i.e., the older women's rage against her daughter for exploiting or abandoning her, or simply for being young. It is still more socially acceptable for the young to reject their parent, than for the parents to reject their children. Gerontologists inadvertently enhance the antagonism of older and younger females when they describe the disadvantage of older widows who seek to remarry *vis-à-vis* younger women. Some older feminists are now expressing anger toward younger women, including younger feminists who neglect them in old age (MacDonald and Rich, 1983). In a review of the MacDonald/Rich book, Colombia University English professor Carolyn Heilbrun wrote:

> 'As an aging (i.e. 58) woman, I have a place in the women's movement because I have a place in the academic world. People ignore me until they know who I am. To watch their faces turn from profound indifference to pleased recognition is to become aware that the aged, until labelled unusually valuable, are assumed worthless. Through longevity I have acquired power, and I can use it in aid of younger academic women. If younger women did not need me, would they bother with me? I think not.' (Heilbrun, 1984: 3).

WOMEN'S LIVES ARE INTERTWINED

Rather than dismissing issues causing distress to subgroups of women —such as ageism, racism, antisemitism, heterosexism, prejudice, against the handicapped—feminists have struggled to understand the forces that unite and divide women. This is because a feminist perspective involves seeing women as a group despite differences, as well as seeing the differences among women despite similarities. When feminists organize intellectual events or artistic gatherings, women of all ages are involved, not just represented:

> 'In the fall of 1977 I went to Washtenaw Community College's festival in celebration of International Women's Year. . . . There were women of all ages and backgrounds, women from all over the world, booths displaying sophisticated political tracts and booths of earnest women showing skills of canning and sewing. All sorts of women were

represented; all sorts of women were there in order to be part of the celebrations. That day "the movement" spoke to everyone and reaffirmed the ideal that this movement can embrace all its great constituency' (Bardwick, 1979: 151).

A celebration of female lives necessarily includes the entire spectrum from before infancy to after death. Feminism views women's lives as intertwined. The young woman needs the older mentor who just as surely needs her.

This can be put another way: the increase in the absolute numbers and proportion of elderly people, particularly in Western industrialized nations, is paralleled by the other major social change with vast consequences—the increase of women in the paid labor force. These two factors mesh: (1) paid caring for the elderly produces new jobs for younger women including the jobs of doing gerontological research, administering programs, and providing physical care; (2) women employed outside the home provide employment for older women who can care for the younger women's children, cook their family's meals, etc.; and (3) the need to care for older women within families places new stresses on younger women who are employed outside the home or raising children inside the home. The dramatic increase in the contemporary labor force participation of women will also yield a dramatic increase in the absolute number and percentage of women retirees. The question is whether women retirees can redefine what retirement meant when it was primarily a male life stage (Stone and Minkler, 1984).

BEING FEMALE IS A CONTINUOUS DEVELOPMENTAL PROCESS

Being female exposes one to degradation throughout development (although perhaps more so among whites than among minorities). First, female fetuses are more likely to be aborted when parents choose to select the sex of their offspring (Jeffery *et al.*, 1984). If she is born, the 'little lady' (the good girl) develops into the 'teenie bopper,' who becomes the 'little woman' (the good wife and mother), who becomes perhaps 'the girl at the office' and finally the 'little old lady' (the good older woman). The recurrent use of 'little' is a hint at socially approved belittling, i.e., the mandate for females to be small and dominatable. Referring to older women as little is an extraordinarily common practice. Even distinguished fighters and leaders become little when they age, if they are women. For example, in *The Boston Globe*'s editorial eulogizing Florence Luscomb, she was referred to as 'the All-American little old lady in tennis shoes—intelligent and witty, feisty and outspoken, understanding and gentle.' We can see the status of an elderly woman creep into middle-age if we look at the way 'little' is used. From the same newspaper: 'This demure little gray-haired lady, about to retire, has suddenly become a tiger in the seat of our family car' (November 11, 1985: 48). Just this week, columns in *The Boston Globe* degraded the talk of older women as 'gossip,' and degraded the environmental activism of older women as 'little old ladies in sneakers.' Research texts frequently use 'old wives' tales' as a metaphor for ignorance and a straw man (*sic*) against which scientific wisdom is contrasted (Reinharz, 1985). Gerontologists would do well to adopt the strategy of feminists—insist on the elimination of ageist language, just as we insist on the elimination of sexist language.

Feminist and gerontological perspectives provide a much needed antidote to this belittling. They assume there is meaning and function in old women's talk. Their 'bobbe-myseh' and 'old wives' tales' are community building (Hochschild, 1973), forms of 'cultural education' (Myerhoff, 1978) or 'life reviews' (Butler, 1963). Maggie Kuhn sees them as potential for 'consciousness-raising' (Kuhn, 1974).

In our society sexism accompanies the developmental course and is internalized at each age. It does not stop at the doorstep of old age. For many girls and women, feeling dependent on men (fathers, brothers, lovers, husbands, colleagues, bosses, presidents, mentors, clergy, physicians) is consistent throughout the life course, and much energy is expended in attracting and retaining the attention of men. The absence of men frightens some women into thinking they are worthless. Contemporary suburban middle-class white women in their late 20s and early 30s report that if they hadn't married by the age of 21, they would be considered 'an old maid,' a terrifying stigma (O'Donnell, 1985). Among the Ik, when females reach 18, they 'lose their ability to charm the cattle herders, and their fellow Ik have neither the energy nor the affection to spare.' They then begin to 'enter the loneliness and isolation of old age' (Turnbull, 1972: 128). Virginia Woolf considered her 'old maid' status to be one of the major causes of her descent into madness at 29 (Olsen, 1965: 200). The simple card game that children play—'Old Maid'—prepares children for this idea which is reinforced continuously.

Frequently, unmarried women do not understand that this attitude of dependence on males induces vulnerability, not safety. As Jessie Bernard explained, a woman's relationship with a male protector provides only temporary immunity from the consequences of powerlessness.

> '. . . a good relationship with one man—husband or lover—[leads] many older women [to] think they have a good relationship with the male world. They feel safe. Not until the relationship is broken by death, desertion, or divorce do they find that their relationship with the male world was not all that good after all. They are not protected by it. They find themselves vulnerable to all kinds of exploitation. Law, custom, convention offer them little in the way of generous treatment' (Bernard, 1981: 151).

The likelihood that women will divorce in old age is increasing with each cohort (O'Rand, 1984: 126) as is the likelihood that in old age women will live alone. Divorce increases women's economic vulnerability in old age. In 1979, for example, divorced wives of retired workers averaged $153 per month in

Social Security benefits, whereas retired male workers averaged $287, and retired workers and wives together averaged $489 (O'Rand, 1984: 128–129). One-sixth of *all* women over 65 have incomes below the poverty threshold, whereas one-third of *unrelated* women (widowed, separated, or divorced) are officially poor (O'Rand, 1984: 132–133).

Women who choose not to marry are not in a better position. For instance, the stigma associated with lesbianism persists into old age (MacDonald and Rich, 1983). If these women have not reared children, they may feel particularly vulnerable to being left alone in old age. Women who have reared sons only may feel similarly vulnerable because sons are not expected to take care of their mothers. As Matthews writes of Australia (1984: 195–196):

> 'caring for the aged is and has always been "women's work." Sons look after money, not mothers. Thus a woman who had borne only sons would be in trouble when old unless the sons had made enough money to buy her institutional care, or they had married women who could be prevailed upon, as daughters-in-law, to undertake the task.'

Middle-age daughters attempting to take care of their elderly widowed mothers assume extraordinarily difficult burdens if they use the model of the nuclear family as the appropriate arena of care. At the same time, however, the caretaker role provides them a unique vantage point for viewing the inequities of bureaucratic forms of care (Safran, 1979), i.e., another opportunity for consciousness-raising.

If raised consciousness does not come about when one is working at caretaking alone at home, it can happen in support groups which function very much like consciousness-raising groups (Wilner, in press). In these groups women frequently discuss the inadequate services provided by physicians, and try to make visible the socially structured problems that accompany their caretaking role. Some feminists have argued that women must be careful not to fall into the 'compassion trap' of 'suffering for their parents,' as they have 'suffered for their children,' but urge instead that they demand proper, assisted care from the community, whether local or federal. The parallels between the rights of women for day care for their children and the rights of women for senior programs for their parents is obvious. This parallel sometimes propels older women into feminism. One such woman labeled this period of her life the third stage (the first was childhood, the second was marriage).

> 'She was 61. Now, "no one needed me. Being needed as a daughter, a wife, a mother had been my identity. I had lived vicariously. . . . I sought a renewed identity." What did she have to build on? The answer: "I am female and growing older. . . . That was the conscious part. I am now convinced that I also embraced again that childhood self so long smothered in the dark shroud of socialization. This late blooming sense of self is built on those very aspects of outsiderness that I had experienced in my lifetime." ' (Preston, 1980).

ABUSE AND OPPRESSION

The basic assumptions about women's continuities and commonalities have led feminist theorists to the radical conclusion that the problems of women are shared. For example, Susan Brownmiller explained that rape is 'nothing more or less than a conscious process of intimidation by which all men keep *all* women in a state of fear' (1975: 5). Examples of older women's lack of immunity from rape are woven throughout her book. Sexual assault by strangers does not stop when a woman ages, a point graphically illustrated in the distressingly popular movie, *A Clockwork Orange*.

So too the problems of elders are shared, although there is some cultural variation granting elders in some societies greater power than in others. Whereas one might suggest that the oppression of women is a structural factor characteristic of most societies, one might also suggest that intergenerational tension is also nearly universal. In a study I recently completed, I was able to demonstrate that intergenerational tension, abuse, and violence against elders is a pattern one can trace throughout history and is deeply embedded in our cultural heritage (Reinharz, 1986). Perhaps the most extreme example of a culture that abuses its elderly is the Ik, or mountain people of Kenya, described by Colin Turnbull.

> '. . . between men and the precipice, a matter of a few feet, stood an ancient and tiny couple of . . . Ik. . . . They had their hands clasped and were jumping up and down in greeting, oblivious to the drop behind them. Peter and Thomas looked cross and said the old couple were nobody, just the parents of the Mkungu (the chief) . . .' (Turnbull, 1972: 46).

He continues later

> 'For the first time I realized that there really was starvation, and saw why I had never known it before: it was confined exclusively to the aged. . . . Down in Giriko's village the old ritual priest, Lolim, confidentially told me that he was sheltering an old man [Lomeraniang] who had been refused shelter by his son and would have died of exposure if Lolim had not helped him. . . . Lomeraniang's wife had died, and his son . . . had told the old man to clear out of the house the old couple had occupied because he wanted it for himself, to sell. He had promised to shelter the old man in his own compound, but, having sold the house, he denied any such promise, and said he had helped build the house and had the right to sell it. . . . In a very short time Lomeraniang was dead and his son refused to come down from the village above to bury him; his sister hurried over and snatched his few belongings, leaving the corpse' (pp. 123–124).

When physical abuse of females by their family members occurs, it can follow the life-course rather than be age-specific. Incest is the abuse primarily of young girls by their fathers, battering the abuse of girlfriends/lovers/ wives by their dates/lovers/husbands, and elder abuse the neglect and violence primarily against old women by their sons, husbands, and even daughters (Pillemer, 1985). When wife battering occurs, it does not necessarily stop in old age (see *Growing Numbers*, 1980: 48–49). Men who beat their wives before they are 65 continue to do so after they reach 65.

A telling example of women's powerlessness being perpetuated rather than relieved in old age can be found in Gurney's (1985) field research on a district attorney office. Gurney showed that lawyers feel contempt for older women victimized in so-called giggolo cases. After their abuse by the stranger, comes scorn from the law. The parallel between male district attorneys labeling giggoloed old women as gullible and young rape victims as seductive or incautious is obvious. Both are seen as 'asking for it.'

Other evidence for the double jeopardy of age and sex can be found in Stephanie Riger's study of the fear of crime (1984). The group with the highest proportion of people feeling unsafe was *women over the age of 65*: of those surveyed, 49.7 felt very unsafe. The *lowest* proportion of women who feel very unsafe are these between 20 and 24. (This proportion is the same as the percentage of men over age 65 who feel unsafe—the highest percentage among age groups of men.)

The fear of the streets experienced by many older women makes them adopt what they believe is a safe home-bound lifestyle. Just as in the case of younger women, fear acts as a mechanism of social control. Ironically, one study of elder abuse (Pillemer, 1984) shows that some elderly women's 'fear of stranger crime' leads them to choose to put up with 'domestic violence,' seen as the lesser of the two evils.

INVISIBLE OR DEAD-END WORK

The lack of recognition of women's unpaid domestic labor has been documented by feminist sociologists (e.g., Oakley, 1974). Its invisibility persists throughout the age span. The lack of recognition given to family-care and housecare spreads into the lack of recognition for middle-aged women's care for their elderly parents, an unheralded job. Daughters are more likely to take care of aged parents and parents-in-law than are sons. Women do the unrewarded kinwork, the 'interactional shitwork' and community work that keep relationships alive. As wives of corporate executives and professionals, they provide one of the persons in the two-person career as long as the husband retains his role. This work, too, is unacknowledged.

Since women's paid labor clusters in lower-paying retail or service industry jobs, upon retiring they are less likely to receive a pension than are men their age. Moving out of the labor force to raise children as unpaid housewives compounds the problem of low earnings when women return to paid work. Thus it is not surprising that in 1981

'only $\frac{1}{10}$ of women over the age of 65 received money from a private pension, wheras $\frac{1}{4}$ of men did. And the average benefit for men was more than 70 per cent greater than the average benefit for women. Many women depend on their husband's pension to help see them through retirement. But what happens to the pension if the husband dies first? In many cases the surviving spouse will receive no benefits, even if her husband worked 20 or 30 years for the same company.' (*The Boston Globe*, April 2, 1984: 11; see also OWL, Gray Paper No. 4).

Many economists are beginning to document this double jeopardy:

'The woman whose family role has led her to depend economically on her spouse can benefit from his private pension *only* if he is covered, does not die too soon, stays married to her, and/or is willing to reduce his benefit to provide her with a survivor annuity. . . . Homemakers have no individual eligibility and no credits of their own to add to employment credit. Divorced women can qualify for a 50 per cent dependent benefit from their former spouse's account only if the marriage lasted ten years or more and only if the former spouse is actually retired . . . disability supports are unavailable to homemakers.'
(O'Rand, 1984: 137).

Obviously, the financial attributes of different jobs differ not only in their starting pay, but in the rate and quantity of increases over time. Sex-based inequities, large to begin with, increase geometrically with age. In corporations, for example, 'managers moved ahead every three to five years; secretaries could stay where they were for twenty years or more' (Kanter, 1977: 83).

In some instances the economic problems of older women are shared by the older men of their class, but in other cases women's vulnerability is unique: the older divorced, separated or widowed homemaker who has never been employed outside the home has no counterpart in the male world. No wonder that nearly 30 per cent of all widows live below the poverty line. The *mean* income for elderly U.S. females over 65 in 1977 was $5101, and those in middle age were not faring much better. One graduate student supplied me with an economic portrait of her mother's life:

'My mother, a widow, has worked every day of her life at more than one job—working the farm, raising children, producing consumable goods and holding down an outside job (at which she now earns $4.25 an hour) for 20 years. If she retired now (at 62) she would get $235 per month from my father's benefits or $219 from her own. She can't qualify for SSI since she is not totally disabled or age 65. She could sell the farm, if market conditions improved and have a bit of money to live on, but she can't come to grips with that loss. So she keeps struggling to make the mortgage and tax payments on her tiny income. Is she worth only $219 per month? I think her story illustrates the need for a redefinition of work and the benefits that accrue from work in our society.'

From a feminist perspective this older woman is a victim of a double inequity pattern—sexism and ageism, compounded by capitalism. Her story is a typical example of one of the patterns that produce the feminization of poverty.

SURVIVAL STRATEGIES

The secretaries in the corporation Kanter studied 'survived' by adapting to an ungenerous environment. Since the company rewards them with love rather than with money, they learn to work for love, i.e., praise. 'The traditional secretary, usually an older woman, knew her place, served with a smile, was willing to be scapegoated and take the blame for the boss's mistakes, and did not presume' (Kanter, 1977: 90). But even subservient adaptation to powerlessness may not be enough to ensure (economic) survival in a culture that has a body-code. In some situations, if one's body does not meet the body-code, the woman is retained only if she can pass. When women attain the symbolic meaning of 'physically unattractive' (to men) they may be pushed out of visible areas or forced into retirement regardless of their skills. As Kanter was told:

> 'We have two good secretaries with first-rate skills who can't move up because they dress like grandmothers. . . . Even those executive secretaries who are hitting sixty don't look like mothers. Maybe one or two dowdy types slipped in at that level, but if the guy they work for moves, they couldn't be sold elsewhere at the same grade' (Kanter, 1977: 76).

Pauline Bart was not hired as an assistant professor when she got her Ph.D. at the age of 37 because of the same problem of 'image.' The rationale, as she heard it, was that 'We don't want the first woman we hired as assistant professor in fifty years to be a Jewish mother' (Bart, 1975: 4). As prostitutes age, they too become less 'valuable' (Matthews, 1984: 16).

The same older woman or older-looking women who cannot 'be sold' in the corporation, cannot easily sell herself as a marital partner. Whereas in 1975 there were 31.4 marriages per 1000 men 65 and over, there were only 9.1 of women (see Bell, 1979: 235). Of course, this figure may also disclose a lack of interest among older women in marriage. Three-quarters of the white widows interviewed by Lopata (1973), for instance, expressed relief at being released from the homemaking which they felt had been imposed on them during marriage.

THE CONTINUITY OF FEMALE CREATIVITY

While recognizing the continuity of oppression, feminists also recognize and celebrate the continuity of women's often unacknowledged creativity (Reinharz, 1984). Obviously, women participate in and derive rewards from the dominant culture. As members on the margin, however, they are likely to change it if they obtain power, e.g., creating programs to help women return for more education or employment, organizing residents of nursing homes to fight for their rights. In addition, women function in a separate world of meaning (Bernard, 1981). One aspect of this separate world of achievement is activism on behalf of women or the elderly.

This separate world of values is referred to politically as the gender gap. It translates into women being more likely than men to favor federal help for the poor and the elderly (Welch and Ulrich, 1984: 10). Women's advocacy for the poor and elderly is certainly needed. In 1984 the U.S. poverty rate reached 15.2 per cent, the highest level in 18 years. Fifty-seven per cent of American poor in 1984 were women. Among the elderly, women were poorer than men, as has always been the case. Nearly half the women over 65 in 1984 lived on less than $5000, whereas less than 20 per cent of elderly men were forced to survive on such a low budget (Longcope, 1985: 59).

The blending of feminism and anti-ageism can be expected to create new life chances for all—men and women, young and old, in our society. The relation of feminism to anti-ageism is neither uniform nor uni-directional. On the one hand, feminism has contributed much of the terminology within which the anti-ageist movement can develop. It has contributed theory, including theories of human development which for the first time reflect women's experiences as well as men's. These concerns have had implications for rethinking existing social theory (see Reinharz, 1985) and will affect gerontological theory as well. At the same time, advocacy of the elderly helps refine, tests, and in certain ways forces a rethinking of feminist theory by illuminating ways in which it has been conceptualized without regard for age and ageism.

The major contribution that the issue of aging can make to feminism is the mandate to re-examine all feminist theory in light of this dimension. And the major contribution that feminism can make for those concerned with aging is to provide a model and some of the personnel of a successful social movement. Scott (1982) has shown that a fringe benefit of women's activism is longevity. If this is true, we can expect feminists to age well and to contribute to a vibrant anti-ageism movement.

REFERENCES

Bardwick, Judith. 1979. *In Transition*. Holt, Rinehart & Winston, New York.

Bart, Pauline. 1975. Emotional and social status of the older woman. In *No Longer Younger: The Older Woman in America*. Institute of Gerontology, University of Michigan.

Bart, Pauline. 1979. The loneliness of the long-distance mother. In Freeman, Jo, (ed), *Women: A Feminist Perspective*. Mayfield, Palo Alto, CA.

Beeson, Diane. 1975. Women in studies of aging: A critique and suggestion. *Social Problems* 23: 52–59.

Bell, Inge Powell. 1970. The double standard: Age, *Trans-Action* (November–December) 75–80. Reprinted in Freeman, Jo, (ed). 1979. *Women: A Feminist Perspective*. Mayfield, Palo Alto, CA.

Bernard Jessie. 1981. *The Female World*. Free Press, New York.

Brownmiller, Susan. 1975. *Against Our Will*. Bantam, New York.

Butler, Robert, 1963. The life review: An interpretation of reminiscence in the aged. *Psychiatry* 26: 65-76.

Christy, Marian. 1985. Conversations: Diana Menuhin. *The Boston Globe* (March 20): 67.

Daly, Mary. 1978. *Gyn/Ecology*. Beacon Press, Boston.

Datan, Nancy. 1981. The lost cause: The aging woman in American feminism. In Pore, Renate and Betty Justice, (eds), *Towards the Second Decade*. Greenwood Press, Westport, CT.

de Beauvoir, Simone. 1970. *Old Age*. Rpt. 1977. Penguin, New York.

Demetrakopoulos, Stephanie. 1983. *Listening to our Bodies: The Rebirth of Feminine Wisdom*. Beacon Press, Boston.

Evans, Sara. 1979. *Personal Politics*. Random House, New York.

Evers, Helen. 1981. Care or custody? The experience of women patients in long-stay geriatric wards. In Hutter, Bridget and Gillian Williams, (eds), *Controlling Women: The Normal and the Deviant*. Croom Helm, London.

Feldman, Harold. 1975. Consciousness raising as a new life style for the elderly. In *No Longer Young: The Older Woman in America*. Institute of Gerontology, University of Michigan.

Fuller, Marie Marschall and Cora Ann Martin. 1980. *The Older Woman: Lavender Rose or Gray Panther*. Charles C. Thomas, Springfield, Illinois.

Golub, Sharon and Rita Freedman. 1985. *Health Needs of Women as they Age*. The Haworth Press, New York.
Growing Numbers, Growing Force. 1980. A Report on the White House Mini-Conference on Older Women.
Gurney, Joan. 1985. Not one of the guys: A female researcher in a male-dominated setting. *Qualitative Sociology* **8** (1): 42–62.
Hacker, Helen. 1951. Women as a minority group. *Social Forces* **30**: 60–69.
Heilbrun, Carolyn. 1984. Aging and raging. *Women's Review of Books* **2** (3): 3.
Hochschild, Arlie. 1973. *The Unexpected Community*. University of California Press, Berkeley, CA.
Institute of Gerontology. 1973. *No Longer Young: The Older Woman in America*. University of Michigan.
Jacobs, Ruth. 1979. *Life After Forty: Female, Forty—what Next?* Beacon Press, Boston.
Jaggar, Allison. 1983. *Feminist Politics and Human Nature*. Rowman & Allenheld, Totowa, NJ.
Jeffery, Roger, Patricia Jeffery and Andrew Lyon. 1984. Female infanticide and amniocentesis. *Social Sci. Med.* **19** (11): 1207–1212.
Kanter, Rosabeth. 1977. *Men and Women of the Corporation*. Basic Books, New York.
Kuhn, Maggie. 1974. Grass-roots gray power. *Prime Time*, pp. 4–6.
Kuhn, Maggie. 1984. Challenge to a new age. In Minkler, Meredith and Carroll L. Estes, eds, *Readings in the Political Economy of Aging*. Baywood, Farmingdale, NY.
Levin, Jack and William Levin. 1980. *Ageism: Prejudice and Discrimination against the Elderly*. Wadsworth, Belmont, CA.
Longcope, Kay. 1985. How women fared in '84. *The Boston Globe* (January 1): 58–59.
Lopata, Helena. 1973. *Widowhood in an American City*. Schenkman, Cambridge.
Macdonald, Barbara with Cynthia Rich. 1983. *Look Me in the Eye*. Spinsters Ink, San Francisco.
MacPherson, Kathleen. 1985. Osteoporosis and menopause: A feminist analysis of the social construction of a syndrome. *Adv. Nursing Sci.* **7** (4): 22.
Markson, Elizabeth W., (ed). 1983. *Older Women*. Lexington Books, Lexington, MA.
Matthews, Jill. 1984. *Good and Mad Women: The Historical Construction of Femininity in 20th Century Australia*. George Allen & Unwin, Boston.
McFadden, Maggie. 1984. Anatomy of difference: Toward a classification of feminist theory: *Women's Studies Int. Forum* **7** (6): 495–504.
Moss, Zoe. 1978. It hurts to be alive and obsolete: The aging woman. In Jaggar, Allison M. and Paula S. Rothenberg, (eds), *Feminist Frameworks*. Rpt. 1984. McGraw-Hill, New York.
Minkler, Meredith and Carroll L. Estes, (eds). 1984. *Readings in the Political Economy of Aging*. Baywood, Farmingdale, NY.
Myerhoff, Barbara. 1978. *Number Our Days*. Simon & Schuster, New York.
Nett, Emily. 1982. Women as Elders. Resources for Feminist Research/Documentation sur la Recherche Féministe **11** (2).
Oakley, Ann. 1974. *The Sociology of Housework*. Random House, New York.
O'Donnell, Lydia. 1985. *The Unheralded Majority: Contemporary Women as Mothers*. Lexington Books, Lexington, MA.
Olsen, Tillie. 1965. *Silences*. Delacorte Press, New York.
Olson, Laura Katz. 1982. *The Political Economy of Aging: The State, Private Power and Social Welfare*. Columbia University Press, New York.
O'Rand, Angela M. 1984. Women. In Erdman, Palmore (ed), *Handbook on the Aged in the United States*. Greenwood Press, Westport, Conn.
OWL, Gray Paper No. 4: Older Women and Pensions: Catch 22.
Pillemer, Karl. 1985. Physical abuse of the elderly, Ph.D. Department of Sociology, Brandeis University.
Preston, Chuck. 1980. Feminism as a third stage: Profile of Lucile Shuck 'Longview'. *Gray Panther Network* (November/December).
Reinharz, Shulamit. 1984. Women as competent community builders. In Rickel, Annette, Meg Gerrard and Ira Iscoe, (eds), *Social and Psychological Problems of Women*. McGraw-Hill, New York.

Reinharz, Shulamit. 1985. Feminist distrust: Problems of content and context in sociological work. In Berg, David and Ken Smith, (eds), *Exploring Clinical Methods for Social Research*. Sage, Beverly Hills, CA.

Reinharz, Shulamit. 1986. Loving and hating our elders: Twin themes in legend and literature. In Pillemer, Karl and Rosalie Wolf, (eds), *Elder Abuse: Conflict in the Family*. Auburn House, Dover, MA.

Rickel, Annette, Linda Forsberg, Meg Gerrard and Ira Iscoe. 1984. New directions for women. In Rickel, Annette, Meg Gerrard and Ira Iscoe, (eds), *Social and Psychological Problems of Women*. McGraw Hill, New York.

Riger, Stephanie and Margaret T. Gordon. 1984. The impact of crime on urban women. In Rickel, Annette, Meg Gerrard and Ira Iscoe, (eds), *Social and Psychological Problems of Women*. McGraw Hill, New York.

Rubin, Lillian. 1979. *Women of a Certain Age*. Harper & Row, New York.

Safran, Rose. 1979. *Don't Go Dancing Mother*. Tide Press, Manchester, MA.

Scott, Anne Firor. 1982. Old wives tales. In Johnston, Priscilla, (ed), *Perspectives on Aging*. Ballinger, Cambridge.

Shaw, Evelyn and Joan Darling. 1985. *Female Strategies*, Walker, New York.

Shields, Laurie. 1981. *Displaced Homemakers: Organizing for a New Life*. McGraw-Hill, New York.

Silverman, Phyllis. 1986. *Widow-to-Widow*. Springer, New York.

Sontag, Susan. 1972. The double standard of aging. *Saturday Rev.* **55** (September 23): 29–38.

Steinem, Gloria. 1983. *Outrageous Acts and Everyday Rebellions*. New American Library, New York.

Stone, Robyn and Meredith Minkler. 1984. The socio-political context of women's retirement. In Minkler, Meredith and Carroll Estes, (eds), *Readings in the Political Economy of Aging*. Baywood, Farmingdale, New York.

Streib, Gordon. 1976. Social stratification and aging. In Binstock, Robert and Ethel Shanas, eds, *Handbook of Aging and the Social Sciences*. Van Nostrand Reinhold, New York.

Troll, Lillian. 1983. Grandparents: The family watchdogs. In Brubaker, Timothy, (ed), *Family Relationships in Later Life*. Sage, Beverly Hills, CA.

Turnbull, Colin M. 1972. *The Mountain People*. Simon & Schuster, New York.

Verbrugge, Lois. 1985. Gender and health: An update on hypotheses and evidence. *J. Hlth Soc. Behavior* **26** (3): 156–182.

Waldron, Ingrid. 1976. Why do women live longer than men? *Soc. Sci. Med.* **10**.

Welch, Susan and Fred Ulrich. 1984. *The Political Life of American Jewish Women*. Biblio Press, New York.

Wilner, Mary Ann. 1986. How do support groups enhance coping? In Reinharz, Shulamit and Graham Rowles, (eds), *Qualitative Gerontology*. Springer, New York.

THE ATHENE SERIES

An International Collection of Feminist Books

General Editors: Gloria Bowles, Renate Klein and Janice Raymond

Consulting Editor: Dale Spender

243

TEACHING TECHNOLOGY FROM A FEMINIST PERSPECTIVE
A Practical Guide
Joan Rothschild

FEMINISM WITHIN THE SCIENCE AND HEALTH CARE PROFESSIONS
Overcoming Resistance
Sue V. Rosser, editor

RUSSIAN WOMEN'S STUDIES Essays on Sexism in Soviet Culture
Tatyana Mamonova

TAKING OUR TIME Feminist Perspectives on Temporality
Frieda J. Forman, editor

THE RECURRING SILENT SPRING
Patricia Hynes

RADICAL VOICES: A Decade of Feminist Resistance from
Women's Studies International Forum
Renate D. Klein and *Deborah L. Steinberg,* editors